MW00810298

SUSTAINABLE WAC

Sustainable WAC

A Whole Systems Approach to Launching and Developing Writing Across the Curriculum Programs

MICHELLE COX
Cornell University

JEFFREY R. GALIN
Florida Atlantic University

DAN MELZER
University of California, Davis

National Council of Teachers of English
1111 W. Kenyon Road, Urbana, Illinois 61801-1096

Staff Editor: Bonny Graham
Manuscript Editor: The Charlesworth Group
Interior Design: Jenny Jensen Greenleaf
Cover Design: Pat Mayer
Cover Image: StudioM1/iStock/Thinkstock

NCTE Stock Number: 49522; eStock Number: 49546
ISBN 978-0-8141-4952-2; eISBN 978-0-8141-4954-6

It is the policy of NCTE in its journals and other publications to provide a
forum for the open discussion of ideas concerning the content and the teaching of English and the language arts. Publicity accorded to any particular
point of view does not imply endorsement by the Executive Committee, the
Board of Directors, or the membership at large, except in announcements
of policy, where such endorsement is clearly specified.

NCTE provides equal employment opportunity (EEO) to all staff members
and applicants for employment without regard to race, color, religion, sex,
national origin, age, physical, mental or perceived handicap/disability, sexual
orientation including gender identity or expression, ancestry, genetic information, marital status, military status, unfavorable discharge from military
service, pregnancy, citizenship status, personal appearance, matriculation or
political affiliation, or any other protected status under applicable federal,
state, and local laws.

Every effort has been made to provide current URLs and email addresses,
but because of the rapidly changing nature of the Web, some sites and addresses may no longer be accessible.

Library of Congress Cataloging-in-Publication Data

A catalog record of this book has been requested.

CONTENTS

CONTENTS

FOREWORD

BARBARA E. WALVOORD

I am the "Walvoord" that you are going to read about in the first chapter of this book. The authors credit me with an early attempt at theorizing Writing Across the Curriculum (WAC) program development, which, they rightly argue, has been undertheorized. Those of us working to establish effective and sustainable WAC programs and to promote broad changes in higher education are facing ever-changing environments, challenges, and possibilities. We need more than advice from the trenches, though we certainly need that. We need more than theories of pedagogy, though we certainly need those, and we've been generating powerful ones. In addition, as the authors rightly posit, we need a robust theoretical framework for program development, to help us understand what is going on and what the possible future trajectories are for our efforts, our ideals, and our goals.

As the authors note, I published, in 1996, an article entitled "The Future of WAC," in which I used social movement theory to try to understand the WAC movement, to envision its future, and to offer guidelines for achieving its long-term goals for change. In Chapter 1 of the present book, the authors offer a fair assessment of what I was trying to do, and they also note correctly that social movement theory was limited as a framework for building transformative and sustainable WAC programs. Others needed to build on my work and move the theorizing forward. This volume does that in a wonderfully insightful, informed, and intelligent way. This book is a signature work that will make a real difference to WAC and to American higher education. It is essential reading for anyone concerned with WAC or, more broadly, with any effort to make American higher education more humane and learner centered.

My own career illustrates the enormous changes and challenges that WAC has faced, and continues to face. I've been involved in WAC since the early 1970s, when I launched, at Central College in Iowa, one of the first WAC programs of our era, though there had been attempts to address student writing throughout higher education history, and, in the 1970s, others were also launching WAC programs (Russell, 2002). Elaine Maimon (1992) described, in *Writing Across the Curriculum: A Guide to Developing Programs*, her chance meeting in 1975 with Harriet Sheridan, then dean of Carleton College, on a San Francisco cable car, as both were attending a Modern Language Association conference. On the cable car, Elaine heard about the Carleton College WAC program—and went on to establish a program at her own Beaver College. WAC programs arose like this, in response to felt need, fed by the sparks of excitement generated by early pioneers, scratching up funds, gathering interested faculty, meeting in collegial workshops to examine student writing and try to figure out how to more effectively use writing in our classrooms. Elaine and I—along with Toby Fulwiler, Art Young, Susan McLeod, Margot Soven, Chris Thaiss, and other early WAC program founders—became itinerant preachers, traveling from college to college to help faculty members launch WAC programs, thus laying the foundations for the highly decentralized, workshop-based, faculty-driven, pedagogy-focused, passionate, idealistic grassroots WAC of those early days.

Things are much different now. A great deal has happened in higher education and in the WAC movement. In my own career, I established another WAC program at Loyola College in Maryland, a twenty-five-college coordinated WAC effort that served K–university teachers in the Baltimore area, then a WAC effort linked to general education reform at the University of Cincinnati, then a teaching–learning center at the University of Notre Dame, and finally an assessment effort there. All the while, I was consulting with colleges and universities not only about WAC, but also about teaching and learning, and about assessing student learning. I worked in my own programs, and I helped other programs, to move beyond workshops to institutional structures; to support faculty after their workshop experiences; to reach beyond early-adopting faculty; to shape curricular writing-intensive course requirements that would not just turn into check-the-box formalities; to establish writing centers and writing fellows as resources for both students and faculty; to deal with insecure funding; to win the support of new administrators; to interact with other campus reform movements; to meet new assessment requirements; to operate in environments of faculty burnout, cynicism, and exhaustion; and to prevent my own burnout, cynicism, and exhaustion. We badly needed a theoretical framework to guide both our visions and our practical actions. This book provides that framework.

The authors explain eloquently in their first chapter what this volume does and how it is organized, so I won't summarize. What I most admire about this book is the integration of lived experience with the theoretical framework. I admire the specific strategies that arise from the theoretical framework, each strategy illustrated with profiles of actual programs. I admire the ways the authors use a whole systems approach to provide an expansive theoretical understanding that can encompass the complex history, the many strands, and the changing environments that WAC programs face. WAC needs this book, as do others involved in transformative learning. Use it for understanding the big picture of WAC; use it for practical suggestions; use it for long-range planning; use it to inform the vision we share with our many allies and colleagues in higher education—a vision of learning that is richly transformative, a vision of pedagogy that uses powerful, research-based principles for learning, and a vision of institutions that richly nourish that learning.

ACKNOWLEDGMENTS

Many people influenced the development of this book over the three years it was written. First, we are grateful for Chris Thaiss's leadership in keeping the Conference on College Composition and Communication's (CCCC) International Network of Writing Across the Curriculum Programs (INWAC) going for thirty-five years. It was after the 2014 CCCC INWAC Special Interest Group meeting that we started discussing this project. We are grateful to Victor Villanueva, director of the writing program at Washington State University, who generously Skyped with us shortly after CCCC 2014 to discuss our ideas. This important conversation led us to move away from our original plan of writing an advice book for new WAC directors and instead develop a theoretical framework that can guide program development. As Victor told us, advice is short-lived, but theory can transcend context. We are grateful to the anonymous reviewers who provided feedback to the prospectus and drafts, feedback that greatly helped us reshape the literature review and clarify key parts of the theoretical framework. We are grateful to those who attended our conference panels and workshops on this work at the 2015 Council of Writing Program Administrators Conference, the 2016 International Writing Across the Curriculum Conference, and the 2017 CCCC Annual Convention. The audience members' questions and comments helped us figure out how to shape key parts of the work, and their enthusiasm for the project kept us motivated to see this project through. The theories we draw upon can be opaque to those new to them, and thus we are grateful to those who helped us untangle them, particularly Steve Simpson and Jeff's colleagues at Florida State University in the Center for Complex Systems and Brain Sciences: Steven Bressler and Joseph Norman.

We would also like to recognize administrators, faculty, and students who worked with Jeff in 2007 on the campuses of George Mason University and Washington State University, especially Terry Zawacki and Bill Condon. His three-day visits to these campuses laid the groundwork for the visual mapping techniques, a systematic approach to program sustainability, and several of Jeff's conference presentations that inform the whole systems approach. We want to thank Katherine Bridgman at Texas A&M–San Antonio and Elizabeth Renn at Valencia College for allowing us to share details of their programs and their collaborations with Jeff as he consulted on their campuses to help develop their WAC programs. We are thankful for the guidance of Bonny Graham, our editor at the National Council of Teachers of English, who recognized the value of this project early on and maintained unwavering support. We would also like to express our sincere gratitude to the many people who have launched and developed the field of WAC, those included in our bibliography as well as those whose day jobs as WAC program directors have kept them too busy to publish.

Finally, we are grateful to be part of a field that values scholarly collaboration. This book is truly the outcome of three minds working together. Before we started this project, we were acquaintances who might bump into one another at conferences. And now, three years later, we marvel at this work that could not have been completed by any one of us alone, and are grateful for the friendship, trust, and humor that sustained us throughout the project.

CHAPTER ONE

The Need for a Systematic Approach to Building and Sustaining WAC Programs

*How will WAC survive? How will it grow and change—
what new forms will WAC programs take, and how will
they adapt to some of the present program elements and
structures in the changing scene in higher education?
What new WAC theories and research will help lay the
groundwork for future WAC programs?*
(McLEOD, MIRAGLIA, SOVEN, & THAISS, 2001, p. 4)

Writing Across the Curriculum (WAC) is the longest-standing curricular reform movement in the history of higher education in the United States (Russell, 2002), yet WAC programs fail to survive at an alarming rate of more than 50 percent (Thaiss & Porter, 2010, p. 558). One way to understand this phenomenon is to consider how WAC programs are developed and institutionalized. We can learn a great deal about how they develop, grow, and fare across time from the narratives of program directors. The field of WAC has a rich history of lore, which has been important for passing on knowledge based in the wisdom of experience. However, as the field matures, we would benefit from reframing lore through the application of a theoretical framework for program building. For these reasons, we frame this book with both vignettes from WAC directors and the whole systems approach to WAC program development and transformational change, a theoretical framework that we have developed by drawing on overlapping cross-disciplinary theories of complex organizations and sustainability.

This chapter opens with two contrasting vignettes demon-strating different levels of WAC's integration into a university system, from a "failed attempt" at WAC to a fully integrated and sustainable program. While these two examples are not meant to represent the broad range of programs across institutional contexts, they do provide us a starting place for considering what can lead to or detract from program longevity. In the first, "A WAC Failure That I'm Trying to Learn From," Michael Michaud describes steps he took to build a WAC program that are often ad-vised in the WAC lore: he worked with a cross-disciplinary group of faculty who were enthused about integrating writing into the curriculum, he used his expertise in rhetoric and composition to guide conversations within this group, and he expanded expertise in writing on campus through faculty development events. And yet, as Michaud points out, the signs of the writing-intensive (WI) requirement's demise can be seen from the start. In the second vignette, "Handing Over the Reins: Ownership, Support, and the Departmentally Focused Model of Communication Across the Curriculum," Chris Anson and Deanna Dannels share the history of a well-established WAC program. This program took more than fifteen years to develop, including stages of data gathering, innovation, assessment, and, ultimately, a handing over of control of WAC to departments.

We selected these emblematic vignettes to open the book because they provide an opportunity to reflect on the relationship between how WAC is initiated and developed and the sustain-ability of the program—a relationship we explore throughout the book. Following these vignettes, we explain why a theoretical framework for WAC program development is needed and briefly describe the whole systems approach, the theoretical framework and methodology for developing WAC programs that structures the book.

A WAC Failure That I'm Trying to Learn From

Michael J. Michaud
Rhode Island College

You arrive on campus, a newly minted composition/rhetoric PhD, ready to get to work and excited to learn that your school already has an established writing board, of which you are now a member. You are pleased to learn that the board has been around for some time. To a certain extent, the groundwork for WAC at your school has already been laid. While there is no official WAC program, no program requirements, no outcomes or assessment mechanisms, and no program director, there is a small band of faculty members from across the disciplines who have participated in WAC initiatives, made writing instruction a core element of their pedagogy, and made the advancement of WAC part of their work on campus. There is some sense, on the campus, that writing instruction is important and should be taken seriously, and that first-year composition is not the cure-all for students' inevitable ills.

Despite the fact that you have never officially consulted with faculty in the disciplines on matters related to writing instruction and know only a little about WAC itself, you are immediately granted "expert" status on the writing board because of your background in composition. During your early years on the board, you help plan the annual professional development workshop, a tradition that dates back over a dozen years and regularly engages about a third of the faculty in a one-day professional development workshop focused on writing and pedagogy. Occasionally, you and the board are given the opportunity to plan other professional development opportunities and to consult with various campus entities on matters related to writing and curriculum. You go to board meetings, you listen to your peers, you begin to be called on by campus entities to discuss writing. You are starting to become the WAC expert that your colleagues on the board members assumed you were.

As you learn more about WAC and become acquainted with the campus, you begin to realize that, while you are lucky to have a great group of colleagues with whom to collaborate, what you have at your school as far as WAC goes is pretty meager. You begin to wonder what you might help build, but your eye is on your upcoming tenure case and your research, which has nothing to do with WAC.

Then, something amazing happens. A powerful and well-respected faculty member who is heading up the campus-wide revision of general education and who is committed to quality writing instruction manages to persuade the campus community to accept a writing-in-the-disciplines (WID) requirement as part of the new general education program. You never quite learn how this was accomplished (you're still not sure). No one, in fact, seems to know how or why the WID requirement was inserted into the general education overhaul, but it's in there nonetheless, and, as the train that is the new general education program begins to leave the station, WID is on board.

The writing board is happy with this new WID requirement but is not really a part of the conversation. Its members mostly stand along the tracks, waving at the train as it goes by. They try to intervene, to ask what this new WID requirement will include, what its goals will be, how it will be assessed, and how faculty will receive training, but no one has any answers and no one, it seems, wants to entertain these questions. You and your writing board colleagues are told that there are far more contentious issues at stake in the general education overhaul and they will need to be addressed first. No one wants to derail the train, including the writing board. So you sit by, pleased, concerned, and largely helpless.

Later, when the dust has cleared and the train has safely reached the station with the general education overhaul, you and the other members of the writing board attempt to intervene in the WID rollout. You quickly learn that you face a significant new obstacle: faculty and administrative resistance. You and your colleagues ask, "What is a WID course at our institution?" "What should it attempt to accomplish?" "Why?" "Who should teach it?" "How?" No one knows or wants to say. WID, you and your colleagues are told, is whatever each individual department decides it is. When you press for more information, an associate dean refuses to engage. "Will there be course caps on WID courses?" It's up to the departments. "What about outcomes?" Up to the departments. "What about classroom practices—revision?" "Peer workshops?" "Conferences?" Up to the departments and individual instructors. "Training for the faculty teaching WID courses?" Same. Same. Same.

You and the members of the writing board begin to get the picture: the new WID requirement is mostly none of your business. Departments will submit plans for how they will meet the requirement to the committee on general education. They will vet the plans, ultimately approve them, and move on. Everyone will strive for a low bar. You and your colleagues on the writing board start throwing around the phrase "check the box" because that, it seems, is what your new WID comes down to. At some later date, you learn that assessment will be discussed, but, since the outcomes of the new general education program are the first things that need to be assessed, assessment of WID will have to wait.

As Kurt Vonnegut would say: And so it goes. The scenario above is the WID failure that I am trying to learn from. So far, were you to ask me to name five things I have learned, they would be these:

1. Powerful faculty members on college campuses with intentions that may or may not align with your own do have the ability to make change happen.

2. These powerful faculty members may or may not care what you think or want to listen to you.

3. If you yourself lack status and/or clout on your campus, you will likely not be taken seriously or much listened to.

4. If you yourself are just beginning to understand the mechanisms by which your college or university operates, you'll probably be unlikely to advocate successfully for the things you care about.

5. Change is hard (I already knew this, but I'm learning it again).

Handing Over the Reins: Ownership, Support, and the Departmentally Focused Model of Communication Across the Curriculum

Chris M. Anson and Deanna Dannels
North Carolina State University

In 1999 we were hired to be the director (Chris) and assistant director (Deanna) of the newly established Campus Writing and Speaking Program at North Carolina State University. Just a couple of years old, the program had been led by interim director Dr. Michael Carter, a compositionist and WAC expert. Founded after widespread concern that North Carolina State students were not demonstrating adequate abilities in writing, oral communication, or teamwork, the program was designed to provide both generalized, university-wide support and consultations to individual departments and programs.

After the program was established, Mike began consulting with a few eager members in select departments in some of the university's ten colleges, including several in the science, technology, engineering, and mathematics disciplines where writing was both underutilized in coursework and underpracticed. Mike's process (described in Carter, 2003) involved collaborating with several faculty in each department to painstakingly tease out and then formally articulate learning outcomes that included those for writing and oral communication. The outcomes would then drive implementation plans (such as helping faculty to design, teach, and assess more communication activities in their courses) as well as plans to assess students' progress on a course-specific and departmental basis. Further support came from the office of assessment, which was sympathetic to the need for increased attention to writing and speaking, and also highly respectful of the expertise that faculty in writing and communication studies brought to the process (see Anson, Carter, Dannels, & Rust, 2003; Carter, Anson, & Miller, 2003). It took Mike five years to complete the outcomes development process across the university.

The slowly transformative potential of this model cannot be overstated. Outcomes came from each department's own understanding of what strong graduates should know and be able to do, and how communication activities strengthened learning. Everything that followed—every approach to implementation, such as a portfolio system for majors, a "saturation" model that put communication into every course, and a miniature writing- and speaking-intensive course model—came from and was owned by each department. With our help, every decision about assessment—every approach, focus, and type of data collection and analysis—was uniquely shaped by the department, molded to best fit its faculty, students, and curriculum (see Anson, 2006).

In addition to supporting individual departments' efforts to integrate writing and oral communication into their curricula, the Campus Writing and Speaking Program provides support on a more general basis. For example, its popular faculty seminar brings together up to fifteen faculty from across the university to revise an undergraduate course. Meeting every other week for a semester, the participants learn about strategies for designing assignments, supporting their development, and evaluating the results. A stipend provides incentive to produce a before-and-after report on the course improvements and the promise to share something of interest about the revisions during one of the program's noon box-lunch sessions the following year. Other programming includes campus-wide workshops, guest presenters, an "assisted inquiry" option (for faculty to get help running classroom-based research projects involving writing and/ or speaking), and individual consultations. Meanwhile, the program's own research agenda, which usually involves graduate consultants who are doctoral students in the PhD program in communication, rhetoric, and digital media, provides material for ongoing support of various curricular initiatives and reports.

Over time, of course, departmental plans and activities can fall by the wayside. The program conducts "profiles" at the department level— expert consultations, similar to external reviews, designed to provide entirely formative feedback to the department about its status quo with respect to communication in the undergraduate curriculum (see Anson & Dannels, 2009). Through meetings with curriculum committees and individual faculty, analyses of documents, and various inventories of practices, we can gauge the level of activity in which a department is continuing to engage in meeting its writing and speaking goals, and offer suggestions as necessary.

Evidence suggests that North Carolina State was the first large institution to put into place an entire program focusing on individual departments' goals for communication. But slowly, the word has spread. The model now includes programs at both large universities, such as North Carolina State, the University of Minnesota, and the University of North Carolina at Charlotte, and at smaller institutions, such as McDaniel College and Colby College. Surprisingly, however, the approach is still dwarfed by the ubiquitous WI model. The success of the WI model in spreading writing more fully across university curricula is often negated by the failure to sustain the effort, to encourage the program's ownership and development beyond the office that oversees it, and to yield a net increase in writing when everyone not teaching a WI course is forgiven for not including it (see Holdstein, 2000; White, 1990a).

The departmental model requires a kind of community activism that at once respects the autonomy and values of departmental cultures while also providing them with new perspectives, knowledge, and strategies. As WAC or Communication Across the Curriculum (CAC) leaders, we must be willing to give over some authority and control of writing and communication to faculty in the disciplines, and see ourselves as supporting and advising their efforts, rather than, in the role of writing and communication tsars, "certifying" or "approving" their courses or faculty and condescendingly telling them what they can and can't do.

These vignettes illustrate contrasting approaches to building WAC programs within complex institutional structures and speak to the need for a systematic and theoretically informed framework for developing sustainable WAC. Michael Michaud described a WID program lacking in cohesion, oversight, and accountability that was created without consultation with the WAC director or campus writing board. Even though this WAC director followed advice often found in WAC guidebooks, there may have been additional steps that could have been taken to make WAC more sustainable. The WAC director and the writing board may have played a greater role in shaping the WID mandate if they had been positioned with more leverage within the institutional system and as a more central hub in the network of relationships that eventually led to the passing of general education reform. A theory of WAC program building focused on fully integrating into institutional structures might have helped the WAC director and the writing board gain more influence with the general education curriculum—more "clout," as Michaud put it.

A theory and methodology for building sustainable WAC programs could be centered on looking holistically at our institutions and working to change the culture of writing, as Chris Anson and Deanna Dannels described. Their vignette offers an example of a WAC program that was built over decades by leaders with expertise in WAC who were given adequate time and resources to make macro-level institutional changes. These changes were made in part through strategic alliances with important units in the institution's network and in part through highly visible and ongoing faculty development events sponsored by a central hub both in the system of the university and in national publications on CAC: the North Carolina State Campus Writing and Speaking Program. But even a program as successful as North Carolina State's needs to ensure that it retains its leadership and visibility as the responsibility for teaching writing becomes integrated into departments, and it needs to continually assess and revise its projects and processes to ensure it doesn't stagnate. An approach for building WAC programs that have the systemic impact and the sustainability of the Campus Writing and Speaking Program at North Carolina State could help WAC directors act not solely on lore, but also on guiding principles, informed by theory, that can provide a methodology and a set of strategies that apply to a variety of contexts for building WAC. A systematic approach could also help WAC directors decide which initiatives might have the largest effects on the campus culture of writing and what steps to take to move smaller projects toward a fully integrated and sustainable program. Of course, many WAC programs begin with small initiatives—a workshop, a retreat, a book group—and a program doesn't need to be on as large a scale as North Carolina State's to be successful. However, as the two vignettes demonstrate, both small and large WAC programs could benefit from thinking strategically, from drawing on theories that address the complexities of institutions of higher education, and from planning for sustainability from the start.

Why Theorize WAC Program Development?

In WAC literature, theory tends not to focus on the complexities of higher education, but, rather, on the writing pedagogies that are at the heart of WAC programs. Exemplifying this point is Christopher Thaiss's (2001) chapter in *WAC for the New Millennium* (McLeod et al., 2001), "Theory in WAC: Where Have We Been, Where Are We Going?," which provides a comprehensive review of the writing theories and instruction that have informed WAC practice, but does not touch on theories related to WAC leadership or program development. This is not an oversight by Thaiss, but is emblematic of a field that focuses more on theorizing WAC instruction than the administration of WAC programs.

This focus on pedagogy may be inherent to the ways in which the field of WAC has developed and defined itself. Russell (2002) attributed the success of the WAC movement to its focus on pedagogy, as faculty are asked to make a commitment to a "radically different way of teaching," a way of teaching that offers "personal rather than institutional rewards" (p. 295). This focus on pedagogy remains in current definitions of WAC. Thaiss and Porter (2010) defined WAC as "an initiative in an institution to assist teachers across disciplines in using student writing as an instructional tool in their teaching" (p. 538). The "Statement of WAC Principles and Practices" developed by the International Network of Writing-Across-the-Curriculum Programs (INWAC) board of consultants, specifies:

> WAC refers to the notion that writing should be an integral part of the learning process throughout a student's education, not merely in required writing courses but across the entire curriculum. Further, it is based on the premise that writing is highly situated and tied to a field's discourse and ways of knowing, and therefore writing in the disciplines (WID) is most effectively guided by those with expertise in that discipline. (International Network of Writing-Across-the-Curriculum Programs, 2014, p. 1)

In this definition, we see reference to two of the main pedagogies that are promoted by WAC programs, widely referred to as *writing to learn* and *writing to communicate*, as well as an emphasis on the sites of writing instruction—courses across the curriculum and across a student's academic career. However, we do not hear, in this definition, about the programs that promote these notions.

This continuing focus on pedagogy rather than program administration may result from the conceptualization of WAC not as a field but as an initiative limited to the scope of a single campus. As Barbara Walvoord (1996) advocated in "The Future of WAC," if we are to see WAC as a reform movement, as Russell (2002) later described it, then it has been a decentralized movement, existing on individual campuses in response to local needs and contexts, with a "plethora of goals and philosophies" (Walvoord, 1996, p. 62). Martha Townsend (1994) emphasized this localized view of WAC in her entry in the *Encyclopedia of English Studies and Language Arts*, arguing, "No single method characterizes the movement, and wide variations occur in its practice" (p. 1299). The writing pedagogies WAC programs endorse tend to be consistent across campuses, but how WAC programs are shaped and structured is highly variable. This variability, we believe, has prevented a focus in the WAC literature on theorizing WAC program administration, for how does one theorize a process that is dependent on local needs, goals, and contexts?

Literature on WAC program administration thus tends to describe individual WAC programs and specific program elements, such as leading a faculty workshop or starting a writing fellows initiative. From each of these types of literature, new WAC directors are expected to adapt insights to their own institutional contexts. Examples of program profiles include edited collections such as Toby Fulwiler and Art Young's (1990) *Programs That Work*, which presents detailed descriptions of fourteen WAC programs across the United States, and Thaiss, Bräuer, Carlino, Ganobcsik-Williams, and Sinha's (2012) *Writing Programs Worldwide*, which offers descriptions of programs around the world. These profiles also include collections by faculty across disciplines within the same WAC program, such as Mary T. Segall and Robert A. Smart's (2005) *Direct from the Disciplines: Writing Across the Curriculum*, which recounts the development of the WAC program at Quinnipiac University from the perspectives of the program directors and disciplinary faculty who implemented WAC in their classrooms, and Jonathan Monroe's (2006) *Local Knowledges, Local Practices: Writing in the Disciplines at Cornell*, in which faculty from across disciplines describe approaches to writing pedagogy.

Literature providing advice to WAC directors is often based on seasoned WAC director experiences. One of the first of such guides was Susan McLeod's (1988a) *Strengthening Programs for Writing Across the Curriculum*, which includes chapters on moving beyond initial workshops, securing long-term funding, and evaluating the program. McLeod and Margot Soven's (1991) "What Do You Need to Start—and Sustain—a Writing-Across-the-Curriculum Program?" offers writing program administrators (WPAs) tasked with starting a WAC program advice on what to consider before accepting the role, such as time for planning and resources for both the program and the director, as well as steps to take for initiating the program, such as forming and working with a planning committee, bringing in an outside consultant, and building in assessment from the start. McLeod and Soven's (1992) *Writing Across the Curriculum: A Guide to Developing Programs* offers advice from WAC scholars and practitioners on such topics as getting a WAC program started, designing faculty development workshops, and creating WI requirements. McLeod et al.'s (2001) *WAC for the New Millennium* also offers advice from WAC scholars, and includes emerging areas not found in earlier WAC guides, such as the accountability movement, English as a Second Language (ESL) students, and electronic communication across the curriculum. The most recent guide is the INWAC "Statement of WAC Principles and Practices" (International Network of Writing-Across-the-Curriculum Programs, 2014), the lead author of which, Michelle Cox, is also one of the authors of the present book. This statement presents WAC principles, guidelines for program development, advice on topics such as leadership and assessment, and a comprehensive bibliography of resources. All of these texts offer nuts-and-bolts advice for building and developing WAC programs rooted in experience, knowledge of the field, and writing theory and research—but not theory on writing program administration.

Literature on WAC program administration has also focused on challenges to WAC programs and steps WAC directors may take so that their programs persist. In their afterword to *Programs That Work*, Young and Fulwiler (1990) described six "enemies" of WAC: (1) the appointment of WAC program leaders who are not full time or tenure track or do not have background in WAC; (2) the positioning of WAC programs in English departments in which the orthodoxy may work against WAC goals; (3) the difficulty of maintaining a cross-disciplinary enterprise such as WAC within the compartmentalized structure of a university; (4) the traditional reward system that values scholarship over teaching; (5) the tendency for universities to move toward large class sizes in which assessment depends on testing rather than writing; and (6) entrenched attitudes held by administrators, faculty, students, and the public toward writing that undermine the long-term institutional commitment needed to support a WAC program. Young and Fulwiler (1990) then pointed to the program descriptions included in their collection to argue that programs with "a more or less permanent structure whereby writing-across-the-curriculum advocacy is ever renewed and expanded" have a higher chance of survival (p. 294). In "WAC Program Vulnerability and What to Do about It," Townsend (2008) summarized the literature on threats to WAC programs, and then described the features of successful WAC programs at the institutional, classroom, and programmatic level, drawing from the literature, her own experience as a WAC program director, and her observations as a consultant. These features include strong faculty support, strong administrative support, ongoing faculty development, low student-to-instructor caps in WI courses, a well-informed program leader, and regular program assessment. The advice Townsend (2008) provided for achieving these features remains useful to WAC programs today. Notice, though, that the line of research in both lists above are still based in description rather than theory—describing challenges that WAC programs have faced and features of programs that have endured, but not analyzing the reasons behind the challenges or why these program features lead to longevity.

This focus on learning from the features of enduring WAC programs has also led to multiple surveys in WAC. In "Whither WAC?," Eric Miraglia and Susan McLeod (1997) compared survey data from 1987 and 1996 to describe features of WAC programs that have ended and those that have endured. They surveyed again the programs that had responded to their 1987 survey, and found that, of the 138 institutions that replied, a third reported that the WAC program had been discontinued (p. 47). In examining the survey responses, they determined that programs that endured had more faculty development components, had more curricular components, and engaged in more assessment than did the programs that ended (p. 54). They also pointed to the "strong and consistent program leadership" of the enduring programs (p. 55). A 2008 survey conducted by Thaiss and Porter (2010) led to further examination of the features of enduring programs. While this survey provided evidence of how widespread

WAC had become across the United States, with 64 percent of the responding US institutions of higher education reporting either having or planning to begin a program (p. 541), the survey also found that more than half the programs that were identified in McLeod and Shirley's (1988) survey no longer existed twenty years later. Thaiss and Porter (2010) speculated on WAC program sustainability and determined that, in longer-lasting WAC programs, the WAC directors were at higher academic ranks, directors reported to higher-level administrators, directors served in their leadership roles for longer periods of time, the WAC programs had strong connections to other services and offices (notably, a writing center and/or library), faculty development included a focus on the faculty workshop, and curricular elements included WI courses. Again, survey data have led to program features that WAC directors may emulate with the hope that the features themselves lead to program longevity.

In keeping with this trend of observing the features of enduring WAC programs, William Condon and Carol Rutz (2012) introduced a taxonomy for categorizing WAC programs according to their characteristics. Their work was partly motivated by the variability of WAC programs: "WAC as a phenomenon does not possess a single, identifiable structure; instead, it varies in its development and its manifestation from campus to campus" (p. 358). Despite this variability, Condon and Rutz (2012) felt it would be helpful for WAC programs to understand where they stood in relation to other WAC programs and what their next steps might be to strengthen the program. To develop their WAC program taxonomy, the authors led Conference on College Composition and Communication (CCCC) session participants in brainstorming WAC program benchmarks, and then further developed these benchmarks based on their own experiences as WAC program directors and as consultants and on what they observed in the WAC literature. The four program types they identified—foundational, established, integrated, and institutional change agent—differ with respect to their primary goals, funding, structure, and degree of integration into the university (Condon & Rutz, 2012, pp. 362–63). Their taxonomy can be used as a practical tool for developing WAC programs, reflecting on program goals, providing cross-institutional comparisons, and developing a grand narrative of program progress and success. However, like the earlier literature on enduring programs, Condon and Rutz (2012) did not attempt to explain the underlying reasons why WAC programs at higher levels in this taxonomy outlast programs at the lower levels.

The literature we've discussed thus far has been largely descriptive—describing WAC programs, steps WAC directors have taken to develop their programs, and features of WAC programs that have ended and those that endure. This kind of descriptive work is a necessary step in any field but stops short of providing a theoretical framework that can help us understand why programs are shaped in certain ways, why directors take particular steps to develop their programs, why challenges to WAC exist, and why specific features of WAC programs lead to program endurance. Understanding the "why" (theory) can help WAC directors make sense of the "what" (program descriptions) and the "how" (strategies for creating programs that will endure). Without this theoretical framework, WAC directors are left to mimic program elements of other programs and use a trial-and-error approach to program development.

A departure from this descriptive work is Walvoord's "The Future of WAC" (1996), which we see as the first attempt to theorize the vulnerability and endurance of WAC programs. Walvoord drew on social movement theory to analyze WAC's successes and challenges and develop approaches for WAC to persist not only as a movement on individual campuses, but also as a national movement. Drawing on the work of sociologist Benford (1992), she defined a *movement* as a "collective attempt to promote or resist change in a society or group" (cited in Walvoord, 1996, p. 58), and, relying on Benford and an essay by sociologists McAdam, McCarthy, and Zald (1988), she described concepts important to organizations that promote a social movement that may be applied to WAC. Walvoord used social movement theory to analyze the development of the field of WAC and understand why WAC programs and the field at large have been vulnerable to such a wide range of challenges. In attempting to understand the variability of WAC programs, for instance, Walvoord (1996) argued that WAC has been largely decentralized, realized through the development of WAC programs on individual campuses and spread through conferences and a group of "traveling workshop leaders" (p. 61), but never becoming a national movement through a national WAC organization—a fact that remains true at the time of this writing. Walvoord (1996) saw this decentralization as giving individual WAC programs strength, as it allows them to form their own goals in relation to their individual contexts, but also as leaving them "vulnerable to cooptation, becoming special interest groups, settling for narrow goals and limited visions, or simply being wiped out by the next budget crunch or the next change of deans" (p. 62). Indeed, the loss of so many WAC programs as indicated by Thaiss and Porter's (2010) survey is evidence of this continuing vulnerability.

An important concept from social movement theory that Walvoord (1996) used is the distinction between micro-level actions (such as "changing personal behavior") and macro-level actions (such as "changing structures and organizations") (p. 60). For instance, she argued that faculty workshops, long the "backbone of the WAC movement," are effective at the micro level, in that they "generate high energy and enthusiasm" for teaching writing among those who attend (p. 63), but do not lead to changes at the macro level, as they do not affect the wider campus culture or university structures. These workshops and conversion of individual faculty are the very features that Russell (2002) credited with the longevity of WAC in the United States. In other words, Walvoord's (1996) analysis leads to insights that directly oppose long-held beliefs in the field. She then turned her attention to the future of WAC and drew on strategies used by social movements to suggest approaches WAC directors could use to strengthen their programs, including macro-level moves such as coming to a deeper understanding of the wider campus and societal contexts within which WAC programs live, connecting to other institutional and national movements, and connecting to university missions and accrediting bodies' standards.

We see McLeod and colleagues' (2001) *WAC for the New Millennium* as a response to Walvoord (1996), in that the editors take up some of the strategies that Walvoord suggested. Walvoord urged WAC directors to better understand the challenges facing WAC from beyond our campuses, the macro-level landscape of higher education. In "Writing Across the Curriculum in a Time of Change," their introduction to *WAC for the New Millennium*, McLeod and Miraglia (2001) traced threats to higher education "that could spell trouble for WAC programs" such as shifting priorities for state budgets, attacks on the tenure structure, increased use of contingent labor, and a loss of morale among faculty (p. 1). Walvoord (1996) urged WAC directors to connect to wider trends in higher education and collaborate with other offices and organizations on campus, which she described as macro-level strategies. McLeod et al. (2001) developed their collection focused on such trends and organizations (e.g., assessment, technology, service learning, learning communities, changing student demographics, and writing centers). However, while McLeod and colleagues drew on strategies suggested by Walvoord, they did not take up the theoretical work she began or the implications of her work for the field of WAC. Interestingly, while Walvoord encouraged WAC to focus more on strategies for program administration, McLeod and Miraglia's (2001) introduction to *WAC for the New Millennium* returned the focus to pedagogy; a final point they made is that "one of the strengths of the WAC movement has been its work at the [local] level, with individual teachers, on their pedagogical practice, in collaborative workshop settings" (p. 21). Indeed, though Walvoord's article has been widely cited, we do not see scholars taking on her larger claims or more pointed insights about WAC.

Our book, too, is a continuation of Walvoord's germinal work. We build on her goal of drawing on theory to better understand WAC program development within the complex and dynamic contexts of higher education. Like Walvoord, we aim for our work to be both theoretical and practical by providing WAC directors with strategies for developing WAC programs that endure. Like Walvoord, we keep our focus on program administration rather than pedagogy. As WAC program directors, we understand and value the power of WAC pedagogy on faculty, but we believe that WAC directors need to do more than train individual faculty members to transform a campus culture so they can create lasting change. Like Walvoord, we see the sustainability of individual WAC programs as connected to the sustainability of the field of WAC, and, in the final chapter of our book, we take up Walvoord's question about the impact of decentralization on the field. However, departing from Walvoord, we find social movement theory inadequate as a framework with which to fully illuminate how WAC directors can develop transformational and sustainable programs. While it provided her with a useful lens for considering the vulnerability and suggesting strategies, social movement theory cannot provide WAC directors with a comprehensive theoretical framework, methodology, and set of strategies for launching, revitalizing, and reviving WAC programs, which the whole systems approach we develop in this book does.

An Overview of Our Theoretical Framework

We offer the whole systems approach for transformational change in order to provide a theoretical framework, a methodology, and a set of principles, strategies, and tactics for making change to campus cultures of writing and for building programs that are integrated, highly visible, and sustainable. Our approach brings together insights from complexity, systems, social network, resilience, and sustainable development theories. *Complexity theory*, which offers an umbrella framework, provides WAC directors a way to navigate large institutions with many moving parts and to build programs that can grow and adapt as the institution evolves (Norberg & Cumming, 2008; Taylor, 2002). Complexity theory thus compels WAC directors to think at both the micro and macro (institutional) levels if they want to build sustainable programs. Thinking at the institutional level about the way systems shape behaviors is the focus of *systems theory*, which is a type of complexity theory (Banathy, 1992; Checkland, 1981; Senge, 1990). Systems theory helps program directors understand how to integrate new university initiatives into the institutional fabric by identifying points of leverage within the system that will make the most enduring change, rather than only tinkering with parts at the micro level. Another way of thinking about systems is in terms of networks with nodes and hubs that WAC directors need to map to ensure their program is well connected with respect to location and influence. *Social network theory*—which, like systems theory, is a subset of complexity theory—provides a methodology for mapping lines of communication in complex organizations, offering a visual map of the primary conduits through which information passes and thereby revealing efficient pathways and strategies for maximizing effective communication in complex networks. This framework also helps us to ensure WAC programs are hubs and not just nodes within the network (Cross, 2014; Merrill, Caldwell, Rockoff, Gebbie, Carley, & Bakken, 2008). *Resilience theory*, which derives from systems theory, helps us understand the nature of change in systems and the need for constant monitoring, intervention, adaptation, and transformation in order to maintain balance and longevity. In both systems and resilience theories, the emphasis is on making change at higher scales beyond just individual instructors or classes. *Sustainable development theory*—another outgrowth of theories of complexity—provides WAC directors with strategies for program longevity and tools (in the form of indicators and feedback loops) for assessing and improving WAC programs (Galin, 2010; Johnson, 2002; Meadows, 1998).

It is important to note that we are not the first to turn to theories emerging from the ecological sciences to understand writing programs. In *Ecologies of Writing Programs,* Mary Jo Reiff, Anis Bawarshi, Michelle Ballif, and Christian Weisser (2015a, p. 3) borrowed the concept of the "ecological model of writing" from Marilyn Cooper (1986) to discuss the interconnections among writers and texts and to imagine writing as part of a "network, a system, a web—an ecology." While these works invoke this theory as a heuristic, we dig into systems and sustainability theories to build an entire theoretical framework, incorporating a comprehensive set of principles, strategies, and tactics for developing, revitalizing, and sustaining WAC programs. While prior authors have invoked the metaphors of system, we provide a methodology for transforming the system.

Outline of the Book

In the first third of this book, we explain our theoretical framework. In Chapter 2, we bring together insights from complexity theory and the other theories we mention above, all of which depend on principles of complexity. Within the context of these theories, we outline a set of principles that WAC directors can use as a foundation for building sustainable programs. The whole systems principles form the core of sustainable WAC programs, but, in order to help WAC directors move from theory to practice, in Chapter 3, we outline fifteen strategies for building WAC programs. These strategies provide WAC directors with guides for long-term strategic actions. The strategies are organized in the stages of our methodology—a process for program building that is reflected in the organization of the book. The methodology helps WAC directors put the whole systems principles and strategies into practice through a four-part process that encompasses *understanding*, *planning*, *developing*, and *leading*. In Chapter 3, we describe this methodology in detail and connect it to our theoretical framework. The methodology is meant as a tool and not a lockstep process that all WAC directors must follow, and the entire process is recursive in nature.

Chapters 4 through 7 each focus on a stage in the four-part methodology. We open each chapter with WAC program vignettes that allow us to talk in concrete ways about our principles and strategies. The vignettes are from a variety of types of institutions and kinds of WAC programs, and, although our principles and strategies can inform a sustainable approach to WAC program building at any institution, we recognize that the tactics used by WAC directors to work toward those principles and strategies will be context specific. To that end, in Chapters 4–7, we present a variety of short-term, context-specific tactics for meeting the goals of the more generalized whole systems strategies and principles. Throughout these chapters, we also refer to some of our own experiences as WAC program directors to illustrate our points. Michelle launched a WAC program at Bridgewater State University in 2007, which she directed until 2012. She is currently building a writing and speaking program for international graduate and professional students at Cornell University. Jeff initiated Florida Atlantic University's WAC program starting in 2004 after developing the University Center for Excellence in Writing and has directed both since their inception. Dan was hired in 2004 to develop a WAC program at California State University, Sacramento, which he led until 2015. He currently directs the first-year composition program at University of California, Davis. We end Chapter 7 reflecting on the recursivity of the whole systems approach, emphasizing the importance of revisiting each stage of the process for sustaining WAC programs in the context of complex institutional systems that tend toward stagnation.

In Chapter 8, we conclude by reflecting on the significance of our whole systems approach for individual WAC programs and the field of WAC. This chapter includes a discussion of two institutions that have started using our theoretical framework as they launch WAC programs, future directions for developing our framework, and implications of our framework for WAC scholarship. We end Chapter 8, and this book, by using our framework as a lens to analyze how the field of WAC is organized and discuss implications for the field's sustainability.

How to Utilize This Book

Ideally, readers would draw from this book before a WAC program is even started, as the approach we introduce would influence decisions made related to the hiring of the WAC leader, how the WAC leader position is structured, how the program is positioned within the university system, and how the program is rolled out and developed. However, we realize that readers will come to this book at different points in their WAC programs' development and have a range of local constraints. While we advocate that you engage in each stage of our methodology, our approach may also be used flexibly, as a heuristic, with specific stages and strategies drawn on as appropriate. Too often, WAC directors are hired to launch and develop a program quickly, leading them to scramble to get a program off the ground and produce immediate results. We hope this book presents a persuasive argument for slowing down the launching and development process. It is possible to get a program off the ground quickly, but these quick-start initiatives can often lead to programs that fall apart quickly. Once a WAC program is tried and fails, it is difficult to start one again, as just the term *WAC* will leave a bad taste in people's mouths. If a university is investing resources in starting a WAC program, it is well worth the time and effort to roll it out slowly and strategically, using the approach we describe here, as it would lead to more sustainable and substantial change.

We developed this book with four target audiences in mind: WAC program leaders, WAC scholars (or scholars in training), administrators seeking to launch or otherwise support a WAC program, and leaders of other kinds of higher education programs that seek to make transformative and enduring change. We imagine each of these audiences using this book in slightly different ways.

For WAC program leaders, who often have limited time to dedicate to reading scholarship, we imagine that the overview of the methodology and strategies for program development described in Chapter 3 would be of key interest. We imagine that these readers will next move back to Chapter 2 to gain fuller understanding of the theories that undergird the whole systems approach, and then forward to Chapters 4–7, focusing on the chapters that correspond to their campus's current point of program development. We also hope that the book, as a whole, allows these program leaders to better communicate to administrators the resources needed to launch, develop, and sustain a WAC program, with one of the key resources being time. We see our book as equally valuable to WAC program leaders new to WAC, program leaders launching new WAC programs, and program leaders who are revitalizing existing programs. However, we do not spend time discussing the writing pedagogies promoted by WAC, as many other resources do this well (see, e.g., Bean, 2011; Gottschalk & Hjortshoj, 2004; Young, 2006).

For WAC scholars, we imagine that the overall theoretical framework presented in Chapter 2 and operationalized in the rest of the book will be of the most interest, as this framework is substantially different from anything that has preceded it. As we do here, many WAC and writing scholars have turned to theories that originated outside of writing studies. As we mentioned above, Walvoord (1996) turned to social movement theory, and Cooper (1986) and Reiff et al. (2015b) drew on theories related to networks and ecologies in their work. Condon and Rutz (2012) invoked quantum mechanics, particularly the concept of the particle and the wave to outline the characteristics of WAC programs of various types and levels of maturity. However, as we explained above, these scholars tend to use these theories as heuristics or metaphors, but do not dig more deeply into the theories or use them to create a theoretical framework and praxis, as we do in this book. Further, our focus on theorizing program administration rather than writing pedagogy marks a departure in the WAC literature that we think will be of interest to WAC scholars. We also see Chapter 8 as being germane to WAC scholars because here we use our theoretical framework to analyze the sustainability of WAC as a field and consider its future. We imagine that seasoned scholars and those newer to writing studies will be interested in this framework, and thus see our book as contributing to graduate courses in composition studies.

For administrators seeking to launch or otherwise support a WAC program, we believe that the book's cross-disciplinary and practical approach will hold much appeal. We feel that the many vignettes by WAC directors in different programmatic and institutional contexts woven throughout the book will provide concrete examples of programmatic change that can be generalized to other institutional contexts. The overviews of our methodology and strategies in Chapter 3 will provide an administrator with a snapshot of the overall process of WAC program development and steps to take at different points in the process. Indeed, while writing this chapter, we imagined it being distributed to a university-wide writing committee, as well as upper administration stakeholders.

While our book focuses on WAC programs, the theoretical approach, principles, methodology, and strategies will also be informative to university leaders seeking to launch and sustain other kinds of university-wide initiatives. All of these programs exist within the same kinds of curricular ecologies, face the same kinds of challenges, and may use the same kinds of methods, strategies, and tactics to develop initiatives that create real change that endures. Indeed, other initiatives such as service learning programs (see Jolliffe, 2001), quantitative literacy programs (see Hillyard, 2012), undergraduate research programs (Chamely-Wiik, Dunn, Heydet-Kirsch, Holman, Meeroff, & Peluso, 2014), and graduate writing support programs (see Caplan & Cox, 2016;

Simpson, Clemens, Killingsworth, & Ford, 2015) have already drawn inspiration from WAC. The whole systems approach we develop here may provide both inspiration and a framework that leads to enduring change.

CHAPTER TWO

The Whole Systems Framework for Launching and Developing WAC Programs: Theories and Principles

Most new WAC directors start by examining programs and practices that other universities have implemented as a way to choose a model that might suit their own institutions. Perhaps they attend the WAC Special Interest Group meeting at a Conference on College Composition and Communication (CCCC), led by the board of consultants of INWAC, to get practical advice about getting started. They may read a few articles in the field to see what others have said about starting WAC programs. Or they may browse through the description of model programs on the WAC Clearinghouse (see https://wac.colostate.edu/) to find ideas for curricular initiatives or faculty development projects. This process is helpful as it provides a sense of current work in the field and suggests possible options for program development. However, the primary problems with this approach are that it looks outward, away from the institution, rather than inward to understand existing or previously existing WAC initiatives; it tends to focus primarily on teaching practices and faculty development rather than a systematic process for integrating curricular change at a given institution; it tends to focus on discrete WAC initiatives like writing fellows programs, WID, and writing retreats rather than starting with a more integrated model in mind; and it focuses on program initiation but not necessarily sustainability. To address these problems, we need a theoretical model that can build from context and represent the complexity of large-scale reform. This model also needs to be able to provide WAC directors and committees guidance on evaluating needs, setting goals, planning programs, implementing projects, assessing initiatives, and tracking sustainability.

To create such a theoretical model, we turned to whole systems theories: theories that provide tools for describing rich and dynamic systems, as well as tools for creating and assessing change introduced to a system. *Complexity theory*, first used in computational and scientific fields to describe complex phenomena, provides an umbrella framework for our approach and offers ways to study interactions among diverse groups of actors and organizations within a complex adaptive system. As scholars began to extend such analyses to social networks like corporations and other social systems, they desired theoretical frameworks that were not just descriptive, but also predictive and focused on intervention. *Systems theory* focuses primarily at the macro level, looking for leverage points within the system to make small changes that lead to significant impacts. Systems theory also involves mapping representations of the system to better understand the relationships that govern them. To focus more on the micro level, we also draw on *social network theory* (organizational network analysis in particular), which seeks information at the micro level to reveal the network of communication among actors within a system. Social network theory is a derivative of systems thinking that maps communication pathways along a network of nodes in order to identify individuals who serve as conduits and/ or bottlenecks. These three theories primarily offer approaches for describing, visualizing, and analyzing a complex system—critical information for WAC directors. But WAC programs also are interested in introducing change into a system—change in how writing is valued, understood, integrated into the curriculum, and taught. The next two theories build on these strategies and add opportunities to create and track change. To study how adaptive complex systems handle change, we turn to resilience theory, and to track the long-term viability of WAC programs, we turn to sustainable development theory. *Resilience theory* helps us understand how systems handle stresses yet maintain a relatively stable state. Conversely, it helps us understand how even small changes can lead to crossing a critical threshold that may result in an alternative, undesirable state. Resilience is the mechanism that enables a program to adapt to change. *Sustainable development theory* provides a practical whole systems approach for introducing transformational change into a complex system by grounding program development in discrete projects that work through cycles of planning, doing, checking, and improving using sustainability indicators (SIs) to monitor progress.

In this chapter, we explore each of these theories in turn and then introduce ten principles that we derive from the theories collectively. All of the principles should be considered when implementing university-wide curricular reform such as a WAC program. We summarize the interconnections between the theories and our principles to close the chapter.

Complexity Theory

Over the last couple of decades, complex systems theory has been applied outside of the computational and scientific environments from which it emerged, and shifted to social, cultural, and corporate contexts. When scientists talk about adaptive complex systems, they often refer to ecosystems or examples such as flocking birds that make minute adjustments in their own flight in relationship only to the birds immediately next to them. These decentralized decisions among individual birds are driven by feedback loops that either magnify a small action across the system or keep it in check. A flock of starlings, for example, can appear in such numbers that they seem to fill the sky as a swarming tornado of movement. As one watches these large groups, one sees how the micro relationships among individuals can result in a flowing mass that sometimes splinters off but often forms and re-forms amoebic shapes in the sky. Complex systems science works to understand the emergence of coordinated macro behaviors, how local rule-following activity leads to these behaviors, how the system remains identifiable as a distinct system, and how it maintains its relative internal stability.

The US educational system is also a complex adaptive system with a wide range of participants, or actors, and multiple layers of interaction among individual actors and organizations. Furthermore, the behaviors of these actors can adapt over time. These adaptive behaviors introduce the potential for actors within the system to self-organize and reduce the need for centralized control, as well as integrate new functions, practices, and actors as the system adapts. Although the Department of Education is the head of the US educational system, diverse organizations emerge from the bottom up as individuals who form into groups within the system interact, synchronize, and form patterns (Leon, 2014). Hence, a governing organization is not necessarily defined as a central controller of the system because, like the human brain, it does not "rigorously manage or dictate low-level inter-actions," but, instead, "interacts with low-level components as parts of collective pattern-forming processes from which macro-scopic phenomena like cognition emerge" (J. Norman, personal communication, September 2, 2015). Similarly, teachers in the classroom interacting with students are not directly managed by the US Department of Education. Rather, they follow relatively simple sets of rules that are discernible and can occasionally lead to coordinated self-organizing behaviors that introduce change into the educational system from the ground up, but which func-tion within a relatively stable system.

Some scholars have argued that universities themselves are complex systems with multiple levels of stakeholders (students, faculty, administrators, board members) "making many decisions, each with varying interests, interacting with one another and af-fecting one another, forming causal loops and cascading effects . . . differential selection, contagion, competition, cooperation" (J. Norman, personal communication, September 2, 2015). This list represents the typical patterns of behavior in self-organizing systems. For the purposes of this chapter, these behaviors are also important for establishing and sustaining WAC programs.

While a WAC program cannot be understood as a complex system itself, it might lead to adaptive behaviors within the system that both increase its complexity and contribute to col-lective pattern-forming processes of the larger complex system. The greater the diversity and connectivity of the individuals at the lowest levels of the system, the more complex the system becomes and the more likely it is that adaptive behaviors will be introduced. Perhaps this is the reason WAC programs that form and grow as grassroots initiatives tend to gain momentum more quickly, face less resistance, and are therefore more likely to become highly integrated into the university and consequently more successful. When programs are determined and micro-managed from above, there tends to be less of a critical mass of like-minded individuals influencing others to participate, helping the program compete with other university initiatives, fostering greater cooperation, and increasing faculty interactions. A strong WAC program would cultivate all of these types of interactions within the university system.

Such highly connected systems are typically modeled by researchers as "networks that can capture and quantify this information about the relationships between the elements" (Leon, 2014). Later, we discuss how organizational network mapping can help us better understand WAC programs within the larger university system and how we can better track growth and indicators of success and distress. Before doing so, however, we first introduce a few additional aspects of adaptive complex systems that can help us track potential program stresses as well as possible program failure: *feedback loops* and *nonlinearity*.

If we imagine the university as a kind of social ecosystem, we can better understand how adding stresses within the system can lead to behavioral adaptations until the stresses become too great and can lead to program failure. Consider a natural ecosystem to which we introduce an industrial zone that is consuming natural resources, altering the environment, and emitting pollution. One of the key features of an adaptive system is that it is typically driven by feedback loops that propagate through the system. There are two basic kinds of feedback loops: positive and negative.

A positive feedback loop is not, as one might think, "good" per se. Rather, it is a self-amplifying loop that has no mechanisms for adaptation or control (Johnson, 2002). A hurricane is an excellent example of a complex system that is driven by a positive feedback loop: as the towering clouds of a low-pressure system begin to organize and start rotating, more warm air is sucked up off the warm ocean waters. As that moist warm air continues to build in the cooler upper atmosphere, the circulation becomes more defined. As long as conditions remain favorable, the energy feeds on itself until the hurricane reaches its full strength. The cycle can be broken when the storm hits land, reaches cooler waters, or encounters shearing forces in the upper atmosphere, but these cycle-breakers are external to the system and cannot be managed to control it.

In contrast, a negative feedback loop works by self-regulating rather than "amplifying its own signal" (Johnson, 2002, p. 196). For example, a cooling system can test the temperature at the location of the thermostat and adjust its functioning if there is a change in the ambient air temperature. The thermostat intervenes to keep a system from spiraling out of control. At each test interval, the thermostat can change its state. It can either leave the air on, turn it off, or shift to heating the air. Its ability to test and respond makes this negative feedback loop system adaptable.

WAC programs function with feedback loops as well. Examples of positive feedback loops in WAC programs can be represented by belief systems that sustain poor writing support. Faculty notice that student writing is not strong and complain that "students cannot write a coherent sentence." They assert that someone should have taught students grammar before the student arrived in their classes, yet they also contend that it is not their jobs to help students address these concerns. There are at least two positive feedback loops in action here. Faculty equate good writing with good grammar rather than seeing writing as a fundamental process in content acquisition and critical thinking. And faculty perpetuate the problem by blaming others for not "doing their job" to train students while simultaneously asserting that it is not their responsibility to address. There is no assessment of the problem in this scenario because faculty often do not realize that grammar issues have a range of causes, from student inattentiveness, to divided attention when dealing with complex material, to a passing-the-buck mentality. Without effective pedagogical conversations, faculty workshops, syllabus and assignment reviews, or some other form of regulating (negative) input, faculty will continue to perpetuate the poor writing scenario even as they continually point it out.

Nonlinearity is the final characteristic that we draw on from complex adaptive systems, and it is so important to this area of theory that complexity science is defined as "the study of nonlinear dynamic systems" (Levy, 2000). Cause and effect are not obviously related in nonlinear systems because of the interactions of a large number of actors, components, and subsystems. Further-more, this wide array of actors means that control is distributed across the system. Behaviors that might seem random may have cumulative or ripple effects that could manifest in unexpected ways across the system. We can understand nonlinearity best by considering what happens when stressors enter the system. For example, what happens when budgets are reduced, negative feedback loops fail, or other university-wide curricular reform projects are introduced that compete with WAC programs for resources? Given the abilities of elements and the system to adapt, the impact of any given stressor may be negligible at first. So we may overlook the concern or behaviors may shift slightly to minimize its impact. At some point, however, the system will lose its ability to adapt, its resilience, and reach a "critical tipping point with some small additional input being able to propagate through the system, creating a phase transition" as the system collapses (Leon, 2014).

Consider a WAC initiative that is designed to shift the culture of writing from a single department to the university at large. The program emerges from a mutual agreement among faculty that student writing is not as strong as it should be at the insti-tution. Faculty volunteer to attend workshops designed to help them better manage writing assignments in their courses. A small stipend encourages some who might not participate otherwise. The exchange of ideas generates interest and excitement. Faculty ask for follow-up workshops, and the WAC director institutes a faculty fellows program to encourage faculty to share what they have learned with their colleagues in their departments. A set of criteria is adopted for WAC courses across the university. A writing center is redesigned to shift its focus from exclusively supporting first-year writing to supporting the additional writing now occurring across the university. Over time, departments are approached to examine how well their curriculum serves their stu-dents. Each participating department develops a systematic plan to address gaps in their curriculum to better serve their students.

These processes continue for a couple years with a high de-gree of energy and interaction among faculty. But, at some point, there is a serious economic recession and political decisions are made at the state level to reduce funding for state universities.

In addition, a new quality enhancement program is initiated at the university that is focused on research. While writing is implicated in some research practices, that initiative has more to do with pairing faculty with students to foster original research. Faculty are increasingly being asked to do more with students, and energy and resources for the WAC program begin to wane. WAC committee members begin cycling off, but no new members are recruited to replace them. Since no review process was implemented to ensure syllabi meet WAC criteria, courses slowly change and are no longer WAC compliant.

In such a system, we can see that the number of lower-level interactions among actors is falling and that stressors in multiple places are impacting the WAC cultural environment. At some point, the system reaches that critical tipping point at which adaptation can no longer keep up with the pace of change. The WAC program slides into stasis, or, worse, is let go to reallocate its funds. Thus, as Leon (2014) explained, "complex systems can exhibit both extraordinary robustness and extraordinary fragility." This fragility compels us to establish indicators within the system to track its resilience to adapt to stressors, maintain self-organizing practices, and increase the capacity for learning and adaptation, as we will explain when we discuss sustainable development theory within the context of resilience thinking.

Systems Theory

Systems theory emerged in the 1940s in the fields of biology and engineering as a method for understanding the complexities of natural and engineered systems in ways that the reductionist and fragmented approach of classical science could not adequately address. Systems theory encourages us to approach complex natural and human systems by focusing on patterns of relationships and by "using the concept of wholeness to order our thoughts" (Checkland, 1981, p. 4). Bela Banathy (1992) argued, "Considering a part out of the context of the total system, dealing with one thing at a time, isolating variables, and dividing up the system are some of the ways of violating the wholeness of the system" (p. 93). Systems theory encourages us to focus on complex interactions and the ways the different components of a system form an integrated whole.

Originally, systems theory was used as a way to think about what Peter Checkland (1981, pp. 154–55) referred to as "structured problems" in natural or engineered systems and what the literature in systems thinking calls "hard systems." More recently, systems theory has been adapted for "unstructured problems" in "soft systems": social systems like universities with human actors and specific social contexts (see, for example Dan's use of system theory to analyze challenges to a campus writing program [Melzer, 2013]). Checkland and Banathy emphasized that soft systems "cannot be reduced to a method (human activity systems are too complex and situated) but rather a set of methodological principles" (Checkland, 1981, p. 162). Systems theory, then, can be thought of as a methodology: a framework to analyze and transform systems.

This systems theory framework involves a recursive process that begins with actors in the system engaging in a discussion of relationships among system structures and processes in order to paint a rich picture of the system. These actors also create a conceptual model that defines their ideal of the system, and the ideal is compared with the structures, processes, and results of the actual system. Other possible models are then considered, including the possible benefits and restraints of these alternative models. A key part of the process is looking at underlying structures and finding the points in the system that will provide the most leverage for change. This focus requires moving beyond "parochial boundaries" (e.g., in the case of a university, individual courses, departments, and colleges) and finding the points of leverage where "actions and changes in structures can lead to significant, enduring improvements" across the system (Senge, 1990, p. 114).

Although systems theory focuses on the wholeness of systems, Banathy (1973) felt that large, open, and complex systems like schools have a natural tendency toward independence, and that this tendency "moves the system's components toward progressive segregation and isolation and eventually toward the dissolution or termination of the system" (p. 24). Understanding relationships among components of the system is key to a systems view, but, as Banathy (1973) pointed out, all too often relationships at educational institutions can become "rigid and static" (p. 29). Perpetual change is part of any system, and routine and rigidity inevitably lead to problems. A systems thinker would argue that looking at the whole of the system is the most effective way to work against this isolation and rigidity, rather than merely "tinkering with parts" (Banathy, 1992, p. 8).

A WAC director applying a systems approach might begin by focusing not on an individual course, department, or writing requirement, but, rather, by getting a sense of writing across the university, from first-year students to graduating seniors. Creating a rich picture of writing on campus would require gathering stakeholders from across the system, possibly in the form of a WAC committee or advisory board. The stakeholders would consider their ideal goals for writing on campus, and create alternative models of the system, looking for strong points of leverage for making change. Typically, points of leverage are highly connected places in the system where even a small change might have significant ripple effects for the entire system (e.g., changing from a timed test to a portfolio for a graduation writing requirement). These ripple effects are what Senge (1990, pp. 79–81) referred to as "reinforcing processes," whereby a single intervention can have a snowballing effect on students, faculty, and the campus culture of writing.

Although Checkland (1981) argued that systems theory is "intrinsically concerned with conflict and change" (p. 251) and that the use of the methodology can be "emancipatory for the actors concerned" (p. 283), the current evolution of systems thinking—*critical systems thinking* (CST)—makes emancipation and the exposure of inequalities and conflicts an explicit goal. While a goal of systems theory is a balanced system, CST works toward liberation rather than equilibrium. Critical systems theorists Robert Flood (1990) and Michael Jackson (1985) drew on the theories of Michel Foucault, with his focus on how power determines what counts for knowledge in social systems, to argue for a critical systems approach that focuses on "recognition of subjugation" and "the bringing about of . . . liberation" (Flood, 1990, p. 51). Flood felt that, historically, in systems thinking, the ideological is too often not acknowledged. Conversely, with CST, "the ideology is declared at the outset" (Flood, 1990, p. 69). The CST approach includes critical awareness, exposing dominant voices, and freedom from restrictive power relations (Flood & Romm, 1996; Midgley, 1996). A WAC director applying a CST approach would be especially focused on exposing the ideologies that underlie the way writing is taught on campus. For example, a campus writing program that emphasizes timed testing and remediation may be oppressive to multilingual students and students from disadvantaged socioeconomic backgrounds. The feedback loops that might reinforce this ideology—students feeling stigmatized, instructors viewing students as deficient, the focus on writing as product rather than process—will further reinforce an oppressive ideology that will inform the entire system. A WAC director using a CST approach would ask the stakeholders to think critically about the ideologies that inform the campus writing program and consider alternative ideologies that avoid discriminating against specific groups of students. Because systems theory best helps us look at the larger organizational structures of an overall system rather than focusing on its individual parts, we turn to social network theory, and, more specifically, organizational network analysis, to discuss the specific network of human relations that constitute an institution of higher learning and the WAC program's positioning within that network.

Social Network Theory and Organizational Network Analysis

Social network theory originated as a way to understand how ties among individuals form and impact social networks, beliefs, and behaviors. Unlike the sociological theories that preceded it, social network theory prioritizes the "relationships and ties with other actors within the network" rather than attributes of individual actors—"whether they are friendly or unfriendly, smart or dumb, etc." (Cragun & Cragun, 2006, p. 82). While antecedents to the theory have been attributed to the social scientist Jacob Levy Moreno in the 1920s and the social anthropologist John A. Barnes in the 1950s (Knoke, 2009), the model didn't begin to become theoretically rigorous until the 1960s with Stanley Milgram's (1967) article "The Small World Problem," in which he argued that the average path length for social networks in the United States is six degrees, and Mark Granovetter's (1973) "The Strength of Weak Ties," which shifted the focus on network models from strong ties (actors in a network with close and recurring relationships) to weak ties (less-connected actors). Social network theory/analysis considers a group of people (e.g., faculty and staff) as an interconnected system of nodes (each individual as members of the university community) with a wide range of ties, or links, to others. Albert-László Barabási (2002) argued that interactivity with network hubs is key for innovative programs (such as WAC) since, in complex networks, failures predominantly affect the smallest nodes first. Barabási also pointed out that there is a critical threshold (i.e., the tipping point) at which the number of links an innovation connects to begins to increase exponentially, and, correspondingly, if an innovation fails to reach a threshold number of nodes, it is bound to fail. Finding points of interactivity in the university system is also key because of the network analysis concept of *preferential attachment*: actors are more likely to link to nodes that are already well connected and popular than to nodes that are more isolated.

These nodes and hubs—the connections among individuals—can be visually mapped to trace and examine the lines of communication, patterns of interaction, and distribution of knowledge within that system. The methodologies that emerge from this theory are collectively called *organizational network analysis* (ONA). These systematic methodologies are typically complex, scientifically validated techniques using elaborate mapping software that reveal a wide range of data-driven results. The typical methodology for ONA is to develop a survey instrument to which every member of the targeted group responds in order to uncover a specific set of organizational patterns within the group. Once the data are collected, the actors are visually mapped as a set of nodes in a three-dimensional network, with links between actors represented as lines connecting individuals, subsets, and larger groups. An effective example of a visual map of relationships is presented in Cross's (2014) study of executives in a division of a large petroleum organization. We are all familiar with the typical organizational charts that illustrate executive hierarchies; however, information rarely moves along those formal paths in predictable ways. Figure 2.1, originally created by Cross (2014), demonstrates how differently information moves through the informal communications networks of this organization than one might expect from the formal hierarchical structure. Notice that there are several mid-level executives who are fundamental to information flow. Cole, in particular, becomes an important conduit through whom the entire production team communicates with the rest of the organization. Furthermore, one can note easily how peripheral the senior executive (Jones) is to the information network, which often occurs as executives move up in an administrative hierarchy. Finally, such an analysis demonstrates how far removed the production team had become from the rest of the network. Cross (2014) explained that, in this particular example, this team had been physically moved to another floor in the building a few months prior to the study, which led to significantly less informal interactions and a significantly reduced information flow. ONA survey studies can help predict such

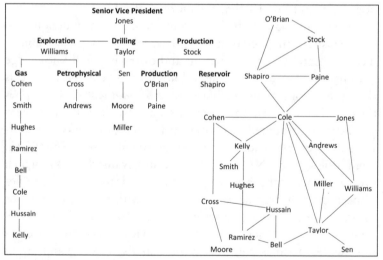

FIGURE 2.1. *Striking contrast between the group's formal and informal structure. From "What Is ONA? Introduction to Organizational Network Analysis" by R. Cross, 2014. Reprinted with permission.*

information gaps and enable organizations to address them by asking questions like to whom one turns for information to get one's job done or how frequently one turns to the people listed.

WAC directors are not likely to use the full ONA survey process, as a sole director could not feasibly survey all stakeholders at a university. As with the other theoretical frameworks from which we draw, we do not expect WAC leaders to conduct scientific studies of university culture before starting a WAC program. However, ONA provides a sense of what WAC directors should look for and a methodology that they can draw from to study the networks of relationships at their institutions and the emergent effects that arise from them. ONA enables directors to visualize and navigate the network of actors as nodes in the university system and identify points of leverage within that network of relationships to facilitate institutional changes. We discuss strategies for approaching this process in Chapter 4, including different types of maps that can be used to reach different goals. Mapping the system and the interactions of its actors is the easiest way to focus on points of high interactivity and leverage to shift the university culture.

Resilience Thinking

We move from theories focused on understanding how complex systems operate—network-based theories concerning complexity, systems, and social network analysis—to theories focused on how complex adaptive systems handle change: resilience theory and sustainable development theory. Resilience thinking derives from systems theory, but also provides the bridge to sustainable development. It studies how adaptive complex systems respond to and manage change, whereas sustainable development theory can be used to track the long-term viability of WAC programs. Resilience thinking, first introduced by Holling (1973), refers to "the capacity of ecosystems to handle challenges or changes to the system while maintaining a relative balanced state or to shift to an alternative, potentially transformational, state" (Folke, Carpenter, Walker, Scheffer, Chapin, & Rockström, 2010, para. 3). For example, ecosystems above and below an existing dam that has been in place for many years tend to reach a relatively stable state. As certain factors change over time, the system can slip over a threshold and reach an alternative stable state, which may or may not be as desirable as the previous state.

Folke et al. (2010) noted that these states and the thresholds themselves can change over time and even shift fundamentally. The key to understanding these system changes are the feedback loops that "determine their overall dynamics" (para. 6). In the example of the dam above, changes in the relatively stable state may be much more subtle and less dramatic, but lead nonetheless to equally significant shifts in the homeostatic state that the system reaches over time. It is not necessary for the dam to fail in order for the lake ecosystem to fail. Over-farming upstream could release enough phosphates into the lake to eventually result in an extensive blue-green algae bloom that causes a mass fish kill. The primary implication from Folke et al. (2010) is that social change is essential to maintain social–ecological systems. They explained that "this is why we incorporate adaptability and the more radical concept of transformability as key ingredients of resilience thinking" (para. 8). Furthermore, this focus on adaptability and transformability introduces the concept of agency, which social network theory cannot address.

Each of these facets of resilience thinking has implications for WAC program adaptation and longevity in relation to the curricular ecology—the relationship between social and curricular practices—of an institution. Typically, when WAC programs are running smoothly, most program directors turn their attention to new program components or other concerns. Resilience theory reminds us that resilience and adaptability are dynamic processes that require constant monitoring and intervention. That initial stable state is going to shift over time as practices are tested and revised, as personnel come and go, and as program elements shift in purpose or function. Think of a WID program that starts with a strong flurry of interest to identify WI courses across departments. Once these conversations slow down considerably and students have been registering for WID courses for several years, the program reaches a relatively stable state of homeostasis. Since so many courses were converted and there is a desire to decentralize responsibility for the program across the university to integrate more into the curricular system, the responsibility for monitoring course syllabi returns to departments. Over time, new tenure-track and contingent faculty teach these courses, departments undertake new initiatives, and syllabi shift away from the original criteria. Without monitoring, intervention, adaptation, and possible transformation, the WID program will eventually slip into an undesirable alternative state. A resilient WAC/WID program will anticipate and typically accommodate such changes by adding new review processes or tinkering with the system itself without crossing a threshold to an unwanted stable state. Because such a significant percentage of WAC programs fades or disappears on such a regular basis, it behooves us to consider resilience as an important factor for the long-term viability of WAC programs.

A key insight from resilience thinking, then, is that dynamic systems change over time and can be significantly impacted by "deliberate transformational change" orchestrated through social action (Folke et al., 2010, para. 17). This point is perhaps the most important notion for WAC programs that we draw from this theory because the introduction of a WAC program within the university curricular ecology can lead to deliberate transformational change in the system itself. This notion fills an important gap for the whole systems approach that complexity and systems thinking could not, helping us articulate what a WAC program actually is, or often becomes. It also helps us make clear why WAC programs themselves are not complex systems but are typically intended as deliberate transformations of existing systems. Finally, it helps us work at multiple levels, or scales, across the system, as we explain below.

Transformational change typically involves "shifts in perception and meaning, social network configurations, patterns of interactions among actors including leadership and political power relations, and associated organizational institutional arrangements" (Folke et al., 2010, para. 16). Deliberate transformational change can be initiated at multiple scales. Think of a WAC director working with a single faculty member on her syllabus, a group of colleagues from a department who have applied for an internal WAC grant to develop a specific course or cross-departmental initiative, or an entire department that is working through a writing-enriched curriculum (WEC) process that maps their curriculum, notes gaps, plans assessment, and develops an implementation plan that addresses the gaps to better achieve the intended outcomes. These different scales have significantly differing impacts. Transformational changes at the lower scales typically involve a learning process that can lead to feedback effects across the system over time. Each colleague with a revised WAC syllabus or support to consider writing to learn rather than focusing on learning to write typically involves a learning process that can lead to changes at other levels. While a WAC director could work to change a university one faculty member at a time, such an approach would not likely be time or cost effective to change the larger system unless the director engages in transformational changes at other scales as well. Folke et al. (2010) have warned, however, that "deliberate transformational change . . . of all the component parts at the same time is likely to be too costly, undesirable, or socially unacceptable" (para. 17).

Forced transformational change typically occurs at higher levels of the system that are beyond the scope of a WAC director or university WAC committee to manage. Legislative acts, state funding, or other university-wide curricular reform projects that compete with WAC programs for resources all typically occur beyond the influence of local actors. Such initiatives can set new standards or call for new programs that can shift a program in an undesirable direction. However, while WAC directors cannot control the forced changes from above, they can have a significant impact on shaping the outcomes that result.

Because there are many forces outside of a WAC leader's control, resilience is needed so that a WAC program may survive the impacts from these changes. A resilience perspective leads to an adaptive approach that initiates targeted transformational interventions across scales. It provides opportunities for cross-learning and is always open for new initiatives to emerge. Its primary constraint is to avoid changes that are not broadly supported, especially those that attempt to cross too many scales at one time or high-level changes that could lead to crossing undesirable thresholds. It is important to note that resilience thinking differs on this last matter from systems thinking. The latter encourages change at the highest levels to facilitate the greatest degree of impact, while the former cautions us that, the higher on the scale we go, the more careful we need to be not to put in motion changes that can spiral out of our control. Resilience thinking presses us to keep in mind balance and thresholds.

Sustainable Development Theory

The theories we have drawn on thus far have provided ways for us to understand and analyze WAC programs and their complex institutional contexts, lenses for studying and introducing transformational change to institutional systems at the micro and macro scale, and means for assessing whether a program is in balance and to achieve resilience. We have not yet, however, offered a theoretical framework for ensuring that WAC programs can limit stagnation and maintain resilience over time and thus be sustainable. We started with the broadest and most abstract theoretical framework and have progressively introduced more granular and practical theories. This final framework, sustainable development theory, provides the most concrete principles and methodologies of the group to help us operationalize the whole systems approach for WAC programs.

While it is grounded in the twentieth-century concern of conservation of renewable resources, the focus on sustainable development can be traced directly to the Brundtland Report, which asserted that "humanity has the ability to make development sustainable to ensure that it meets the needs of the present without compromising the ability of future generations to meet their own needs" (United Nations World Commission on Environment and Development, 1987, para. 27). Sustainability serves as a core value and outcome of any continuous curricular initiative, which is at least as important as the guiding vision of the curricular reform itself. This point may seem obvious, but it is worth emphasizing. No institution would undertake a potentially paradigmatic shift in its mission, with the time, money, and resources it takes to do so, without a desire for these changes to persist. Given the distributed nature of university systems, no such change will likely persist unless sustainability is a core value from the outset of the project. Thus, sustainable development must be a core value of any WAC program that hopes to have a lasting legacy.

As we note above, sustainable development is significantly more project focused and action oriented than the other four systems models. It is also consciously political in its desire to change the ways in which societies worldwide manage their own natural resources. However, it incorporates aspects of the other theories, particularly focusing on complex adaptive systems, which relies heavily on resilience thinking to help maintain adaptability and homeostasis. It shares a focus on mapping networks and relationships, seeking leverage points to maximize change and resisting stagnation. And it extends these frameworks by offering a governing ideology and fundamental methodology for introducing change and using SIs to track the long-term viability of the system. These SIs are the most significant distinguishing feature of sustainable development theory. They are identified early in the planning stages of a program and used to track its sustainability. Ideally, program stakeholders identify key indicators, but only as many as can be tracked, interpreted, and reported effectively.

Since sustainable development theory is founded on the process of identifying and tracking SIs, but this practice has never been applied to WAC programs, we provide some historical context of their emergence. The first broadly accepted articulation of SIs and their guiding principles in sustainable development was introduced in *Assessing Sustainable Development: Principles in Practice* (Hardi & Zdan, 1997). Two years later, the principles were further explained and procedures provided for implementation in *Indicators for Sustainable Development: Theory, Method, Applications* (Bossel, 1999), but had shifted away from individual projects and programs to the assessment of global sustainability dynamics. This global turn was finalized into 100 global monitoring indicators presented in *Indicators and a Monitoring Framework for the Sustainable Development Goals* (Leadership Council of the Sustainable Development Solutions Network, 2015). By this point, the implementation process had morphed into a political document of internationally shared goals for global sustainability.

For the purposes of the whole systems approach, we draw from the two reports from the 1990s to introduce the broad principles of SI development and the general procedure for implementation, and later, in Chapters 5 through 7, we turn to *Sustainability Indicators: Measuring the Immeasurable?* (Bell & Morse, 2008) to operationalize SIs at the project and program levels.

Unlike the other theories that are mostly descriptive and analytical, sustainable development emerged to solve serious global challenges. The Brundtland Report laid out the need for building a future "that is more prosperous, more just, and more secure" (United Nations World Commission on Environment and Development, 1987, para. 3). This ambitious political agenda requires buy-in from stakeholders at every level of the system and has thus slowly evolved over time.

The initial Brundtland Report noted the global and national challenges in conceiving sustainable development across a range of human and ecological concerns. This call for principles and policies to manage natural resources in the face of human development was echoed at the 1992 Earth Summit. But it was not until 1996, at a conference in Bellagio, Italy, that "measurement practitioners and researchers from five continents came together" to develop a set of assessment principles for selecting, designing, interpreting, and communicating SIs that could be used to track sustainable development across global projects (Hardi & Zdan, 1997, p. 1).

The ten unanimously endorsed principles for assessing SIs (see Hardi & Zdan, 1997) were essential for the sustainable development movement, but it took eighteen years from the time that the Bellagio conference report was published to the development of a full sustainable development framework with ten new global principles, seventeen global monitoring goals, and 100 universal indicators, as presented in *Indicators and a Monitoring Framework for the Sustainable Development Goals* (Leadership Council of the Sustainable Development Solutions Network, 2015). The reasons for this long delay are not surprising, given the shift in scope and scale between the two reports. The initial principles were designed to guide the management of a single project, situated in a specific region of a given country. The latter was designed as a set of universal principles that all nations would use in addition to national, regional, and thematic indicators of choice. While we do ultimately pose the question of what SIs might look like for WAC programs nationwide in this book's final chapter, our whole systems approach is built on the earlier principles, as they focus on individual WAC programs in specific institutional contexts.

From Bellagio Principles to Principles for WAC

As the principles we developed for WAC echo the original Bellagio principles, the latter are worth summarizing here. They state that sustainable development must:

1. create a vision and goals that engage the whole system;

2. develop from a holistic, whole system, perspective;

3. emphasize essential elements such as equity and disparity;

4. adopt an appropriate time horizon that builds upon historic and current conditions;

5. maintain a practical focus that directly links vision and goals to a limited set of indicators and assessment criteria;

6. rely on openness of data sharing and analysis;

7. communicate effectively assessment of progress, using indicators that engage decision-makers;

8. engage broad participation to create strong ties from assessment of indicators to decision making and policy adoption;

9. foster ongoing assessment that enables iterative, adaptive, and responsive measures; and

10. support institutional capacity for data collection, maintenance, and documentation, as well as clearly assigned responsibilities and ongoing support in decision-making processes (Hardi & Zdan, 1997, pp. 2–4).

By "whole system," these Bellagio principles are referring to complex adaptive systems that are concerned with indicator development based on complex systems theory. Hardi and Zdan's

(1997) *Assessing Sustainable Development: Principles in Practice* explained the first principle, "guiding vision and goals," by noting that a core element of the approach is "the idea of the 'whole' system which can co-evolve successfully in a changing environment" as a result of emergent properties, hierarchical structure of nested systems, and feedback loops that shape adaptation in response to stress (p. 12). In addition, indicators are needed to assess the "performance of the constituent parts, controls, feedback loops, and the whole system" (Hardi & Zdan, 1997, p. 12). Furthermore, the power of a whole systems approach derives from a realization that some system properties are "not evident from simply looking independently at the parts" (Hardi & Zdan, 1997, p. 12).

For example, many WAC programs have as their goal shifting the campus culture of writing. In attempting to achieve this goal, program directors have paid significant attention to distinct program components, such as training faculty, developing WI courses, partnering with writing centers, and developing assessment rubrics and student portfolios. In some cases, these foci have led to shifts in campus ideologies away from high-stakes testing and assigning of writing rather than the teaching of writing. However, WAC programs have not typically paid attention to the collective impacts of these program components across the scales, at the levels of the individual, department, college, and institution. At the level of the individual, we might ask how often specific faculty teach WI/WAC courses, how many more adjuncts tend to teach them over time, or how such courses impact international students. While program leaders usually focus on high-impact practices when starting up programs, they often do not identify existing departmental- or college-level initiatives where the various writing and assessment initiatives already reside, or determine how to include those stakeholders in university-wide conversations. Furthermore, few if any programs focus on curricular stressors that would conflict or compete with WAC initiatives, such as an emphasis on ethics, critical thinking, research, or other university-wide curricular changes. Finally, practically no programs begin by identifying indicators to track program visibility: How many departments have developed capstone or honors courses that rely on significant writing? How many students are publishing work as undergraduates? What are stakeholders from outside of the university saying about the quality of thinking and writing of the graduates they hire? These webs of interconnected feedback loops need to be considered integrated parts of a larger system.

This focus on feedback cycles and SIs provides the practical bridge from the Bellagio principles to a framework for our own principles, as well as a rationale for why we gave our book the title *Sustainable WAC: A Whole Systems Approach to Launching and Developing Writing Across the Curriculum Programs.* While the Bellagio principles focus entirely on SI development, we use them to provide a theoretical underpinning for the strategies that we lay out in Chapters 4 through 7 within the context of vignettes of WAC programs. SIs become one piece of our overall whole systems set of principles, but echoes of the Bellagio principles are obvious:

1. *wholeness*—understanding a WAC program as a significant intervention within a complex system with competing ideologies and many levels, actors, and practices;

2. *broad participation*—engaging stakeholders from all levels of the institution to help plan, approve, implement, and assess program goals, outcomes, and projects;

3. *transformational change*—identifying points of leverage for introducing change to the university system at multiple levels, including changes in ideologies and practices as they relate to writing culture;

4. *resilience*—adapting to program challenges, maintaining self-organizing practices, and increasing the capacity for learning and adaptation to sustain desirable pathways for development;

5. *equity*—working to minimize disparities in current and future generations of WAC faculty and student writers;

6. *leadership*—identifying leadership that can serve as the hub for the program, with the authority on campus to lead a cohesive effort of planning, launching, developing, and assessing WAC;

7. *systematic development*—building a WAC program incrementally over time with a clear mission and prioritized goals;

8. *integration*—building program components that synchronize with national and local mandates, integrate into existing structures and practices, and facilitate collaborative campus relationships;

9. *visibility*—ensuring that program development, assessment, and change are transparent, regular, and public, as well as promoting program events and successes through multiple means of reporting; and

10. *feedback*—identifying indicators and repeated measures to reveal trends, stimulate recursive and adaptive change, promote collective learning and feedback for decision making, and determine whether a WAC program is in balance and whether individual WAC projects are sustainable and achieving their goals.

How the WAC Principles Reflect Complexity Theories

These principles provide a summary of the whole systems approach by emphasizing key features of the theories presented in this chapter. *Wholeness* emphasizes systematic relationships. WAC programs that consciously work across scales have the capacity to change the curricular ecology of a university. But the narrower the focus and the lower the levels of scale that a WAC program impacts, the less curricular change will occur and the less likely the program will be sustainable. Seeing a university as a complex adaptive system means that, the more one understands about institutional relationships and how they support and perpetuate practices, the more likely one can design effective interventions to transform that system. All five theoretical frameworks are dependent upon whole systems thinking.

Broad participation becomes important when intentional *transformational change* is the goal. A complex adaptive system has negative feedback loops that help maintain pattern formation of emergent behaviors, but these feedback loops do not create change on their own. Resilience theory introduces the concept of transformational change. The intent to create such changes occurs when a broad array of stakeholders across system scales set goals, identify leverage points, plan program development, and identify, track, and share results of SIs. In addition, these stakeholders, and particularly WAC directors, need to draw on social network theory to map out the network of relationships on campus to understand the organization through which communications and procedural change need to move. Finally, resilience theory cautions that forced transformational change too high on system scales can lead to changes that spiral out of control. Thus, it tempers systems theory, which seeks leveraged changes at these highest levels.

CST and sustainable development theory provide the justification for addressing issues of *equity* within the whole systems approach. The former expects stakeholders to examine existing campus writing program ideologies for discriminatory practices and encourages them to intervene to shift these practices. The latter helps stakeholders plan new programs or projects with equity in mind. Furthermore, unlike the other theories, sustainable development combines agency, intentional transformational change, and sustainable use of vital resources. For sustainable development, equity typically means addressing disparities that can jeopardize resources for future generations. In communities, such issues as overconsumption, poverty, human rights, and access to services are balanced against the "ecological conditions on which life depends" (Hardi & Zdan, 1997, p. 14). In WAC programs, issues of equity typically concern how a WAC program impacts students and faculty as a result of changes in the curricular ecology. A sustainable WAC program takes into consideration who teaches the WI courses on a given campus, how often, and for what percentage of their assignment. Likewise, such a program considers how curricular changes introduced by WAC programs affect the ability of students to enroll in the classes they need to maintain progress toward their degree, the quality of support for second language (L2) learners, the ease of access for transfer students to complete requirements, the support for faculty to respond effectively to student work, and the recognition of participation for tenure and promotion purposes. Without attention to such issues, as well as those addressed by the other principles, the system will lose *resilience* and, thus, adaptability in the face of system challenges.

Leadership for sustainable growth draws from several of the theories. Complexity, systems, and network thinking help us understand that leadership is distributed in a complex adaptive system. No one leader controls all aspects of the system. The very nature of emergent coordinated behaviors helps us understand that WAC programs may fit within the strategic mission of an institution, but the most sustainable programs typically evolve from grassroots concerns that student writing is not meeting expectations, rather than from top-down initiatives. Furthermore, systems thinking helps us recognize that distributed leadership is necessary to leverage desired change. WAC directors and stakeholder committees typically rely on a network of others to sustain a program, including but not limited to individual students and instructors, directors of composition, curriculum committees across departments and schools, department chairs, writing centers, and campus libraries. And network theory helps us realize that university organizational charts do not necessarily represent the most common lines of communication within an institution that are necessary to sustain campus-wide curricular change.

The distributed nature of leadership; the complexity of instituting significant curricular change; the need for multiple WAC program components; ongoing, iterative, and adaptive assessment; and identification and tracking of SIs all point to the need for *systematic development* over time. Moving to implement too quickly may make it unlikely to *integrate* the WAC program into the curricular ecology of the institution and ignore curricular expectations at higher scales in the system, such as state, regional, or national mandates. Lack of integration reduces broad impact, resilience, and systematic development.

The notion of *visibility* is specific to sustainable development theory in part because the other four theories are primarily descriptive of complex adaptive systems, while sustainable development is proactive. Visibility affects perception of a WAC program across its networks and projects. Even with a focus on the whole system, broad participation, transformational change, equitable practices, program adaptability, distributed leadership, systematic development, and strong integration, WAC programs tend toward stagnation and institutional entropy if program visibility is not a priority. Sponsored events, university-wide assessment, data sharing, program review, faculty support, student and faculty recognition, curriculum grants, department-by-department planning, and other such features help WAC programs stay current, vital, and visible. They also help WAC to compete with other university initiatives that garner attention and university support.

Finally, *feedback* is a fundamental feature of all five theories. They all include positive feedback loops that amplify out of control and the negative feedback loops that monitor systems to prevent them from breaching their equilibrium. Feedback informs networks of communication and decision making at every stage of a WAC program. It also drives inputs and outputs such as faculty training and evaluation of student writing. In other words, feedback is the backbone of adaptive transformational change.

While these ten principles provide the framework for the whole systems approach, we distinguish among principles, methodology, and strategies in the next chapter, a step that the Bellagio principles did not make. In doing so, we establish how the theories discussed above lead to praxis.

CHAPTER THREE

The Whole Systems Process for Launching and Developing WAC Programs: Methodology and Strategies

In Chapter 2, we described a group of complexity theories and a set of principles derived from those theories that can provide the foundation for building a WAC program. We emphasized that complexity, systems, and social network theories provide WAC directors with ways of analyzing institutional systems. Resilience theory, which draws on the other three, provides strategies for introducing transformational change and measuring its continuity. Sustainable development theory helps us translate these theories into praxis, providing us with a foundation for our whole systems methodology.

The methodology forms the core of our approach and offers a new way for the field to think beyond just the nuts and bolts of creating WAC programs toward a systematic process for creating sustainable interventions that lead to transformational change. We realize that not all readers will be in a position to use our approach in its full form, but we hope that its full articulation will be informative as you consider options as you advocate for and develop programs. We begin this chapter with a discussion of this methodology and its origins. We then focus on the development of SIs, as this part of our methodology is fundamental to our approach and will likely be new to most readers. Next, we list and discuss the fifteen strategies that constitute the whole systems approach to WAC program development. We close with a summary of how our process and practices connect to the principles for developing sustainable WAC programs that we discussed in Chapter 2.

The Whole Systems Methodology for Launching, Revitalizing, and Reviving WAC Programs

One of our goals in developing a methodology for WAC program development is to create an iterative and participatory cycle with which to establish institutional change. Another goal is to track program resilience and sustainability by developing and assessing SIs. This methodology is designed for the development of entire WAC programs as well as particular WAC projects (e.g., WI programs, faculty seminars, etc.). It draws primarily on two models from sustainable development: (1) the "plan–do–check–improve" (PDCI) model developed as part of Canada's Federal Sustainable Development Strategy (Environment Canada, 2013, p. 12) and (2) Bell and Morse's (2008) "Imagine" approach, developed to create projects using SIs.

Canada's Federal Sustainable Development Strategy is a national policy introduced in 2008 to create "an environmental decision-making system that is transparent and accountable and supports the continuous improvement of the management of sustainable development" (Environment Canada, 2010, p. 3). Every three years, the Government of Canada publishes a federal plan for sustainable development, which draws from sustainability data, goals, and targets gathered from across sectors and departments, and creates systematic approaches for measuring and monitoring sustainable development. Adapted from "plan–do–check–act," an iterative problem-solving process used in business for quality management, the Federal Sustainable Development Strategy model uses a PDCI system that incorporates a "plan" stage to define the change desired and the approach to take, a "do" stage for project implementation, a "check" stage to analyze and evaluate the results, and an "improve" stage to take action on the results (see Figure 3.1). In adapting the PDCI method toward meeting sustainable development goals, Environment Canada (2013) integrated a participatory process for establishing goals and targets into the "plan" stage, the development of measurement frameworks into the "do" stage, and the public sharing of results into the "improve" stage. This broad cycle provides a mechanism for introducing change, but it neglects an essential stage prior to planning: understanding. Before transformational changes are introduced into a complex system, it is critical to understand the network of relationships that govern current practices, the ideologies that inform them, the points within the system where changes are likely to have the greatest impact, and a method for assessing indicators of sustainability. The Federal Sustainable Development Strategy cycle also fails to provide specific strategies for implementing change. Therefore, we borrow from Bell and Morse's (2008) "Imagine" approach to introduce an *understanding* stage to our whole systems methodology and to develop strategies for each of the four stages.

In *Sustainability Indicators: Measuring the Immeasurable?*, Bell and Morse (2008) drew on systemic sustainability analysis

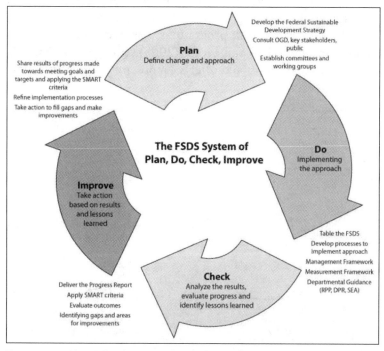

FIGURE **3.1.** *The Federal Sustainable Development Strategy's PDCI model. From "Planning for a Sustainable Future: A Federal Sustainable Development Strategy for Canada 2013–2016" by Environment Canada, 2013, p. 12. Reprinted with permission.*

to offer a process model for developing projects with SIs. Their five-step process, the "Imagine" approach, is represented as a Möbius strip (see Figure 3.2). Here, the Imagine approach involves understanding the context, agreeing on SIs and the band of equilibrium that defines sustainability (see Chapter 5, Strategy 7), creating AMOEBA diagrams (spider graphs using SIs to assess projects) to help understand sustainability over time and to envision a sustainability scenario, revising sustainability scenarios, and publicizing the message.

Bell and Morse (2008) argued that sustainability cannot itself be assessed, only its parameters (indicators). Furthermore, they asserted that "the approach to measurement is always based on an individual's vision of sustainability, which in turn can be changed depending upon the measurement mindset" (pp. xvii–xviii). Because the mindset of program leaders is subjective and can be shaped by a range of inputs, the broader the participation from stakeholders, the more likely the measurement mindset will be shifted for the overall program as a shared vision. In order to fulfill this goal, Bell and Morse (2008) set out to evaluate SIs critically so that they could offer a "more holistic, realistic, par-

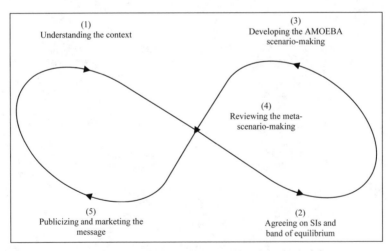

FIGURE 3.2. *The five steps of the Imagine approach. Adapted from* Sustainability Indicators: Measuring the Immeasurable? *(p. 156) by S. Bell and S. Morse, 2008, New York: Routledge. Reprinted with permission.*

ticipative and systematic approach to gauging sustainability" (p. xviii). Our whole systems methodology (see Figure 3.3) combines the strengths of the PDCI and Imagine approaches to focus on a process for creating change that helps shift the mindset of program assessment in our field by introducing a practical and systematic approach to gauging sustainability that is holistic, inclusive, concrete, transparent, and practical to implement (see Figure 3.3).

Separating understanding from planning forestalls a conversation on mission and goals until stakeholders have a clear idea of conditions preceding program development. The *understand* stage is critical for planning an intervention that will have a transformative effect. Understanding context includes assessing campus mood for WAC, mapping the system in order to understand its

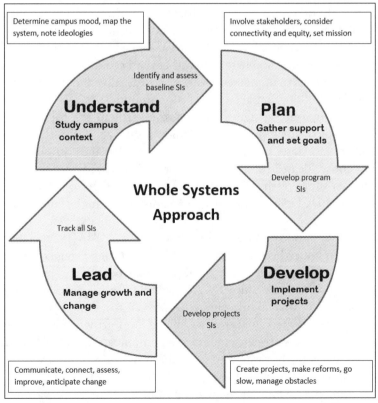

FIGURE 3.3. *The whole systems methodology for transformational change.*

broad network of relationships, identifying stakeholders, locating points of leverage in the system to introduce change, understanding the ideologies that underlie campus programs, policies, and attitudes related to student writing and writing instruction, and establishing baseline SIs that mark the pre-implementation status of WAC programs. We incorporate the vision development process into the *plan* stage so stakeholders from different parts of the system can come together to create a mission, goals, and expected outcomes, imagine program development scenarios, and determine which cluster of SIs should be used, as well as the range within which actions will be sustainable based on the SI measurements (the band of equilibrium). Determining which program initiatives, or projects, should be undertaken, across what time frame, and in what order offers realistic scenarios for transforming a university's curricular ecology. In stage three of our methodology, *develop*, we focus on implementation (akin to the PDCI "do" stage). This stage includes strategic project design, thinking in terms of both the micro and macro levels, aiming for gradual and sustainable reform rather than rapid reform, dealing with obstacles to implementation systematically, and implementing SIs, checking impact as the program builds.

In our fourth stage, *lead*, we've integrated the fourth and fifth steps of Imagine ("review" and "publicize") with the third and fourth stage of the PDCI cycle ("check" and "improve"). We chose "lead" rather than "improve" in part because it is a broader concept that encompasses the later stages of the Imagine and PDCI cycles, and in part because we want to emphasize the role of WAC leadership in program publicity, assessment, and sustainability. As we argue in Chapter 7, WAC leadership has been undertheorized by the field, and our *lead* stage offers a theoretically informed way to think about both WAC program leadership and leadership of WAC as a field. *Leading* encompasses the strategies that should guide the WAC leaders and stakeholders as the program matures, as change and growth need to be managed. These strategies include communicating regularly and at all levels of the system to keep the program visible, connecting to systems beyond the institution that could benefit WAC, planning for sustainable leadership to help ensure the program's long-term success, and assessing and revising the WAC program using SIs. Note that we are not implying that a single leader needs to initiate all of these functions. As we discuss in Chapter 7, in programs with distributed leadership, these responsibilities can be distributed as well.

Developing SIs in the Whole Systems Approach

Bell and Morse (2008) provided a comprehensive historical review of SIs from indicator species in ecological systems to indicators that measure "driving force," "pressure," "state," "impact," and "response" drivers of change (p. 31). These five types of indicators are all connected. A driving force is a need (Kristensen, 2004) that creates pressures, which results in a state that has significant impacts on a system that warrant response. For instance, in the United States, there is a state of high linguistic diversity among undergraduates and graduate students, as US universities are enrolling high numbers of international and permanent resident multilingual students. This state is creating pressure on the curricular ecology, as faculty without training to support multilingual writing may become frustrated at what they perceive as "substandard" writing. The driving forces behind this pressure are a combination of the government divestment of higher education and the corresponding search for new revenue streams. One impact may be dropping course availability because of faculty reluctance to teach WI courses, particularly in degrees that attract linguistically diverse students. Another could be decreased attention by faculty to sentence-level concerns in student writing because of the perceived complexity and time required. Responses may be to decrease the driving force (i.e., decrease the number of multilingual students) or to decrease the pressure (i.e., by providing more faculty development and multilingual writing support services).

While Bell and Morse (2008) spent several chapters tracing the development of the driving force–pressure–state–impact–and response framework, they also emphasized that state and impact SIs are the primary measures for sustainability projects, with impact SIs being the easiest to identify. The other three types may be developed later to help the project team understand what the state SIs describe and how to mitigate impacts. We define *state SIs* as measurable conditions of the curricular environment that are shaped by drivers and pressures before, during, and after project initiation. *Impact SIs* are results of state changes that alter the well-being of students and faculty. To simplify, we combine these driver types together in what Jeff has called indicators of distress or success (Galin, 2010). Indicators of distress are the warning signs that a project is becoming unsustainable, and indicators of success are the signs that a project is sustainable.

To aid in the identification of SIs, we turn to a model introduced by Hardi and Zdan (1997) and extended by Bossel (1999). Their model focuses on three major systems, two of which include subsystems: (1) the human system (consisting of individual development, the social system, and the government system), (2) the support system (comprising the economic system and infrastructure system), and (3) the natural system. These systems are outlined in Figure 3.4, which Jeff adapted from Bossel (1999, p. 18) to reflect WAC concerns (Galin, 2010).

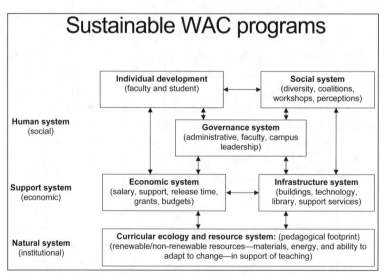

FIGURE **3.4.** *The three major systems of the anthrosphere and their relationships. Reprinted from "Improving Rather Than Proving: Self-Administered Sustainability Mapping of WAC Programs" by J. R. Galin, 2010.*

Considering the three major systems of the university anthrosphere can help WAC stakeholders think about program viability across all scales at the university level as they begin to brainstorm indicators. We believe it may be easiest for WAC stakeholders to start identifying SIs by focusing on indicators of distress, as they may be already aware of points of concern in the program. Further, identifying indicators of distress early in the process provides stakeholders a quick means to identify the links in the current system with the greatest vulnerabilities and potential places at which to intervene to create change. Below, we list example indicators for each system. Variations of the following example indicators can be used at stakeholder meetings for programs that are just starting or well established by shifting the language slightly and including only the SIs that might apply.

At the individual level, indicators may include:

◆ quality of student writing leveling off or dropping;

◆ student or faculty perceptions shifting negatively;

◆ participation of faculty/students dropping unexpectedly;

◆ syllabus review process stalling;

◆ compliance of WI syllabi dropping significantly;

◆ WAC director's position not identified or filled;

◆ director's position not classified at high enough a rank to negotiate university politics;

◆ publication or teaching effectiveness of director dropping significantly;

◆ director's level of commitment shifting noticeably (overcommitment to national service, publication, service elsewhere at the university);

◆ amount of time director/assistant director commits to program management and growth dropping significantly;

◆ numbers of courses taught dropping unexpectedly;

◆ support for director waning (concerns over promotion or program effectiveness).

At the level of the social system, there could be shifts that challenge resilience:

- no departments applying for WAC grants;

- marked decrease in program communication to university community;

- no oversight committee designated to recommend and implement policy;

- significant shift in faculty participation on the WAC committee;

- key potential campus partners excluded unintentionally or intentionally;

- recent transitions in leadership (director, department chairs, director of assessment, or other key partners);

- marked increase in administrative obstacles to program management or growth;

- increasing resistance (faculty, students, or administrators);

- realignments of support;

- marked drop in faculty participation.

At the level of the governance system, indicators might include tracking:

- significant university policy changes;

- significant increase in challenges to program governance;

- perceived drop in importance/impact of WAC program;

- program becoming too centralized around a dynamic director;

- shifts in primary relationships that define the program (director, dean, provost, departmental claims for control);

- significant change in program mission or a shift away from stated mission;

- realignment of WAC program with parallel and competing programs;

- expectations for writing assessment change at the state or local level;

- state writing mandates change markedly;
- realignment of WAC responsibilities;
- program becoming too decentralized or losing track of its core mission.

At the financial level, it is important to track:

- increased pressure on budget from competing unit(s);
- new costs and/or projects without commensurate budget increase(s);
- shift in control over foundation or endowment funds;
- state or university budget crisis;
- other unforeseen economic challenges;
- significant changes in ways that budget is allocated;
- change in funds available to support WAC events;
- grant funding nearing end;
- change in commitment to faculty stipends; and
- shift in administrative stipend or release time for program director and/or assistant director.

Finally, at the level of the university curricular ecology, there are resources that can derail sustainability and resilience, including:

- merging/fracturing of college departments or divisions;
- missing/aging digital resources for effective course delivery;
- institutional realignment/change of student support services;
- relocation of offices or other physical resources;
- shift in use of shared resources (special equipment, technological support, multiuse centers in libraries);
- substantial changes in allocated space (loss of storage, use of meeting rooms, or sharing of office space, limited availability of classrooms).

Working through human, support, and curricular ecology systems provides an easy way to isolate essential indicators. It is less important to distinguish between state and impact indicators than it is to ensure that the selection process is systematic and indicator sets are predictive of program longevity. Furthermore, indicators of distress more accurately identify the purpose of actionable SIs and offer opportunities to communicate positive changes when distresses can be shifted to successes.

The burden for SI development should not fall solely on the WAC director. It is critical that the process of SI development be participatory (with a large stakeholder group, or at least a representative one such as a WAC committee) to ensure that the SIs encompass the visions and values of the community for which they are developed. Bell and Morse (2008) encouraged the SI discussion facilitator to help stakeholders explore the explicit and implicit dynamics of the group, recognizing underlying reasons for statements and recommendations. They also cautioned facilitators not to drive the process in a "particular direction" (p. 175). This group should first *brainstorm* all possible SIs without concern of practicality. The group then needs to *narrow* the set by noting which can be quantified and assessed and whether they are predictive over time, not overlapping, and long lasting. Further narrowing can be done through considering feasibility in terms of difficulty, financial costs, and time commitment. The last step is to *operationalize* the chosen set by determining the range of functioning for each. Boundaries should be defined below and above which the indicator marks unsustainable practice (e.g., not enough WI classes available for student needs or too many to cover with available faculty). Also, it is important to determine what will likely influence or drive the outcomes for each SI. For example, if the SI is to determine whether student writing is improving as a result of work completed in WI courses, what is causing this change and how can those drivers be managed? The goal is to identify a numeric scale for each SI. As SIs move above or below these thresholds, adjustments should be made to bring them back into the sustainable range. AMOEBA graphs should be developed periodically to visualize SI ranges in relationship to one another. (See Chapters 5, 6, and 7 for examples of how to create and use AMOEBA graphs; see also Appendix A.) As new projects are added or existing ones shift purposes or scales, SIs should be revisited. And, once the AMOEBA graphs are established, periodic checking should take place throughout the planning and leading stages.

The whole systems approach makes these initial discussions concrete and the process manageable. SIs should focus not on all the concerns but on the major concerns, and the number of SIs should be as small as possible to capture what is critical to track and assess; the stakeholder group can narrow this list further to five to ten SIs for the imagined WAC program and five to ten for each additional project, with some SIs likely overlapping across projects. Furthermore, indicators must be clearly defined, reproducible, unambiguous, understandable, and practical. It should be possible to deduce, from a look at the set of chosen indicators, the visibility and sustainability of current program developments in comparison to alternate development paths. We discuss SIs more fully in Chapters 4 through 7. Next, we introduce the strategies that emerge from the whole systems methodology.

Whole Systems Strategies for Launching and Building Sustainable WAC Programs

At each phase in the whole systems methodology, there are strategies WAC directors can use to help turn principle and process into practice and projects. Just as our whole systems principles provide a foundation for our methodology, they are also the framework for a set of fifteen strategies for building WAC programs that work with the stages of our methodology. Before discussing these strategies and the way they evolved from our principles and connect to our methodology, we differentiate between *principle* and *strategy*.

Our definitions of these terms are based on Linda Adler-Kassner's (2008) work in *The Activist WPA: Changing Stories about Writing and Writers*. Adler-Kassner encourages WPAs to begin with a set of core ideals that guide actions, since understanding principles is the starting point for WPAs as activists (p. 124)—or, in our case, WPAs as WAC program directors tasked with making transformational change to complex institutional systems. These core ideals are guiding principles, and they are based on both theory and personal experience. Adler-Kassner (2008) argues that WPA work should be strategic action and that the strategies should connect to core principles. She feels that neither "actions without principles" nor "ideals without techniques" are effective modes of operating for the activist WPA (p. 128). She defines "strategies" as long-term plans and contrasts them with "tactics," which are short-term and context-specific actions. Principles are ideal guidelines for action, strategies are approaches for enacting the principles that can work in a variety of institutional contexts, and tactics are site- and situation-specific ways to achieve strategic goals. Our fifteen strategies are enumerated below.

Strategy 1: Determine the Campus Mood

WAC programs are initiated in a range of ways; sometimes, out of grassroots concerns, and, at other times, from top-down directives. If a program had been active in the past and then went dormant, any number of reasons might emerge to revitalize the program that could influence the overall mood of the institution to participate. The mood of an institution tests the status of interest on campus for supporting a university-wide curricular initiative and determines how the program is initiated and developed. One of the best tactics for analyzing the mood of an institution is to use a SWOT analysis in which the strengths, weaknesses, opportunities, and threats for developing the program can be weighed against one another (see Chapter 4). Another tactic is for the director to talk to stakeholders across campus, from faculty and upper administrators to department chairs and college deans. If the upper administration wants a WAC program, but will not provide funds for a dedicated director, faculty support, or assessment processes, the mood for WAC might be judged slightly hostile. Such a context would warrant a slower process of development, broader outreach, coalition building, and possibly pilot projects that can be evaluated and then reported back to the upper administration. Hence, timing is another key feature affecting program development, which is determined primarily by campus mood.

Strategy 2: Understand the System in Order to Focus on Points of Interactivity and Leverage

Institutions of higher education are complex entities that have both connectivity through a variety of network nodes and hubs (such as academic senates and centers for teaching and learning) and also segregation and isolation (the siloed structure of departments and colleges; the division of staff, administration, tenure-line faculty, and contingent faculty). Before building toward a sustainable WAC program, it is beneficial to map out the facets of institutional complexities. There are numerous ways to map programs, each of which has specific advantages (see Chapter 2). Although not every WAC program engages in mapping the institutional landscape at the outset, this kind of mapping can focus on a particular project or initiative to limit the scope of the map. At a minimum, the map could identify key nodes and central clusters of nodes (hubs), and then could be further filled out as the program develops. Creating rich visual maps of the places where writing occurs, student demographics, the requirements involving writing, the sequence and processes of writing requirements, and hubs of writing instruction that have the most connectivity within the system will help WAC directors choose interventions and reforms that will have leverage to make significant and sustainable change. WAC directors should locate points of leverage and connectivity where even a small influence or change could have wide-ranging effects throughout the system. In academic institutions, these points might include graduation writing requirements, college-wide assessment and placement for writing, general education requirements, academic technologies adopted by the campus, and cross-curricular events such as new faculty orientation or academic senate meetings.

Strategy 3: Understand the Ideologies That Inform the Campus Culture of Writing

The ideologies that define campus writing will inevitably shape the individual behavior of faculty and administrators in regards to the teaching of writing. It is important to understand the ideologies that inform the campus culture of writing in order to locate ideological reinforcing processes that have a snowball effect because they reinforce a certain kind of attitude or behavior. For example, an institution that is focused on timed writing tests is informed by a theory of writing as a product, and a climate of timed testing will create an ideology and a process that reinforces to teachers and students that a writing task can be completed and assessed in a single draft. Shifting from timed writing to portfolio assessment would not only change the theory of writing under which the system operates, but could also reinforce positive changes to both students' conception of writing processes and teachers' writing pedagogy. Understanding the ideologies of writing at work at the institution will help WAC directors make visible assumptions that underlie practices, anticipate points of resistance, determine which existing ideologies might be candidates for change, identify ideologies that clash, and plan strategies for handling those differences.

Strategy 4: Involve Multiple Stakeholders in the System

Building sustainable WAC programs that have a high level of connectivity and influence throughout the institution requires the involvement of multiple stakeholders across the system. Curricular change is university-wide, so buy-in and influence are essential. Ideally, this involvement would be both formal and structured as well as grassroots: a writing advisory board or an academic senate committee are two common formal structures for building collaboration and input from multiple stakeholders, but informal relationships developed through outreach to departments, individual consultations, faculty development workshops and retreats, etc., are also critical to establishing credibility and garnering support. Sustainable WAC programs typically involve stakeholders from a variety of scales across the system, from individual faculty to department chairs, to academic senate committees to deans and provosts. Throughout the WAC program development process, these stakeholders will collaborate to map the system, establish the mission and goals, determine SIs, and set the agenda for program development.

Strategy 5: Work toward Positioning the WAC Program for Greater Interconnectivity and Leverage in the Institution

WAC programs that do not fully integrate into existing institutional structures and do not move beyond a small core group are rarely sustainable. From their inception, WAC programs should aim to be a hub within the network and not just a node, or to at least connect to hubs. When considering where to locate WAC, hubs that connect across disciplines, like writing centers, centers for teaching and learning, independent writing departments, and academic affairs administration, are typically superior to a less connected node like a traditional English department. Writing committees of academic senates provide an enduring connection to shared governance and make it easier for WAC directors to help facilitate reform of curricular and institutional writing requirements. WAC directors can also connect to the structure of the institution through collaborations with highly connected units such as libraries, academic assessment, or institutional diversity. Connecting the WAC program in such a way will ensure WAC is perceived not as marginal or temporary but integral—part of the fabric of the institution and a key player in faculty development and student retention and support.

Strategy 6: Consider the Impact of WAC on Faculty and Student Equity

Achieving equity and minimizing disparities in current and future generations is a key component of sustainability. How WAC affects the students the program serves and the faculty that it implicates should be considered in the early stages of program development. If WAC programs increase the amount of writing in classes and the emphasis on writing assessment, WAC directors need to be aware of the impact these changes have on faculty, departments, curriculum, and students. The creation of a WAC curriculum as part of, for example, first-year seminars or upper-division WI courses, could unintentionally lead to the hiring of more adjunct faculty and TAs or create an unreasonable increase in workload if course caps are not enforced or if the same faculty are expected to teach the WAC courses for a given major or program. Such a change would also require that faculty development on teaching writing within their own disciplines is offered. Indeed, this area of WAC has been well theorized, as there is a great deal of literature on WAC pedagogies that involve writing to learn, revision/recursivity, and scaffolding student learning with carefully written assignments. Less discussed is the impact of WAC initiatives and policies on particular groups of students, such as students who use English as a second or additional language. It is important to keep in mind that positive changes to one part of a system may create unintended disparities for actors in other parts of a system, and that inequalities sharpen when systems become dysfunctional or stagnant. Power disparities can also be traced to certain groups (such as students or adjunct faculty) having less of a voice within the structures of communication of the university as a network of actors.

Strategy 7: Set Mission, Goals, and SIs

WAC programs often grow organically from an initial workshop or retreat, or develop in fits and starts as a director experiments with various projects or connects with different campus units. However, a WAC program that sets a mission statement, goals, outcomes, and set of SIs in the planning stage is more likely to have a more significant system-wide effect, since it will be more coherent and goal driven. A focused mission will also help keep the WAC director from being spread too thinly. To ensure that a mission statement is representative, it should be formed by a stakeholder group such as a writing committee or a WAC advisory board. Such groups should also consider both the broader mission of the institution and the issues and concerns that faculty across disciplines are most focused on. Consider as well issues of student retention and support, and include student voices in the discussion.

Strategy 8: Maximize Program Sustainability through Project-Based Development

The concept of a "project" comes from sustainable development theory. Typically, a problem is perceived—perhaps a waterway is being polluted—and a project is mobilized to solve the problem that includes both human and environmental factors and agents. Planning for a sustainable WAC program requires a similar intentional project-based approach to translate a program mission and goals into action. In WAC programs, example projects include WI initiatives, writing fellows programs, and faculty development retreats. Each project is self-contained and moves through the entire whole systems cycle of understanding, planning, developing, and leading. Focusing on program elements as projects enables directors to manage program growth and complexity with an eye toward integrating WAC-sponsored initiatives into existing university functions. SIs are developed in the initial stages and evaluated regularly to establish threshold boundaries within which each project can be expected to function successfully. Taken together, a set of projects is used systematically to fulfill the WAC program mission and goals. Using a project-based approach enables the WAC director or committee to prioritize which programs should be developed, in what order, and on what timeline to most impact the system.

Strategy 9: Make Reforms at Both the Micro and the System Levels

In WAC programs, working at the micro level (e.g., consulting with individual faculty, giving a presentation on peer review in a class) and working at the systems level (e.g., working with a department to create a departmental writing assessment plan or institute a WI requirement) go hand in hand. Typically, when WAC programs start, the director focuses on the micro level. This work is rewarding, and can help the director establish relationships with faculty, create credibility, and build critical mass. However, if directors spend most of their time at the micro level, then they can't spend much of their time at the systems level, which is necessary for making enduring and transformative changes to the campus culture of writing. Thus, while working at the micro level, think toward the systems level. For instance, if a department is interested in working with a director to pilot a writing fellows program, think of this pilot as a means for convincing broader audiences of the value of this type of program. As a program director, take time to reflect on where you are putting your time and energy, and aim for balance between working at the micro and systems levels.

Strategy 10: Plan for Gradual Rather Than Rapid Reforms to the System

Academic institutions are complex organizations that do not change course easily. WAC programs seek to shift the culture of writing at the institution, and this kind of change happens slowly and incrementally. From the example of established WAC programs, we know it can take decades to transform the culture of writing of a campus. Even specific projects can take years to fully develop. For example, a shift to building a WEC model that involves departments making multiyear commitments to curriculum analysis and change might take several years to gain footing barring a substantial external grant. The WAC committee might take six months to a year studying models; a faculty learning community might follow; a pilot department or two may go through the process. It is important for WAC directors to understand this principle, for two reasons. First, quick change can end in disaster, as such changes do not allow time for cross-institutional buy-in or an understanding of the potential impact on other parts of the system. Second, thinking that sustainable change will happen quickly will only lead to frustration on the part of the WAC director and perhaps those to whom the WAC director reports. Furthermore, quick change can often mean time-limited funding to the upper administration. Funding models need to be built on sustainable efforts.

Strategy 11: Deal with Obstacles to Program or Project Development Systematically

Every WAC director faces a wide array of obstacles that must be overcome for a program or project to proceed. Sometimes these obstacles are technical, like getting a WAC designation on a transcript. Such problems often take more time than seem warranted, but are typically manageable by working through appropriate institutional channels. At other times, problems may emerge that the director might perceive as intentional roadblocks. For example, a dean may decide that WI sections of large lower-division history and philosophy courses may not be pedagogically sound, and therefore a WAC program cannot work in her college because these classes are college staples.

We recommend using a systems approach to solving most significant problems. Systems theory reminds us that the ideologies that underlie systems structure the behaviors of individual actors within the system. A systems-thinking mindset includes not taking things personally, exercising patience, listening carefully, thinking logically, involving multiple stakeholders, and using common sense when negotiating conflicts. A systems process for resolving conflicts necessitates a broader understanding of the objection, which includes the collection of any necessary data, consideration of the scope of its reach, attention to primary stakeholders, a desire to balance the concerns that need to be considered, a willingness to compromise, and clear models or simulations to help predict the system's performance before the changes are implemented. Often, it also includes the ability to anticipate pressing objections and to develop contingency plans for addressing problems like the one identified above when they arise.

Strategy 12: Communicate Regularly and at All Levels of the System to Keep the Program Visible

To be seen as part of the fabric of the institution, WAC programs need to stay visible and on people's radar through good PR, politicking, and reminding other units of the relevance of the

WAC program. Visibility may be maintained through a variety of channels, such as WAC websites, newsletters, and event announcements. Visibility can also be maintained through different activities, such as preparing annual reports, attending campus meetings, joining university committees related to teaching and learning, making implementation processes transparent, following up with faculty who have participated in workshops and consultations, and publishing results of WAC initiatives both locally and nationally. Creating visibility is also about branding: creating signature events that happen at regular times each year (e.g., a yearly pedagogy retreat), naming a workshop series (rather than offering individual workshops that can appear as one-offs), or creating venues that are campus-wide in nature (e.g., a writing guide for students, a guide to teaching writing for faculty, a journal of student writing, National Day on Writing events). A WAC program can also become more visible by partnering with groups or initiatives on campus already garnering attention or focusing on topics currently of interest to faculty.

Strategy 13: Be Aware of Systems beyond Your Institution and Connect to Those That Are Beneficial to the WAC Program

Changes in systems beyond your institution may affect the campus culture of writing. Some of these effects may be negative, such as a state government slashing funds for basic writing programs. Other such effects may be positive, such as disciplinary accrediting bodies like the Institute of Electrical and Electronics Engineers, the Accreditation Board for Engineering and Technology, or the Commission on Collegiate Nursing Education increasing emphasis on written communication in their assessment of programs. And some effects have yet to have played out, such as the recent adoption of the Common Core State Standards across K–12 in forty-two states, a curricular reform mandating writing in the disciplines. In addition to being aware of such suprasystems, WAC directors can also make a point to use connections to larger disciplinary systems to help positively influence their institution's support of writing. These larger systems could include INWAC and its advisory board; the CCCC's WAC Standing Group; International Writing Across the Curriculum (IWAC) conferences; the Council of Writing Program Administrators' (CWPA) consultant-evaluator service; and position statements by the National Council of Teachers of English (NCTE), the CCCC, and the CWPA. In addition to these broader disciplinary systems, WAC directors in the United States can look to connect to systems outside of composition studies, such as the US Council on Undergraduate Research, the US Department of Education, and the Association of American Colleges and Universities.

Strategy 14: Assess and Revise the WAC Program

Systems tend toward segregation and stagnation, and compre-hensive writing programs are susceptible to becoming static rather than dynamic if feedback loops in the form of assessment activities aren't built into the development of the program. For example, a WI requirement without oversight or regular faculty development will most likely face dwindling enthusiasm and less coherence as a program. Even the most thoughtfully designed, systematic writing programs will have a tendency toward stagna-tion, so the WAC director needs to be perpetually reflective. In addition to the typical forms of assessment that include formal and informal measures of student work or curricular change, there is a particularly important form of assessment of program health and sustainability suggested by a whole systems approach: tracking the indicators of success and distress that were estab-lished in the planning stages of each project. For example, early in the development of a program, it may be important to track the number of WI-designated courses needed to reach critical mass for university-wide implementation. Later in the development of a program, it may be necessary to track numbers of faculty contacts in training or workshop contexts to determine whether they are decreasing and warrant intervention. Ideally, at every stage of program development, WAC directors should identify a set of questions based on organizational and program maps, identify the necessary but sufficient set of indicators to track program sustainability, develop an assessment model that keeps track of the full picture, and revisit the pool of questions and indicators as programs grow and change. There are wide ranges of potential indicators at several levels within the university system. Identifying and tracking them can help guard against program stagnation and provide the institution with key measures of program viability over time. Such practices also prevent us from being simply reactive to program threats.

Strategy 15: Create a Plan for Sustainable Leadership

All successful WAC directors know the joy of building projects and implementing institutional change. That excitement and desire to continue is a finite resource that must be acknowledged and directed carefully. It can be limited by an inadequately defined position, lack of adequate compensation (financial and course release), lack of acknowledgment by supervisors and upper administration, overcommitment, interference with teaching, research expectations/goals or progress toward tenure, overbearing supervisors or micromanagement, university politics, competing university-wide initiatives or mandates, health, and even family concerns. The sustainability of WAC leadership does not rely only on the director's ability to manage the number of commitments, but also on the distribution of WAC leadership. From a systems perspective, leadership that is located at only one point in the system and that comes from only one perspective is not as effective as leadership that is collective and disbursed throughout the system. The emerging area of leadership theory known as *complex systems leadership theory* (CSLT) argues that leadership is a system function and should have the goal of changing and improving the way actors in the system interact. CSLT posits that this improvement should be achieved primarily through transforming the structures and processes of the system, in order to attain richer interactions and greater sustainability and equity. According to CSLT, leadership is not solely within individuals but emerges through interactions among actors. Disbursement of WAC leadership may mean developing a critical mass of individual teacher-leaders across disciplines, working with a WAC advisory board or committee, creating graduation writing requirements that are overseen by cross-disciplinary committees, or collaborating with other campus units on signature faculty development events. Even when leadership becomes distributed, it creates more layers of oversight for the WAC director and thus does not necessarily decrease the WAC director's workload. Given the ever-expanding nature of a WAC program, the director needs to balance commitments to avoid burnout and maximize efforts. Finally, directors need a succession plan built into the program, so that, if they leave the institution, someone else is in a position to pick up where they left off.

How Our Process and Practices Connect to Our Principles

It is critical to emphasize that the methodology and strategies we present in this chapter are not solely derived from WAC lore or just our lived experiences as WAC practitioners and consultants. The whole systems methodology of *understand*, *plan*, *develop*, and *lead* and the strategies associated with each stage of the methodology represent praxis: theory connected to action, principles informing reflective practice. The principle of *wholeness* requires a methodology that begins with understanding the context and aiming for change at both the micro and macro level and strategies for mapping the system and finding points of leverage. *Integration* and *broad participation* are principles that lead to a process that involves stakeholders from across the system at every step, from understanding to planning to assessing, and strategies for how to involve multiple stakeholders are critical. The principles of *transformative change* and *equity* and the goal of changing not just a few courses or departments but institutional ideologies and practices require a more complex process than simply offering a few workshops or working with a handful of teachers in isolation from the rest of the system. Transformational change requires strategies for understanding and changing ideologies and improving equity for teachers and students. The whole systems methodology also supports the principle of *systematic development*, since the process emphasizes setting goals and building strategically and incrementally rather than rapidly and in an ad hoc manner. The principle of *feedback* applies to every stage of the whole systems methodology, but it is especially important in planning and in assessing. Strategies for assessing both individual projects and the WAC program are important for feedback and for ensuring the program doesn't become stagnant. In the final stage of the methodology, the principles of *visibility* and *leadership* are foundational: sustainable projects and programs must remain visible across the system, and the entire whole systems methodology should be facilitated by a leader with time, expertise, and support. Strategies for planning for sustainable leadership are key to the longevity of WAC.

The whole systems methodology for transformational change and the corresponding strategies discussed in this chapter represent a recursive and flexible process, rather than a set of discrete stages that we think all programs should follow. Even though we don't expect WAC directors to follow the methodology and strategies presented in this chapter lockstep, we offer them in an order that presents a possible process for program development. New WAC directors often feel overwhelmed by the scope and complexity of building or reviving a program, especially if they aren't given adequate release time or budget, as is too often the case. We want to stress that, although we're arguing for a whole systems approach that emphasizes systems-level thinking and sustainability, new directors might wind up starting small, and possibly just adopting elements of our approach and not enacting the entire methodology. The methodology and strategies we outline can be used as either a road map for designing a complex WAC program or a heuristic for starting small but aiming for long-term growth. Whether you are starting small with a single project or launching a formal WAC program, Chapters 4–7 provide descriptions of our whole systems principles, strategies, and tactics in practice through vignettes of a variety of different types of WAC programs and institutions.

CHAPTER FOUR

Stage One of the Whole Systems Methodology: Understanding the Institutional Landscape

In the first three chapters, we described the theoretical framework for a whole systems approach and presented principles, a methodology, and strategies for developing sustainable and transformative WAC programs. In Chapters 4 through 7, we detail the strategies and tactics associated with each stage of our methodology. In this chapter, we discuss the first stage, *understanding*, which focuses on gathering stakeholders and working together to understand the institutional landscape before planning a WAC program. Each of the following vignettes connects to this initial stage. Maury Elizabeth Brown, Germanna Community College, emphasizes the value of gathering data and surveying faculty to gauge the campus mood regarding the teaching of writing. Stephen Wilhoit, University of Dayton, emphasizes the importance of understanding the ideologies that inform faculty attitudes and practices regarding writing as a first step to leveraging change. Bryan Kopp discusses his systematic approach to analyzing a new "Writing in the Major" requirement at University of Wisconsin–La Crosse. In the final vignette, Michael J. Cripps, University of New England, describes his process for understanding why a WI requirement was failing and what steps he took to intervene. The vignettes are followed by discussions of the strategies connected to the *understanding* stage: Strategy 1, determining the campus mood; Strategy 2, understanding the system in order to focus on points of leverage, and Strategy 3, understanding the ideologies that inform the campus culture of writing.

Whither WAC at the Community College

Maury Elizabeth Brown
Germanna Community College

I was having difficulty finding an entry point to discuss WAC at my community college. My English faculty colleagues raised valid concerns that such an initiative was beyond the scope of the department and represented voluntary extra work without an institutional imperative or compensation. These concerns about time and labor are real and cannot be discounted. But, when you believe wholeheartedly in something, like I do regarding the importance of literacy and the shared responsibility for developing it in students, you continue to try to find an in, a place where the value of WAC can be asserted to the right people at the right time.

A redesigned developmental education initiative provided an opportunity when we noticed that it included a new placement test, coupled with a co-enrolled support course for students who formerly required a semester of developmental reading and/or writing. These changes meant that hundreds more students were now college composition eligible, allowing them to enroll in other courses and potentially shorten their time to degree. As a result, teachers in other disciplines were now teaching students who had noticeably lower reading and writing skills and who lacked the benefit of a semester in developmental English to help them learn to access and produce college-level content.

It became apparent that I needed hard data. Anecdotal conversations about student skills could quickly turn into unproductive gripe sessions. Presenting general research about the benefits of WAC programs or writing program administration was met with a bevy of reasons why such coordination was either unneeded or could not be accomplished with available resources. To break through the assumptions held by colleagues, I needed to know what expectations about writing our college faculty held, and what assignments they gave to students. Only by looking at data across our own college could I challenge long-held assumptions.

With the support of our president, vice president of academic services, office of research, and a system-level research grant that gave me the time to develop and administer a qualitative and quantitative survey instrument to our faculty, I was able to collect information about the length, type, and frequency of writing assignments faculty assign, and their expectations for student composing skills in their courses. The data gave us starting points for continued conversations, and are providing a means to analyze and align learning outcomes in first-year composition and the writing students are being asked to do in their other courses. In addition to the learning days, I have been given time on faculty meeting agendas to present some research findings. There is a core group of faculty who have self-identified as being interested in pursuing this work further, and they are beginning to talk writing in their own department meetings. Full-time faculty institution-wide are at least aware now of wide disparity among their colleagues in writing assignments. Furthermore, there is near-universal concern among respondents regarding students' writing skills and a strongly held belief in the connection between writing and student success in a course, in degree attainment, and in the workplace. These shared faculty concerns have not escaped the notice of administration, who, along with faculty, will be choosing the next institutional quality enhancement plan (QEP). WAC has been suggested as a QEP focus; a committee will make the final decision later this year.

So the moral of this story is four-fold: (1) persist; (2) talk, and keep talking; (3) obtain primary data; and (4) capitalize on higher education reform changes. College administrators tend not to listen unless a solution meets their needs; they are under considerable pressure from boards, chancellors, politicians, and donors to demonstrate value in measurable terms. Implementing WAC in the twenty-first century means using data to demonstrate the value of a WAC program to all constituents. To do so, we need to tie WAC to institutional initiatives, which, today, are about student success: metrics about student retention, transfer, and degree attainment that, in more and more states, are becoming the data points that drive funding.

As composition and rhetoric scholars, we have long known there is a connection between literacy and student success. We feel it in our bones, and, for many of us, this implicit understanding that what we are doing matters to our students, our economy, our society, and our democracy is the driving force for our interest in the field. But we have to be able to speak those convictions to those outside our field and especially to those who hold institutional or societal power. The language of those discourse communities is the language of data and return on investment. We need to speak it, and we need to be aware of higher education reform efforts and how to align our WAC work with those institutional and political imperatives.

WAC *without a* WAC *Program*

Stephen Wilhoit
University of Dayton

In 2008, I received a telephone call from a reporter at *USA Today*. He was working on a story related to some recent National Survey of Student Engagement results. The reporter told me that, on the survey, students at the University of Dayton gave particularly high marks to questions concerning the amount of writing required in their classes, and he wanted to know more about our apparently successful WAC program. I told the reporter that the results surprised me because we don't have a WAC program at Dayton.

Instead, since 1999, we've had a very successful semester-long seminar for faculty that examines WAC principles and practices, particularly the relationship between writing and student learning. When I received that call in 2008, about a hundred faculty members had already completed the seminar. The seminar is still going strong at Dayton, which has shown me that you don't need a fully articulated WAC program to promote WAC at a school.

Like a lot of other WPAs, in the late 1990s, I began to think seriously about establishing some sort of WAC presence at my institution. I was intrigued and excited by all the WAC-related success stories I was reading about in journals and hearing about at conferences. However, I'd been at Dayton long enough to understand its dominant ethos and culture, and that I would need a strategy built both to introduce WAC at my institution and to encourage faculty to embrace it.

Faculty at Dayton are deeply committed to being effective teachers and open to instructional practices that promote student learning. However, a longitudinal study of student writing I conducted during my first six years at the university indicated that faculty primarily saw writing as a way to test student learning rather than to facilitate it. The most common writing assignments students completed across the curriculum were essay test answers. The study also showed that faculty who included writing in their classes relied heavily on formal, graded assignments: research papers, book reports, and abstracts, for example. My yearly interviews with the students taking part in the study further revealed that faculty who assigned writing in their classes rarely offered their students any instruction or assistance—just an assignment sheet (maybe) and a due date. In short, faculty across the curriculum had a limited view of the role writing could play in helping them achieve a valued goal: promoting student learning. I believed that providing faculty with some training in WAC theory and practice could bring about a significant change in how they employed writing in their classes and would help them teach writing more effectively.

Second, academic departments at Dayton value their independence and are highly skeptical of top-down program requirements. Moving WAC forward on campus would have to be a retail enterprise, not wholesale—I'd have to work with individual faculty to bring about the changes I thought were needed. The pace of change would be slow, but I believed the results would be long lasting if, over time, my colleagues came to see the value of WAC in their classes. To gauge interest in the topic, I offered a few one-hour introductions to WAC as part of our university's "Faculty Development Day." They were well received—during the sessions, faculty quickly began to identify ways they could apply writing-to-learn practices in their classes.

About that time, I was asked to serve on a committee charged with developing new general education requirements. The committee ultimately agreed on language that encouraged departments to include discipline-specific writing instruction in upper-level classes—not a WAC or WID program or requirement per se, but certainly a big step in the right direction. Once that language was adopted, I argued that, if departments were going to include more writing in their classes, faculty needed to be prepared to teach it. The provost agreed and asked me to propose a way to accomplish that.

While the one-hour workshops I'd already tried could generate awareness of and interest in WAC, they alone were unlikely to alter faculty practice. That kind of deep change takes time to accomplish. So, instead, I proposed a semester-long seminar that would bring together a small group of faculty from across the curriculum to share ideas and learn from one another. My hope was that, over the course of the semester, the participants could develop applications of WAC theory that made sense in the classes they were teaching, actually have students complete those assignments and activities, and report back to the group on the results. I knew I would win faculty buy-in if they experienced firsthand how these new ideas and practices could benefit their students.

I made workshopping a part of the seminar as well. At several points, participating faculty submitted their assignments for peer critique. Faculty loved having colleagues suggest revisions to their assignments and being able to provide feedback in return. In addition, the participants felt they left the seminar with a greater understanding of expectations for student writing across the curriculum.

The inaugural WAC seminar succeeded beyond my expectations. The faculty were enthusiastic during the sessions and praised it in assessments conducted at the end of the semester. More important, though, they encouraged colleagues in their departments to participate the next time the seminar was offered.

When the provost saw the assessment results and heard personally from some of the participating faculty, he proposed that we offer the seminar every year, open it to all faculty (including lecturers and part-time instructors), and hold it in the university's newly opened learning teaching center.

I still host the seminar every fall term, with ten to twelve participants. Over time, it has positively impacted teaching across the curriculum at Dayton. Part of its success had to do with timing—I proposed it as our learning teaching center was taking shape and could link it to a new general education program. However, as I told the *USA Today* reporter in 2008, I also learned that, when faculty are interested in improving student learning and willing to experiment with their teaching in the company of peers, WAC initiatives can thrive even at a school that doesn't have a formal WAC program.

The Elusive Whole: From Writing Emphasis to Writing in the Major

Bryan Kopp
University of Wisconsin–La Crosse

As a writing programs coordinator, I am constantly reminded of the plural "s" in my position's title. Any statement I make about writing on our campus has to be highly qualified because it may apply to one writing program but not another. This would not be a problem if there were not a need to articulate what grants coherence and consistency to WAC on our campus, and to assess whether the whole is more—or less—than the sum of its parts. At the current moment, our WAC initiative seems to be suspended in the liminal space between general education and major degree programs, existing in and owned by neither entirely, and yet, potentially, by both, in the broader university context. After sharing background on the history and structure of WAC at University of Wisconsin–La Crosse, a mid-sized regional comprehensive university located in the upper Midwest, I will reflect on those elements that have been most and least sustainable.

In 1991, University of Wisconsin–La Crosse adopted a writing emphasis (WE) requirement as part of its new general education program. Since then, all students are required to take first-year composition plus two WE courses, one of which must be in the major and one upper division. A WE course includes fifty pages of writing (approximately forty writing to learn and ten formal writing) and is taught by a certified instructor. To become certified, instructors complete a training session and submit an approval form. Approximately 250 instructors have been certified and can teach any course in a WE manner without gaining further approval.

The problems with this instructor-based approach to WAC are perhaps too obvious in hindsight: (a) individual instructors tend to carry the burden of teaching WE courses; (b) the quantitative definition of fifty pages per course (over two courses) is sometimes perceived as an empty requirement; (c) there is no mechanism for monitoring future compliance or conducting assessments. Further undermining the sustainability of this approach is the questionable assumption that taking two unrelated courses adds up to improvement in students' writing. Although students do more writing outside of English composition, they do not necessarily produce better writing. Indeed, students may be experiencing contradictory advice, conflicting standards, and incompatible pedagogies. Included in the "basic skills" section of our general education program, the WE requirement expanded our institutional commitment to writing, establishing in effect a graduation requirement, but it did so as an add-on.

As writing is integral to learning in all disciplines and the development of writing abilities is a longer-term goal that extends beyond individual courses, we created "Writing in the Major" (WM), a more systematic and sustainable approach to WAC. Located within fields of study rather than general education per se, WM is a coordinated, collaborative effort to improve students' writing abilities and to promote student learning through writing. Effective since 1998, undergraduates completing their major requirements in approved WM programs automatically fulfill the WE requirement. A WM program has six interrelated characteristics: (1) clearly defined goals, outcomes, and standards for student writing; (2) a shared evaluation framework; (3) effective writing processes throughout the major; (4) integration of writing to learn throughout the major; (5) development of mindful writers; and (6) assessment of student learning and writing. To gain WM status, departmental teams must integrate writing into their major curriculum, define formal writing competence in their discipline, articulate department-level learning goals, and create an assessment plan. Significantly, these departmental goals have no explicit connection to the general education program and yet they are a way to fulfill a general education requirement.

To date, more than thirty-three programs have been approved as WM, providing evidence that student writing has become a collective responsibility—one that is developmentally oriented, qualitatively defined, learning focused, and discipline based. Like WE, WM presents challenges, though—namely, how to track overall compliance and see the bigger picture. If goals are articulated and progress is assessed within departments, how is a WAC coordinator to know what is happening at the university level? Moreover, how is the general education program to understand where writing, now with a decidedly non-general focus, fits into its requirements?

Such problems require multiple solutions, some of which we have tried: for example, (a) construct a university-level portrait of the effects of our diverse WAC efforts through surveys of students using National Survey of Student Engagement–WPA survey questions and other instruments, such as the College of Liberal Arts survey; (b) clarify in faculty development sessions how WE/WM fulfill both general education and major goals; and (c) require reporting of WM assessments in academic program reviews and, as applicable, general education assessments.

The greatest challenge has been for us to conceptualize how multiple, department-level WAC/WID systems function together, harmoniously or not, in the larger university system, including lower-division general education experiences *and* upper-division major experiences. An important next step is to map course, general education, and departmental student learning outcomes related to writing, with the hope that university-level outcomes and a multitiered approach will emerge. For us to achieve for the whole university what individual WM programs have already—namely, a coordinated, systematic, developmental approach to WAC—we will need to be able to imagine multiple systems at play, because that is, after all, what our students experience.

Wrangling Writing Intensives

Michael J. Cripps
University of New England

For three years (2007–2010), I served as the WAC program administrator at a midsized four-year public college with a three-course WI graduation requirement. Taking the reins in the sixth year of WI implementation, I led a program confronting many of the challenges known to plague WI-based WAC programs: insufficient WI offerings relative to the undergraduate population, a nearly broken WI course proposal and review process, and skyrocketing waivers of WI requirements for graduating seniors. I inherited a program that had already seen two WI coordinators fail to wrangle the problem of course review processes and WI waivers, a fact that signaled the possibility that it might be time to completely rethink the WI component of the WAC program. Knowing the institution and the WAC program, however, I had the strong sense that the institution's WI challenges could be addressed by bringing together institutional and outcomes data; such stakeholders as the advising and registrar's offices, the deans, the academic departments and faculty who would deliver WI courses; and respected faculty who regularly taught WI courses.

Working with the college's institutional research office, we secured information about WI completion rates by class. Our WI requirement called for two such courses at the lower (100 or 200) level, primarily in the general education curriculum, and at least one in the upper level in the major program of study. It quickly became clear that undergraduates were not starting their WI sequence in their first year or completing their lower-level WIs by their second year, which meant they had to scramble to pick up lower-level WI courses while focused on completing coursework in the major. Putting together data on cohort sizes and the number of WI courses offered at the 100 and 200 levels, we quickly determined that the college was not offering enough WI courses to meet demand. And, by tracking WI graduation waivers by WI level and major, we were able to confirm that the college needed more lower-level WI courses to identify the academic programs responsible for the majority of graduation waivers. Although lower-level WI waivers were sprinkled throughout the college, upper-level waivers were concentrated in just a couple programs. The data called for a three-pronged approach to WI completion: (1) improved advising and communication with students, (2) expansion of lower-level WI offerings, and (3) work to get at least one WI offering in every major program of study.

Meetings with the advising office revealed an advising pattern at odds with the recommended curriculum. First-year student advisors, it turns out, were directing students away from WI courses because they perceived them to be more difficult and wanted students to experience success in the first year. Faculty advisors, not surprisingly, were often focused on prerequisites and coursework for the major, and WI requirements easily dropped off the radar. Working with the registrar, we found that it was difficult to make the WI offerings for a given term visible to students and faculty in a way that would encourage registration. To address these advising and registration challenges, we met with departments and advisors to remind the community of the requirements and the reasons for the recommended sequencing of WI offerings: one WI in year one, one WI in year two, one WI in the major. We also published (in print, via email, and on the WAC website) a one-page list of the upcoming term's WI courses that many inserted directly into the schedule of classes. Information about current WI offerings and the goals of the recommended WI sequence was certainly necessary if students were to know about and register for WI courses. But the institutional data revealed that advising was hardly sufficient.

The college did not offer enough WI courses to meet student need. Not enough lower-level WI courses were being offered, and a couple major programs had yet to identify appropriate upper-level WI courses for their majors. More faculty would need to offer their courses as WI, a designation with requirements that committed them to providing more feedback on student writing, assigning more writing, and including in-class attention to the writing process. WI courses came with a reduced course cap to permit such attention, which required a department to offer additional sections. A chair committing to more WI courses in his or her department would need to shift faculty around and possibly hire some adjuncts to teach courses. And the dean's office would need to commit resources (instructional compensation and classroom space) if more WI courses were to run. It is here that the interconnected nature of the challenge comes most clearly into view.

Armed with data, we had the support of the dean's office for added sections of lower-level WI courses, provided the college had a visible, rigorous review process for WI offerings. As the dean was fond of saying, "How do you know the WI is really WI?" In asking the question, the dean exposed another weak link in the WAC program: the WI review process, while clear and approved by college governance, had not been followed in years. In fact, an earlier effort to require a formal WI review process to align practice with the process outlined in the governance documents had failed amid faculty opposition to the WAC police. This time, we sought out highly respected faculty with considerable WI experience to serve on a "WI advisory committee." We intentionally drew a faculty member from each disciplinary area of the college. That group, led by the WAC program administrator, vetted every WI course proposal that came in and offered peer-reviewed feedback to each instructor as well as individualized guidance in some cases. By drawing on their disciplinary networks, committee members encouraged faculty to consider offering

WI courses and communicated the importance of the committee. The dean's office committed to supporting WI offerings for every course recommended for approval by that committee.

In under two years, the college moved to reviewing a proposal for every WI offered on campus, expanded by 50 percent the number of lower-level WI offerings and mostly addressed the issue of upper-level WI courses, and doubled the number of first-year students completing their initial WI course in the first year.

Strategy 1: Determine the Campus Mood

In the principles we derived from theories of complexity, we emphasized the importance of *wholeness*—of approaching WAC programs as interventions into complex systems with many actors. These actors—faculty, staff, administration, students—have perspectives on writing that WAC directors need to be aware of before they act. Whether launching WAC on a campus where WAC hasn't existed, restarting a dormant program, or revitalizing an existing program, before enacting change, it is critical to first determine the campus mood. Simon Bell and Stephen Morse (2008), leaders in sustainable development theory, have observed that exploring "mood" can help one gauge whether "the context is one of historic hope and goodwill, or one of despair and anger, or if there is a mixture of both with neither predominating" (p. 158). Gauging mood is an important step in assessing the overall readiness of an institution for increased commitment to student writing across the curriculum—whether it's the "right time" to introduce change, as discussed by Maury Elizabeth Brown in her vignette. Brown had been interested in initiating WAC for some time, but had been warned by her colleagues in the English department that doing so would amount to "voluntary extra work" as she did not yet have "institutional imperative or compensation." Brown thus waited until the institutional imperative arrived—in the form of a redesigned education initiative—which she used to apply for a grant that gave her the time and resources to gather data, information that would help her determine the campus mood on student writing.

Determining the campus mood is a mix of collecting data, talking to stakeholders, reflecting on current writing practices across university contexts, and identifying points of conflict and support concerning possible WAC program models. The kinds of data one collects and the tactics used to collect it depend on a number of factors: where the impetus for increased emphasis on student writing is coming from, the history of WAC and other writing programs on campus, the familiarity of the WAC leader with the campus culture and system, and the scale of the intervention to be introduced.

Brown's tactic of administering a faculty survey on the kinds of student writing assigned and faculty expectations is one approach to assessing campus mood. She used the survey results to initiate discussions on student writing with stakeholders, a move that led to the formation of a faculty group focused on student writing and the recommendation that WAC become a QEP focus the following year.

But faculty surveys aren't always feasible or appropriate. Brown was not a newcomer to her campus when she decided to use this tactic. Those who are new might choose to take a more ethnographic approach, such as attending faculty development events and meetings related to teaching and learning, and meeting individually with faculty, department chairs, and administrators to learn more about current and past student writing-related matters. These ethnographic tactics would allow for an informal assessment of campus attitudes toward student writing and a sense of the oases and deserts of writing support on campus.

To determine the mood in relation to a particular intervention, Bell and Morse (2008) recommended using a SWOT analysis. The SWOT method offers a heuristic for brainstorming the potential strengths, weaknesses, opportunities, and threats as related to a specific project at a specific point in time (Bell & Morse, 2008, pp. 158–59). A SWOT analysis would be a useful tactic for reflecting on the campus mood regarding particular WAC initiatives, such as a writing fellows program or change in a policy. While Bryan Kopp did not conduct a formal SWOT analysis, we can see, in his vignette and in Figure 4.1, that he used a similar heuristic for thinking through the problems and potentials of the existing WE program. SWOT analyses offer snapshots of a project or program at a particular moment in time. However, they are heuristics, not systematic assessments of individual projects or analyses of the larger institutional landscape. SWOT analyses can allow WAC directors to identify gaps in their understanding in order to identify data that needs to be collected. In Kopp's case, his analysis of the WE approach allowed him to plan an intervention—the Writing in the Majors (WM) program—that built on the benefits and addressed the drawbacks of the present curricular structure. This intervention would likely not have been as effective had Kopp not taken the time to assess the campus mood.

	POSITIVE	NEGATIVE
NOW	**Strengths:** Long history at the institution (initiated in 1991); widely institutionalized (250 faculty have been trained in WAC pedagogy and thus approved as WE instructors; the WE courses are graduation requirements); promotes multiple opportunities for students to write across their career (students must take first-year composition plus two WE courses, one of which must be upper level and in the student's major)	**Weaknesses:** A subset of instructors carry the burden of teaching WE courses; the quantitative requirement for a certain number of assigned pages of writing in WE is sometimes seen as an empty requirement; there are no mechanisms for ensuring compliance after a faculty member is approved as a WE instructor; the program is grounded in the perhaps faulty assumption that more writing equals improvement as a writer; student may experience conflicting writing advice, pedagogies, and standards
LATER	**Opportunities:** The existence of the WE program lays the groundwork for a more systematic approach to student writing development	**Threats:** Since the students are taking apples-and-oranges writing-enhanced courses that may not actually lead to improvement in writing, faculty perceptions of poor upper-level student writing may threaten the continuation of the WE program; and, as WE courses are owned by individual faculty rather than departments or majors, system-wide support for the program can't exist

FIGURE 4.1. *SWOT analysis of a WE program, based on Kopp's vignette.*

Bell and Morse (2008) warned us that mood is fickle, can change quickly in relation to other factors in the context, and is subjective (p. 159). Indeed, it may be dangerous to place too much faith in a determination of campus mood, as is illustrated in Michael Michaud's vignette, which opens Chapter 1, in which he first describes the many positive signs of campus mood he had identified, but then his deep disappointment that the WAC program proposal ultimately wasn't supported. Assessing mood is, as Bell and Morse (2008) asserted, "limited and partial, but a starting point" (p. 161), adding, "once the researcher feels a degree of comfort and familiarity with the context and the mood of the actors, the analysis can go on to describe the range and type of stakeholders" (p. 162). In the rest of the current chapter, we describe additional strategies that may be used in conjunction with determining the campus mood. Despite its limitations, we value the strategy of determining mood because it can provide, as Bell and Morse (2008) emphasized, a "baseline condition of the context" (p. 159). Understanding mood can help a WAC leader determine the extent to which the conditions are right for introducing new WAC interventions—important information before dedicating further time and resources.

Determining the Campus Mood: Questions to Consider

1. In what contexts is student writing being discussed on campus, why is it being discussed, who is discussing it, and what attitudes about student writing or teaching with writing are expressed?

2. How visible is student writing on campus? Where and how is student writing featured?

3. What is the culture of faculty development at your campus, what kinds of faculty development are happening, and how are they being received? Where is the exigency for WAC coming from, who is behind it, and why is it happening now?

4. What kinds of student writing initiatives have existed on campus? Regarding past programs, what were their successes, and what led to their demise? For present programs, what are their strengths, weaknesses, opportunities, and threats?

5. Given institutional realities (e.g., teaching loads, pressure to publish, working conditions for adjunct faculty, value of teaching in tenure/reappointment), what kinds of interventions would likely be the best received?

6. Given the student body (e.g., preparation for writing in K–12 and first-year composition, linguistic and cultural diversity, goals post graduation, number of credits carried each semester, workload outside of studies), what kinds of interventions would students find the most beneficial?

Strategy 2: Understand the System in Order to Focus on Points of Interactivity and Leverage

In Chapter 2, we discussed resilience theory to introduce the notion of WAC programs as interventions for deliberate *transformational change*. Our contention is that WAC programs, by their very natures, are designed to shift the curricular ecology of the given institution. New WAC directors need to keep this in mind, as knowing how to create manageable, deliberate, and sustainable change in a complex system to shift its culture is neither simple nor obvious. Furthermore, while WAC directors can learn from strategies used by other WAC programs, each institutional context is unique and requires a clear understanding of its specific lines of communication, vested stakeholders, policies and practices, expectations, current status of conditions on campus, and goals, as well as pathways of least resistance before and after its initial development. In fact, given the levels of scale across which WAC programs function—faculty, student, classroom, course, program, department, college, university, state, accreditation boards, etc.—it behooves WAC directors to understand, map, and determine key measures of the state of the system across time, where and how student writing takes place, how that writing is introduced and supported, what system elements focus on writing and writing outcomes, how writing manifests across curricular contexts, and how to build writing support systems that can be integrated into the pedagogical ecology of the university. These levels of understanding help program stakeholders identify what interventions should be made, at what levels, in what order, and on what scales. Such information also helps stakeholders prioritize what initiatives might best enable an emerging WAC program to have greatest impact/leverage and simultaneously achieve maximum buy-in. Mapping can be undertaken at any point in a program's development, but is particularly instructive at moments of change such as the development of new initiatives, a change of director, or a realignment of financial support. Effective strategies include quick institutional diagrams, process maps, and full-scale institutional network maps, as well as determination of state SIs that can be used to understand the existing curricular ecology.

Quick Institutional Diagrams

In her vignette, Brown provides an example of a program that would have benefited from a quick institutional diagram early in their planning processes. She begins by noting that she was having a hard time finding an entry point to discuss WAC at her community college until a "developmental education initiative provided an opportunity." She noted that a new placement test, coupled with a co-enrolled support course for students that replaced a developmental writing course, led to hundreds of students entering college writing sooner. Teachers in the disciplines noticed weaker skills and were concerned. Brown's response was to survey faculty, a tactic that allowed her to better understand campus mood, but a quick institutional diagram could have helped her explore WAC in relation to different factors at the university. Such a map would look something like Figure 4.2. This figure does not represent a WAC program, but, rather, a historical record of steps taken to gain support to start a WAC program. The numbered dark gray items are university agents, factors at the university level. State SIs could be defined for each to determine the starting environment for introducing curricular change. The other, light gray items are pre-WAC program agents. Notice how few links and nodes appear here. A significant number of additional agents and their connections would need to be identified even for a quick institutional map to indicate the various places where writing is mandated, taught, supported, assessed, and discussed in programs, departments, and college and university levels. Once mapped, the nodes would need to be prioritized for most significant impact on writing, a step best taken with a group of stakeholders, as we discuss in the Chapter 5. Figure 4.2 demonstrates that many node types can serve as agents for change in the system, including the collective concerns of faculty. In this map, it is obvious that the QEP would be the single greatest point of leverage for change in the system, as QEPs are designed at the institutional level, must receive significant funding for an extended time frame, and can provide opportunities to study the impacts of change in the curricular ecology of the institution. If, however, a different topic is chosen for the QEP, that should not mean that WAC is dead at this institution. But a much more complex institutional web would need to be developed to identify other points of leverage.

Process Maps

As we explained in Chapter 2, ONA involves detailed surveying and mapping of processes used by organizations to create more efficient paths for communication and workflow, but, for WAC purposes, a less formal version of this tactic is sufficient to enable what we call *process mapping*. The first step involves conversations with stakeholders across scales like selected faculty, chairs, campus committee representatives, and perhaps a dean to get a broad perspective of how information flows through the system and where to start when beginning a new initiative. The

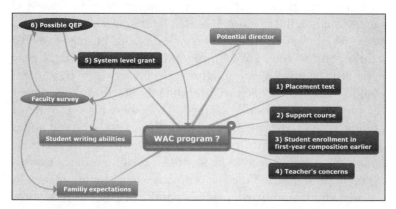

FIGURE **4.2.** *Exploratory WAC initiative at a community college, based on Brown's vignette.*

more specific work of process mapping identifies the actors and communication pathways important to a particular project, as demonstrated by the steps that Brown and Wilhoit both took to initiate their university-wide studies. To survey the faculty, each had to figure out who had the authority to grant permission, who specialized in survey development to review the draft, to whom the completed survey should be sent for approval, how the survey would be distributed, and to whom results would be reported. In many cases, these process maps are created on the fly when needed and thus are rarely recorded, though documenting them can greatly facilitate the transition from one WAC director to another.

Full-Scale Institutional Network Maps

The final mapping process we discuss identifies not only the human conduits in the flow of information and production, but also other, non-human agents. This type of mapping may work best in established WAC programs to reveal patterns of organization and lines of connection that the stakeholders could not fully visualize without a comprehensive map. In 2006, Jeff researched the WAC programs at Washington State University and George Mason University to begin understanding and theorizing what sustainability means for such well-established programs. He interviewed stakeholders across all scales at each institution, collected a range of institutional documents, and developed full-scale institutional network maps to represent each program. The map of George Mason's WAC program (Figure 4.3) demonstrates how central a role the director played at the time of the research project. Notice how many links stem from the WAC director. In fact, there are no major nodes (represented as "clouds") without direct links to the director. The map of Washington State's program (Figure 4.4), on the other hand, reveals that the WAC program is decentralized, as the WAC directorship was eliminated when the office of undergraduate education was formed soon before Jeff arrived on campus.

It is important to note that these type of maps are best made by an outsider to the system, who can come in, study the program in all its facets, and then develop the visual map in mind mapping

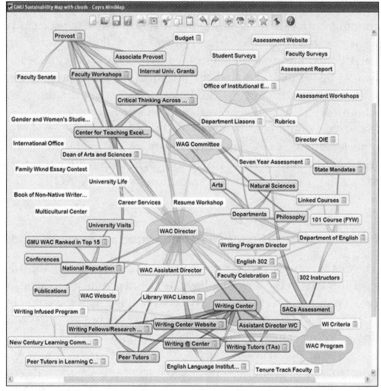

FIGURE **4.3.** *George Mason University's WAC program, institutional map (August 2006).*

software (in this case Cayra, which is no longer supported). That said, a WAC director can create such a map, as long as it is shared and verified by the major stakeholders in the program. This kind of map would have helped Kopp with the challenge he identifies in his vignette: conceptualizing how "multiple, department-level WAC/WID systems function together, harmoniously or not, in the larger university system, including lower-division general education experiences *and* upper-division major experiences." Furthermore, such a map would help stakeholders in the program figure out state SIs to track general education and departmental student learning outcomes related to writing with university-wide outcomes to develop a "multitiered approach." If mind mapping software is used to create the map, users can select a node within

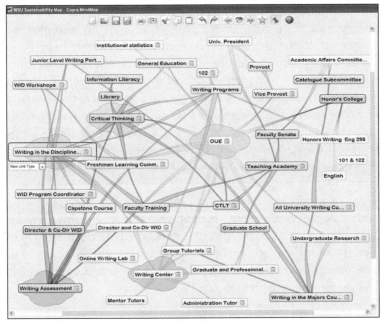

Figure 4.4. *Washington State University's WAC program, institutional map (September 2006).*

the system and orient the system around that node as the center. Being able to manipulate these visual networks in this way provides an insider's perspective of how that agent perceives its place within the system, and allows the stakeholder group to ask questions that mark the state of current curricula and conditions of the curricular ecology. For example, knowing the state of student writing upon matriculation can help program planners understand the difference between preparedness of first-time-in-college students and transfers. Similarly, knowing the state of teaching loads across departments can provide opportunities to identify programs in which WAC courses might be most successful.

Similarly, the WAC program at the University of New England (described earlier) would have benefited from institutional mapping. Cripps notes in his vignette that two WI coordinators before him had failed to "wrangle the problem of course review processes and WI waivers, a fact that signaled the possibility that it might be time to completely rethink the WI component of the

WAC program." Cripps succeeded where others had failed, in part because of his intuition for problem solving, his management style of broad stakeholder involvement, and his ability to perceive the necessary steps by leveraging key agents in the system. Notwithstanding, a visual presentation of the network, a clear process for tracking the state of current writing practices, the location of problems in the system, and an accompanying narrative of how the problems impact the system would have helped Cripps represent the reinforcing feedback loops, lapses, and bottlenecks that were causing the system to fail. Furthermore, because such maps create a snapshot of the institution relationships within a WAC program at a moment in time, future WI directors of the same program could greatly benefit from seeing how this network changed over time. Future WI directors could use the map to help identify additional aspects of the system that could be changed to institute future reforms, prevent potential bottlenecks and failure, and thereby ensure greater sustainability.

Understanding the System in Order to Focus on Points of Interactivity and Leverage: Questions to Consider

1. Who are the stakeholders in the institution who must be consulted to build a WAC program? (Provost, vice presidents, deans, chairs, faculty, students, student support services, etc.)

2. What are the pathways that policies, official WAC documents (like rubrics or WI criteria), and decisions must follow for approval?

3. Who or what are the conduits and bottlenecks?

4. Where on campus does student writing regularly take place?

5. How is that writing introduced and supported?

6. What is the state of writing by first-time-in-college students and by transfers?

7. Where are there gaps in support for writing or teaching of writing?

8. What programs, initiatives, and departments overlap with or compete for resources with the WAC initiative?

9. What existing committees or programs (e.g., undergraduate curriculum committee, faculty senate, assessment committees) currently support writing-related initiatives?

10. What are the current lines of funding and support, and what are their sources?

11. What are the current teaching support services (e.g., center for teaching and learning, e-learning, critical thinking initiative)?

12. What resources are devoted to writing on campus (e.g., computer labs, library, writing center, undergraduate research grants, first-year composition workshops)?

13. What assessment instruments and processes are currently used to assess writing on campus?

14. How do all of these elements link to one another?

15. Which type of map (e.g., quick institutional diagram, process map, or full-scale institutional network map) would be most helpful for understanding the institutional landscape at this point in the development of the WAC program?

Strategy 3: Understand the Ideologies That Inform the Campus Culture of Writing

Our whole systems principles emphasize WAC as a change agent, and the principle of *transformational change* focuses on the importance of changing ideologies and practices as they relate to writing culture. Understanding ideologies that underlie campus writing programs and faculty attitudes is different from understanding the campus mood, as discussed in Strategy 1 (above). Understanding mood is about the overall readiness and willingness of the campus to increase its commitment to WAC, and it can help WAC program directors with timing, deciding on types of initiatives, and recognizing stakeholders who may provide support. Ideology, on the other hand, is focused on assumptions about writing that are already in place and that reflect the way writing is defined and understood by the campus. For example, a common ideology that WAC works against is the view that good writing is grammatically correct writing. Understanding ideology is also about analyzing how assumptions about writing are reflected in—and reinforced by—processes, practices, and programs.

There is a complex and codependent relationship between the structure of campus writing programs and faculty ideologies regarding writing. As Cripps's vignette illustrates, a broken WI requirement can create problematic reinforcing processes that will begin to shape faculty's attitudes about the teaching of writing. At the University of New England, too few WI courses were offered to meet student demand (state SI), which was coupled with a lack of oversight of WI requirements (state SI). These are common problems that can lead to WI class sizes being increased (impact SI) and WI courses being added at the last minute (impact SI) and assigned to contingent faculty who may or may not have training in teaching writing (impact SI). This could affect both administrator and faculty attitudes about student writing, creating a process that reinforces the ideology of writing as a burden that should be shouldered by composition teachers. As Cripps investigated the problems with his campus's WI requirement, it was important for him to understand not only what was broken about the requirement, but also what reinforcing processes resulted from the problems with the requirement and how those processes shaped faculty and administrators' beliefs about writing.

Kopp discusses in his vignette how his campus addressed similar problems with a course-based WI requirement by shifting to integrating writing throughout a major. As Kopp argues, this WM approach emphasizes that writing is "a collective responsibility—one that is developmentally oriented, qualitatively defined, learning focused, and discipline based." Shifting from a WI to a WM model (or WEC model, as Anson and Dannels discuss in their vignette in Chapter 1) can create a reinforcing process that can help change a campus ideology that writing is the responsibility of the English department or of a handful of teachers in a department who are willing to take on the "burden" to an ideology that assumes writing is everyone's responsibility.

In his vignette on the development of a WAC seminar for faculty, Wilhoit mentions how he explored writing on his campus through the tactic of a longitudinal study of student writing he conducted over his first six years at the institution. Ethnographic, longitudinal studies are a labor-intensive but rich way to investigate student writing at an institution, and it was through this research that Wilhoit unearthed a common ideology among faculty across disciplines at many institutions: "Faculty primarily saw writing as a way to test student learning rather than to facilitate it." This ideology of writing as a tool for testing rather than a tool for learning manifested itself in the assigning of a large number of essay tests. It's not hard to imagine the way the ideology of writing as testing can turn into reinforcing processes: essay tests becoming the norm in the culture of departmental curricula as more and more instructors rely on tests, the campus adopting timed writing tests at the institutional level since they are widely accepted by faculty across disciplines, and even the future acceptance of standardized tests like the Collegiate Learning Assessment for accreditation purposes. Wilhoit's faculty development seminar was a WAC project that intervened to revise faculty ideologies regarding writing and prevent reinforcing processes that could undermine assumptions about writing as a mode of learning. Because of the power of reinforcing processes, a shift in the ideologies that inform campus attitudes about writing can have compounding effects. This is why it's critical, when understanding the institutional landscape, to analyze not just the mood of the campus and the networks of writing, but also the ideologies that underlie programs and practices.

As we suggested in Chapter 2, Critical Systems Thinking (CST) provides a useful way to think about ideology when trying to understand the culture of writing at an institution. CST focuses on emancipation and the exposure of inequalities, and it helps us move toward liberation rather than simply equilibrium. CST methodology includes critical awareness, exposing of dominant voices, and freedom from restrictive power relations (Flood & Romm, 1996; Midgley, 1996). CST emphasizes that, as we look to understand systems and create models of alternatives to the current system, we should include equally the voices of all stakeholders in the system, expose oppressive power relations, and find alternative models of more liberatory systems. Coming to an understanding of the ideologies of writing at work at the institution will help WAC directors make visible assumptions that underlie practices, anticipate points of resistance, determine which existing ideologies might be candidates for change, identify ideologies that clash, and plan strategies for handling those differences.

To illustrate tactics WAC leaders might use to make visible these ideologies, we discuss an example of a CST approach to WAC that Dan applied at his former campus. From years of building informal networks through WAC faculty development and departmental outreach, Dan knew that the campus writing requirements and the sequence of tests and remediation courses that students were tracked into were creating conflict and struggle for students, faculty, and administrators. He and his writing program colleagues used a faculty senate retreat on writing as leverage to ask the senate to charge the existing reading and writing subcommittee (a subcommittee of the senate's curriculum policies committee) with proposing reforms to the comprehensive writing program. This subcommittee was made up of stakeholders from across the system (writing specialists, faculty across disciplines, administrators), and Dan's first step was to ask the stakeholders to create a rich picture of the comprehensive writing program in the form of a flow chart. The flow chart—a complex maze of testing, sorting, remediation, and barriers for students from the moment they entered the system to the moment they graduated—exposed a number of ideologies at work. The amount of testing and remediation exposed the system as working on a deficit model, and data on the types of students most likely to be caught in the web of remediation (first-generation students of color from disadvantaged socioeconomic circumstances) further emphasized the systemic oppression at work in the structure and processes of the system.

Dan asked the stakeholders to create a comprehensive writing program's outcomes statement for student reading and writing, and he then contrasted the positive language of the outcomes statement with the language of the current comprehensive writing program, which labeled students as "remedial" and placed them into "basic writing" using a "writing proficiency exam." The students who were least confident in their writing often postponed taking what was intended as a rising junior exam until they were graduating seniors (state SI), and, if they "failed" the exam, they had to take a series of non-credit-bearing "remedial" courses, even though many of them had completed the rest of their undergraduate coursework. The cycles of testing and remediation created oppressive reinforcing processes for students and faculty: students labeled remedial by a timed test and tracked into a long series of non-credit-bearing courses became distraught and frustrated, and faculty associated writing assessment with weeding out students who were "deficient" and needed to learn "the basics." Administrators saw these students as a drain on the system, costing the university money and dragging down the graduation rate. The "rich picture" of the system created by the flowchart, as well as the stark contrast between the stakeholders' ideals (the outcomes statement) and the actual system in place helped Dan and his writing program colleagues facilitate a discussion that focused on exposing the ways that racism and inequality permeated the comprehensive writing program.

The tactics Dan and his colleagues used in this situation can be applicable to any WAC leadership team faced with the challenge of understanding and exposing the ideologies that underlie the institutional system. These tactics include using flowcharts to expose structural barriers facing students and faculty, focusing on oppressive reinforcing processes, naming practices that label and track underrepresented students, considering the ways that language reinforces oppressive ideologies, contrasting the outcomes and processes of the current system with the stakeholders' ideals, identifying state SIs that could be shifted to impact students and faculty productively, and working with the stakeholders to imagine other scenarios—other versions of the system—that would be less oppressive to students and faculty. Additional tactics that Dan did not implement but that could have been effective include inviting the students who are negatively affected by the system to become part of the conversation, including allies such as student multicultural centers and teaching and learning centers, and consciously forming stakeholder groups that are pluralistic and not dominated by voices that might seek to preserve the status quo or that might lack awareness of problems such as systemic racism due to white privilege.

Understanding the Ideologies That Inform the Campus Culture of Writing: Questions to Consider

1. Based on your investigation of the campus mood and the institutional network, how would you describe the ideologies that underlie campus writing practices and attitudes?

2. What campus stakeholders/units do you anticipate will be most resistant to WAC ideology?

3. What types of writing assessment and placement are happening at your institution, and what theory of writing informs the assessment and placement?

4. What faculty attitudes regarding students' writing abilities are reinforced by campus writing assessment and placement?

5. What are the consequences for students—and, especially, for students of color, students from disadvantaged socioeconomic backgrounds, and multilingual students—of campus writing assessment and placement?

6. What types of writing requirements, in general education and in the majors, are included at your campus, and what ideology informs those requirements?

7. What kinds of reinforcing processes are created from campus writing requirements, and how are attitudes about writing shaped by these reinforcing processes?

CHAPTER FIVE

Stage Two of the Whole Systems Methodology: Planning a Program

During the planning stage, information gathered during the understanding stage is used to position the WAC program in the network strategically, ensure equity, and create a shared vision for the program—steps illustrated by the four vignettes that open this chapter. Timothy Oleksiak, Bloomsburg University, discusses how he convened a cross-campus committee and worked with it to establish a mission and goals for a WID program—important steps before launching a program. Speaking to the challenges of launching a WAC program at a community college, Marla Hyder, College of Lake County, describes the steps she took from a position with little institutional power (non-tenure-track and part-time) to gain momentum for a WAC program initiative, successfully securing it as one of three of the college's yearlong quality-improvement projects. Kerri Morris, Governors State University (GSU), describes the launching of a WAC program in a unique context, a four-year institution that recently expanded from a two-year institution, and how she grew support for WAC "organically." Christian Weisser and Holly Ryan, Penn State Berks, describe the approach they have taken to support faculty teaching WI courses on their branch campus that are overseen by the main campus, Penn State University Park.

Following these vignettes, we discuss strategies associated with the *planning* stage of the whole systems methodology: Strategy 4, engaging multiple stakeholders from across the university; Strategy 5, positioning the WAC program so that it becomes a hub within the university network; Strategy 6, considering the impact of WAC on student and faculty equity; and Strategy 7, setting program missions, goals, and SIs so that the WAC program has a clear direction.

Creating a Mission and Goals for WID

Timothy Patrick Oleksiak
Bloomsburg University

My English faculty colleagues hired me as the WID coordinator in part on the strength of my job talk: "The Ideal Writing-in-the-Disciplines Program." In this talk, I articulated a three-pronged approach to WID that consisted of a classroom-level writing fellows program, department-level WEC programs, and a university-level advisory committee.

I was new to the university culture and creating the WID advisory committee was crucial to learning the institutional context in which I found myself. Though a high-level administrative council approved the committee on November 6, 2014, we met for the first time on February 16, 2015. The late start date meant I had less than three months to lead the WID advisory committee in creating a living document that would guide the committee's future work and announce to the university community who we are and what we do.

On May 1, 2015, I reported to my dean that the WID advisory committee had created the following document:

Mission

The mission of Bloomsburg University WID advisory committee is to function as a resource for faculty teaching students to write well within disciplinary and interdisciplinary contexts.

Vision

We believe that good writing is theoretically grounded, ethical, and responsive to changing disciplinary, interdisciplinary, and sociocultural contexts. We foster a campus-wide environment where writing to learn and learning to write are a part of Bloomsburg University's culture.

The WID advisory committee is charged with:

♦ identifying best practices for the teaching of writing as well as opportunities and challenges relating to the teaching of writing;

♦ collecting resources for faculty related to WID;

♦ creating points of contact among faculty for sharing information regarding the teaching of writing;

♦ offering recommendations to individual faculty, departments, and colleges related to the teaching of writing;

- ◆ assessing the effectiveness of its programs, initiatives, and outreach;
- ◆ seeking internal and external funding to meet the needs of previous charges.

How did a sixteen-member committee consisting of myself, eight faculty members from four colleges, one university council chair, three directors, two assistant vice presidents, and an associate dean reach consensus on the language and content of these documents over the course of five one-hour-long meetings?

First, we played to our strengths. Committee membership is, by design, made up of administrators and faculty. College deans nominated each of the faculty members. The administrators were selected because of their relationship to writing, assessment, and/or institutional expertise. We were allies working together on something we all believed in. We wanted WID initiatives to be successful because we saw, from different vantage points, the need for them.

Second, we focused on goals while encouraging free-form conversation. Our first two meetings were largely dream sessions—open, free discussion of what we would like to see our students do with writing during and after their time at Bloomsburg University. Further, we considered concerns that the committee might not last beyond the energies of the first sixteen members and anxieties about faculty resistance. We had to clarify that interested parties would be welcome to take advantage of WID initiatives rather than be forced into them. I archived our conversations in shared Google Drive documents and reminded committee members to review these notes frequently.

I made sure that each meeting ended with specific deliverables toward which members of the committee worked. The deliverables ranged in complexity from "comment on the current draft of the mission" to "please vote for or against approval of the final document." Making sure we had work between meetings, however, was how we demonstrated our progress. I adapted when different deliverables than I anticipated emerged and relied on my expertise in rhetoric and composition to help make connections and keep us moving.

Two important questions became central during these first meetings: Who is our audience? What is the committee to do? The answers were not initially apparent, but we concurred that we had to be a faculty resource that supports their teaching undergraduate writing effectively and efficiently.

During the third meeting, we created a word bank: research driven, community of practice, interdisciplinary, scholarly and practical writing, recommending body, inclusivity, ethics, collection of resources, identify challenges and opportunities, support faculty and students, create "points of contact" among faculty, writing to learn and learning to write, sharing of information, efficiency and proficiency, resources. I revised the mission statement based on these phrases and developed a specific list of charges. Meetings four and five included a collaborative revising of the mission and charges. We wordsmithed in real time and face to face.

In a short time, we had created a document that guides WID at Bloomsburg University. Although in its nascent stages, we have begun necessary work that moves us toward implementing specific WID programs. Our vision for year two is to focus on implementing these programs in manageable ways and with an eye on data-driven assessment.

Beyond Status: Forming Alliances for Student Success

Marla L. Hyder
College of Lake County

I was an adjunct composition instructor when my large midwestern community college asked me to develop and pilot a part-time WAC program in January 2013—following two years of planning by faculty across the disciplines. Though I began with a newly furnished office, enviable support from the assistant vice president for educational affairs, and an established faculty advisory committee, I possessed no status or clout. My fledgling WAC program joined numerous new initiatives being shot at the target of "student success," and I knew it would get crowded out if I didn't find ways to quickly build visibility and momentum.

So I started making calls. I wanted to identify allies of WAC and, more important, offer myself as an ally to existing programs, departments, and initiatives. I began by asking simple questions: What are you doing? What role does writing play? How can we partner to advance both missions and, ultimately, student success?

Obvious allies were the writing center, faculty development center, reference librarians, and literacy specialists. We found common ground and offered joint workshops, while maintaining our unique mandates. For example, the writing tutors used their frontline perspectives to help me train faculty in assignment design, and I trained the tutors in disciplinary approaches to writing.

The faculty themselves were the most important allies to court, and I found them to be generous colleagues when I took the time to listen *first*. I heard that heating, ventilation, and air-conditioning's employer focus groups wanted graduates to come out with better written communication skills. I learned from architecture faculty that an architect's sketchbook is similar to exploratory journal writing. Automotive technology told me their students needed to be able to translate—in writing—between the customer ("Why is my car is going 'wheeeeee-clunk'?") and the professional technician. Health and wellness corroborated writing studies' claims that reflective writing decreases stress. In short, I found that WAC work was already happening across the college, including in the places I least expected.

I also listened to the buzzwords flying around campus—and around budget and grant proposal meetings—and looked for intersections with WAC work. The *flipped classroom* lends itself to exploratory writing and peer workshops; writing is a key *active learning* and *classroom assessment* strategy; classes that involve writing enhance student *engagement* and *retention*; and writing is inextricably linked to the *accelerated model* of developmental education. Attaching WAC to these and other movements helped faculty see them as connected pedagogical strategies, rather than one more fad to either ignore or squeeze into an already overstuffed syllabus.

And then there were the meetings. Oh, the meetings! I visited large division meetings, small department meetings, governing councils, faculty senates, and anyone else who would have me. I strategized with our ESL specialists and collaborated on projects with the general education assessment coordinator. I founded a faculty writing group and provided "Tips for Writing in College" for new student orientation. I developed resources with our office for students with disabilities for faculty wrestling with the reading and writing challenges of deaf and hard-of-hearing students.

A year after initiating the WAC program, we successfully proposed WAC as one of three yearlong quality-improvement projects—part of the college's accreditation. This propelled WAC into institutional priority status and brought additional funding and exposure. It led to a close partnership with the institutional effectiveness, planning, and research team, which helped run a comprehensive faculty survey and campus-wide assessment of student writing.

My focus on forming strategic and diverse alliances is neither revolutionary nor any great credit to me: it was a matter of survival for a young program and a part-time faculty member with no previous WAC expertise and no institutional power. I hope my story demonstrates one way to get WAC off the ground when there simply is not enough money at the outset to hire a full-time outside specialist. In fact, we have found that using an adjunct may be *more* sustainable because it is more flexible: if necessary, the position can ebb and flow with particular WAC projects and institutional priorities, whereas a fixed full-time position—and the bigger chunk of change it represents—would more likely end up on the chopping block at every budget discussion.

But this model comes with a warning label: such a tenuous part-time position is highly dependent on the person in it (who might be hired away at any time), the pool of adjunct faculty to choose from, and the whims of higher-level administration. An adjunct-led program will always be limited in scope and effectiveness if the institution doesn't maintain and grow its investment.

Regardless of our status, we all need allies. If WAC reaches out to form a web of partnerships, then, whether we enjoy huge budgets or have to fight for survival every semester, we are more likely to achieve our ultimate goal of being allies of our *students*.

WAC and General Education at GSU

Kerri K. Morris
Governors State University

GSU admitted its first freshman class in fall 2014. It was among the last of the nation's senior colleges, institutions that offered only upper-level undergraduate courses and graduate programs. I was hired four years ago, in part to help with the transition to a four-year program. In addition, I was hired to reinvigorate the WAC program that had begun at GSU more than a decade ago. Initially, these two aspects of my job seemed separate from each other. As we have created this four-year program, however, it became evident how interrelated the two are.

First, let me explain how timing separated, at least in my own mind, the two tasks of building a general education program (and our inaugural first-year students' writing program) and revitalizing a languishing WAC program. When I arrived, GSU had already committed to admitting first-year students, and a general education task force was established at the end of my first semester of employment. We were in the initial stages of creating our general education program. However, WAC seemed the more immediate need.

A year before I arrived on campus, GSU had also established its first general education assessment program. While we offered some courses that could fulfill the intent of general education, we didn't technically have general education. Still, our accrediting agency believed we should be assessing general education outcomes. The assessment committee's initial project was assessing student writing in capstone courses. When I arrived, that committee's work had already revealed a consensus on campus that our students needed much more support for writing.

Further, as I learned from the committee once I joined, though we had many courses designated as "writing intensive," few were taught as such. In many cases, instructors weren't even aware that their courses were considered as such. Oddly, we had a requirement for WI courses and courses designated to meet the requirement, but the faculty senate had never approved an official WAC policy.

My initial work focused on having conversations with as many people as I could, sketching out a history of WAC from documents and policies, and clarifying where writing was already being integrated into the curriculum. From this research, I discovered an institution that had pockets of exemplary WI programs, particularly the graduate programs in occupational therapy and physical therapy.

I relished the notion of putting flesh on the bones of our WI requirement. I knew that I'd need the approval of the faculty senate to move forward and would need the support of key faculty members. I began talking to folks about putting together an advisory board. Much to my surprise, this plan met with strong resistance. If the faculty senate doesn't officially approve WAC, then it's hard to establish a WAC board. Further complicating the matter was the fact that I did not have a title. I was just an English professor, hired to do a job but not officially tasked to do it.

However, I did have resources, information, and insight that could support colleagues who were already committed to integrating writing into their courses or who were looking for support. And I knew that we had at least two exemplary and long-standing programs that could serve as models for others. With the generous support of our administration, I became a faculty-in-residence with the faculty development program, which helped me clarify my role. I was vetted without being "official," and so my attention turned fully to faculty development and away from policy and structure.

Policy and structure, however, have occurred organically through the work of the general education task force. Our general education program is committed to WI courses. Faculty from across campus on the task force, without my prompting, argued passionately from the beginning that WAC was a critical part of the general education program. We require one WI course at each level of the general education program, including our junior and senior capstones. With that requirement, we also established exactly what "writing intensive" meant. Because WAC was integrated into the general education curriculum, the faculty senate had no resistance to approving the WAC policy. Instead of layering WAC over existing programs, the creation of a general education program has integrated WAC into the curriculum.

I have learned firsthand what most folks involved with WAC have always known: WAC takes hold when it emerges from the ground up. And the unique context of GSU's past history with WAC, combined with the creation of a general education program, have reminded me to have faith in that process. At its most successful, WAC is organic, and WAC leadership is most successful when it is responsive to meeting needs and solving problems.

Shifting from Curriculum to Faculty to Create a Sustainable WAC Program

Christian Weisser and Holly L. Ryan
Penn State Berks

WAC programs thrive and remain sustainable when they support the local goals and material circumstances of the faculty and students they serve. In fact, many scholars have written about the need to tailor WAC programs to institutional contexts and explicit objectives rather than to broadly defined criteria or guidelines. In their article "Clearing the Air: WAC Myths and Realities," Susan McLeod and Elaine Maimon (2000) reminded readers that WAC curriculums are varied and contextually driven: "Because WAC programs are site specific by nature . . . no single curricular element is more advisable than another" (p. 581). Simply put, each WAC program must make decisions about what works best for its own faculty and students, adapting to the material conditions at hand.

This value is challenged, however, in situations in which one entity within a geographically dispersed university system makes decisions about writing course criteria for all campuses within its purview. In these settings, where diverse campuses are subjected to a set of uniform WI guidelines, individual WAC coordinators are often hard-pressed to negotiate the requirements of the institutional system with the immediate needs of faculty and students at their campus. Andrea Davis and Vanessa Cozza (2014) addressed this point more fully in their article "WAC/WID Campus Concerns: 'Growing Pains' or Perspectives from a Small Branch Campus," highlighting their "struggles to accommodate the branch campus' needs, and, at the same time, meet the main campus' policies and expectations" (p. 1).

Davis and Cozza's experiences reflect the tensions we faced in negotiating the institutional WI course policies in our state university system (Penn State) and our own campus's goal of creating a faculty-centered WAC program (Penn State, Berks Campus). Penn State requires undergraduates to complete at least three credits of WI coursework (referred to as "W" coursework) prior to graduation, regardless of campus or major. The policies and criteria for "W" policies are administered through a committee at the flagship campus (Penn State, University Park), which also approves all "W" course proposals throughout the system. Each campus in the system is responsible for offering a sufficient number of "W" courses, and the academic divisions and majors at each campus are tasked with creating and offering such courses within their individual curriculum.

When we began our campus WAC program seven years ago, it was under the premise of helping Penn State Berks faculty through the "W" course proposal process. Our first workshops focused on writing "W" course proposals and guiding faculty through the "W" course proposal process. From an institutional perspective, this model was successful; several "W" course proposals were submitted and accepted within the first year of the Berks WAC program's creation. However, we quickly realized that faculty needed more than an explanation of the prescribed WI course criteria and help with the proposal process; they needed broader and more comprehensive guidance in creating effective writing assignments and in responding to student writing in a way that would facilitate critical thinking and learning.

As a result, we shifted the focus of our campus WAC program from an institutionally driven model to one grounded in writing pedagogy and best practices. We realized that focusing on institutional criteria was unsustainable, since it offered faculty little that would help them adapt their pedagogy to student writing situations beyond those prescribed, designated "W" courses. Consequently, our program has grown into one built on faculty development workshops, in which we discuss the broader goals and objectives of WAC, the relationship between critical thinking and writing, and effective strategies for responding to student writing. This faculty development model supports the continued growth of writing at our campus by helping teachers develop methodologies they can apply to their other courses rather than simply designing a single-course curriculum. Research shows that many WAC programs offer faculty development workshops and seminars as a way of supporting faculty writing initiatives across disciplines (Thaiss & Porter, 2010, p. 554), and this model has enabled us to focus on the local goals and material circumstances of our faculty rather than institutional constraints.

Our experience echoes that of McLeod and Maimon (2000), who argued that faculty development must be a "starting point" for transforming writing and teaching pedagogy (p. 580). We have found that this orientation allows us to circumvent the top-down nature of WI curriculum at our campus by focusing on the best practices of writing pedagogy and creating faculty-driven workshops. This process offers a much more sustainable approach because it provides the tools for future growth of writing in our curriculum rather than focusing on transitory curricular requirements. We have found that focusing on best practices—rather than institutional criteria—has been a more sustainable and successful approach to our WAC program.

Strategy 4: Involve Multiple Stakeholders in the System

It may seem that the strategy of involving multiple stakeholders in the system is a commonplace approach in WAC. As Marla Hyder commented in her vignette, "My focus on forming strategic and diverse alliances is neither revolutionary nor any great credit to me." Indeed, we saw this strategy displayed in many of the vignettes we received from our call, and it has long been part of the standard advice given to new WAC directors (see, e.g., McLeod, 1988b, p. 8; Walvoord, 1992, p. 13). However, we are viewing this concept through the lens of a whole systems approach. The principle of *broad participation* emphasizes engaging stakeholders from all levels of the institution to help plan, approve, implement, and assess program goals, outcomes, and projects. The importance of involving multiple stakeholders is emphasized in both systems theory and sustainable development theory. These theories recommend gathering stakeholders from different scales and with diverse perspectives on the system and allowing them the time to gauge the mood of the institution, map the system, develop SIs and sustainable projects, and assess these projects. Resilience theory adds another perspective on the necessity of involving stakeholders from across the system, emphasizing the importance of making "deliberate transformational change" through social action (Folke et al., 2010, para. 17). We argue that WAC programs should have a plan for making *transformational change* to an institution from the start. In order to create university-wide curricular change, buy-in and influence at different scales across the institution are essential. Not only does the upper administration need to be on board—the academic senate, deans, and provost—but also those who interact with student writers, promote WAC curriculum, and enact WAC pedagogy—advisors, writing center staff, teaching assistants, adjunct faculty, and tenure-track faculty.

The principle of *broad participation* applies to every stage of our methodology, but we stress involving multiple stakeholders in the *planning* stage—after learning the lay of the land (and identifying stakeholders at different scales) and in anticipation of the next strategy we discuss: positioning WAC for leverage and connectivity.

In fact, involving multiple stakeholders during the planning stage can help position WAC for leverage, as it did when Michelle used this strategy to launch the WAC program at Bridgewater State University. The assistant vice provost to whom she reported perceived of WAC narrowly—as a quick fix to the temporary problem of a few faculty not knowing how to teach writing. He saw WAC as consisting of one-to-one consultations with faculty and perhaps a couple of workshops. He didn't see it as a "program," award WAC its own budget line (though Michelle could ask for funds on a piecemeal basis), or see a need for a cross-curricular steering committee. Despite these challenges, Michelle could see that, if she could get a WAC program off the ground, it would be well received by faculty, and this success might change the administration's perception of the scope of WAC. The faculty were committed to teaching and sought out opportunities to learn how to better serve their students and improve their craft. The teaching mission of the university meant that faculty spent most of their time in the classroom (i.e., 4–4 teaching loads) and hungered for time to reflect on their pedagogy and for community with colleagues. They were also hungry to learn more about teaching with writing, given the implementation of a new Core Curriculum that year, which introduced WI first- and second-year seminars and a WI upper-level course in the student's major. And Michelle knew that the assistant vice provost had a good reputation on campus for being supportive of faculty development. But she first needed to garner energy, support, and input from across the Bridgewater State University community.

To gather this support, Michelle initiated a program that would become known as the "WAC Network." For the first year of the program, she obtained funding to bring an outside speaker to campus and small stipends for twenty-four faculty participants, whom she recruited through an open call paired with invitations to faculty who regularly participated in faculty development programming. That fall, Toby Fulwiler gave a full-day workshop, leading the participants through foundational WAC concepts and pedagogies. A month later, Michelle met with the participants for a follow-up workshop. After they had each discussed changes in their teaching inspired by Fulwiler's workshop, they discussed the direction of the program. They decided to expand the group to include staff and administrators, that members should be able to stay on as long as they wanted, and that the group should grow each year, like a network—and, thus, the name the WAC Network was born. They also decided that the Network should offer short, monthly workshops—"WAC coffee breaks"—with the topics brainstormed by Network members and led by them. This idea took off. Five years later, the Network had 105 members, including department chairs, part-time faculty, administrators (e.g., the director of undergraduate research), staff from different programs (e.g., advising), and teachers from area K–12 school districts. This group functioned as an informal steering committee for the WAC program, as it held regular meetings to make decisions about WAC programming and initiatives. And, by the end of these five years, WAC was perceived, by administration and faculty alike, as part of the fabric of the institution.

Timothy Oleksiak's vignette on the beginnings of the WID program at Bloomsburg University also provides insight into the value and process of involving multiple stakeholders in the planning stage of WID. Even before he arrived on campus, Oleksiak was thinking in terms of working at different scales of the system, proposing in his job talk "a three-pronged approach to WID that consisted of a classroom-level writing fellows program, department-level WEC programs, and a university-level advisory committee." One way to gather stakeholders at different scales is to form an advisory committee, and, in Oleksiak's case, the WID advisory committee reflected his multiscale approach, with faculty members from different colleges, a university council chair, three directors, two assistant vice presidents, and an associate dean. Oleksiak observes that "creating the WID advisory committee was crucial to learning the institutional context in which I found myself." WAC directors that are new to an institution will have difficulty planning sustainable WAC projects if they lack the perspective of stakeholders from across the system, and a WAC advisory board or committee is one way to gain this perspective quickly.

Unlike the open call Michelle used to bring together WAC Network members, the WID advisory committee assembled by Oleksiak was carefully chosen to provide support for WID and for himself. Oleksiak says of the way the advisory committee was formed, "administrators were selected because of their relationship to writing, assessment, and/or institutional expertise. We were allies working together on something we all believed in. We wanted WID initiatives to be successful because we saw, from different vantage points, the need for them." One benefit of gathering stakeholders in the planning stage is drawing not only on different vantage points, but also on allies who can help the WAC director make connections and garner support. These allies can help form a critical mass to overpower threats to WAC initiatives. It is important for stakeholders to understand the barriers and pockets of resistance WAC initiatives might face. A tactic such as a SWOT analysis (discussed in Chapter 4) can help stakeholders identify the constraints, barriers, and threats that are an inevitable part of trying to make interventions meant to transform large bureaucratic systems that tend toward stagnation.

It is also helpful to include those actors whose perspectives are not always fully considered in campus initiatives, such as students, staff, and contingent faculty. These groups will provide different perspectives from those of the tenure-track faculty and administrators who typically populate WAC advisory boards. Oleksiak's WID advisory board is already quite large, with sixteen members, and, pragmatically speaking, it would be easy to become bogged down if representation from students, staff, and contingent faculty were added to the board as permanent members. But it is possible Oleksiak could have invited members who represent these other important actors in the system during some of the "open, free discussions" of the initial meetings and again for feedback on the vision statement. In both systems theory and sustainable development theory, the ideal is to gather stakeholders from across scales of the system in order to engage in substantial mapping, goal setting, modeling, planning, and establishing of optimal thresholds for program success/sustainability, but the constraints of academic institutions may lead WAC directors to consider alternative tactics for including multiple perspectives, such as surveys or focus groups.

Marla Hyder's vignette presents a different and less formal process for reaching out to stakeholders from across the system. Unlike Oleksiak, who came into the WID position as a result of a national search and was given leadership of an advisory board made up of influential faculty and administrators, Hyder was an adjunct composition teacher "without status or clout" who was tasked with starting a WAC program. Her strategy was to be proactive in reaching out to stakeholders across scales of the system in a grassroots effort by attending different types of campus meetings, founding a faculty writing group, and collaborating with organizations that focused on key groups, such as ESL students, students with disabilities, and first-year students. As she noted, she met with "anyone who would have me." Hyder's strategy of planning WAC projects with stakeholders across the system lead to more influence and buy-in for WAC.

This informal reaching out by an energetic individual is typical of how many WAC programs develop, but it is also a tactic that many WAC programs never move beyond. To move toward greater sustainability and connectivity, Hyder's next move might be to formalize stakeholder relationships and find ways to get these various stakeholders into communication long term. A WAC advisory board of the kind that supports WID at Bloomsburg University may be one way for Hyder to involve multiple stakeholders for the long term, as well as to plan WAC projects not only in the context of individual relationships, but also across programs and units to enable interventions in the system as a whole in order to make transformational change. The development from informal connections with individual stakeholders to more formalized and regular conversations with groups of stakeholders from across the scales of an institution is critical to planning sustainable WAC projects.

One more component of involving multiple stakeholders from across the system in planning WAC projects is considering different types and levels of involvement. Administrators may be more likely to attend a one-off event that connects to issues that are centers of gravity for the campus, such as assessment or writing requirements. Contingent faculty who are working at multiple institutions may have difficulty committing to a semester-long learning community, but a summer retreat might be more accessible. However, a learning community may appeal to faculty who want to explore WAC pedagogies in more depth than one-off workshops can provide. Offering consultations and workshops directly to departments to enhance writing in the disciplines, such as through a WEC initiative, will help WAC directors move up the scale from working with pockets of faculty to working with entire departments. The formation of an academic senate writing committee (or a writing subcommittee of a senate curriculum committee) could provide leverage for WAC directors to develop writing policies that affect not just individual faculty or departments but the entire institution.

WAC directors should aim to work with stakeholders at every scale of the institution. Working with individual faculty, programs, departments, and schools are all important. However, if the WAC director is working primarily at lower scales—such as one-on-one consultations with individual faculty—then they are less likely to build a WAC program that is sustainable or that leads to transformative change in the culture of writing at their institution. There may be times when a focus on grassroots faculty development and intense individualized work is what is most needed, as seen in the vignette by Christian Weisser and Holly Ryan that describes a grassroots response to a top-down WI initiative at Penn State Berks. However, even successful grassroots efforts may not be sustainable or have a transformative effect on an institution if they don't eventually reach larger scales. Although WAC stakeholder groups will shift as the program is planned, implemented, and matures, WAC directors should aim to spend more and more of their time and effort gathering stakeholders at higher scales of the institution, even as they continue to nurture relationships at lower scales and value the perspectives of those who are not always included in the conversation—a point we will revisit in Chapter 6, when we discuss the strategy of making reforms at both the micro and systems levels.

Involving Multiple Stakeholders in the System: Questions to Consider

1. What current institutional structures or events involve participation by multiple stakeholders at different scales of the system? How can WAC connect to these structures or events?

2. What kind of committee or advisory board model would work best within the institutional context? At the outset? As the program is implemented? When the program changes?

3. If there is an existing WAC committee or advisory board, does it represent perspectives of multiple stakeholders from across the scales of the institution?

4. Which actors are not often included in campus conversation? How can WAC include the perspectives of underrepresented actors?

5. Which actors might be skeptical or hostile to WAC projects? How can the WAC program anticipate and understand those perspectives in the planning stage?

6. What types of WAC projects will appeal to multiple stakeholders?

7. How might stakeholder participation be leveraged to consolidate program support?

Strategy 5: Work toward Positioning the WAC Program for Greater Interconnectivity and Leverage in the Institution

The principle of *transformational change* encourages us to identify points of leverage for introducing change to the university system at multiple levels, so that the change affects the wider campus culture and lasts past the initial burst of energy. The literature and lore on WAC is rife with stories of programs that began with enthusiasm but failed to sustain momentum, such as those that never made it beyond a small group of "true believers," that never moved beyond the occasional workshop or consultation, or that were located in an English department and became a casualty of being a low priority to the department when budget cuts hit. Many of these stories have to do with a lack of positioning for interconnectivity and leverage within the institution from the inception of the program, or a lack of access to higher scales and institutional hubs in order to make the transition to sustainability over time. The research on how innovations develop and become sustainable in complex networks can provide strategies to help ensure that a WAC program doesn't become yet another tale of initial excitement followed by a decline in interest and influence. One key to avoiding this decline is highlighted in our whole systems principle of *integration*, which emphasizes building program components that integrate into existing structures and practices and facilitate collaborative campus relationships. The theory that most informs this principle is social network theory.

Social network theory focuses on "relational ties (linkages) between actors" (Wasserman & Faust, 1994, p. 4). For those looking to introduce a sustainable project, these relational ties should be a more important consideration than the role of any individual within the network. Wasserman and Faust (1994) argued that "relational ties among actors are primary and attributes of actors are secondary" (p. 8), echoing the systems theory mantra that structures shape behavior more than individual personality. Networks of relational ties in an institution are made up of nodes, hubs, and clusters of hubs. The nodes have little connectivity and leverage within the network, but the hubs connect to multiple parts of the network. The most powerful connectors can be found where there are clusters of hubs. WAC programs that are merely nodes—for example, a program run by a single dedicated faculty member doing WAC as something "extra," or a program located in an English department that is perceived as part of the discipline of literary studies and not campus wide—are less likely to be sustainable and less likely to create successful innovations that impact the institution as a network or system. WAC programs that are located in or connected to institutional hubs like a writing center, a center for teaching and learning, an independent writing department, an academic affairs unit, or an academic senate are more likely to be resilient, sustainable, and lead to *transformational change*. WAC directors should think about connecting their programs to clusters of hubs right from the inception of the program and should continuously work to connect to other academic units. Programs that begin as nodes—for example, as an underfunded mandate given to an English department professor—should look to move toward both connecting to network hubs and becoming a hub. WAC directors should also look to form sustainable partnerships. An informal, temporary tie such as collaborating on a workshop or coauthoring an article is helpful, but better still are more formal, long-lasting ties such as ongoing partnerships or annual cosponsored events.

It is important for WAC directors to understand the science behind the ways that complex networks behave. For example, research shows that each link made can create exponential connectivity. Even a few extra links can drastically decrease the average separation between nodes (Barabási, 2002, p. 53). Furthermore, failures within networks are more likely to affect the least connected nodes first. Failure is also common when the most connected hubs resist an innovation. Conversely, actors in a network are more likely to link to nodes that are already popular—what is referred to in social network theory as "preferential attachment." By linking to clusters of hubs, actors in a network introducing an innovation are more likely to have success gaining the critical threshold where an innovation begins to exponentially become adopted. Remaining below this threshold means the network will never fully adopt the innovation, making it likely to die out (Barabási, 2002, p. 131).

This science informing how complex networks behave points to the importance of the network mapping strategies discussed in Chapter 4. In his vignette, Oleksiak mentions that, when the stakeholders from across campus on the advisory committee began discussing the WID program, they focused on coming to consensus on what they would like to see students do in their writing and how to deal with faculty resistance. Both of these are important areas to consider, but the WID advisory committee might also have considered ways to position their work within the complex network of Bloomsburg University. Faculty resistance would be less pronounced and less likely to spread, for example, if the WID program could connect to clusters of hubs, or could start as a hub itself. The WID advisory committee decided that one goal of the WID program was to create "points of contact" among faculty—an important goal for most WAC/WID programs. The advisory committee could have created an institutional network map to help them focus their efforts on the parts of the network with the highest percentage of points of contact and the most well-connected individual actors. A map outlining the network processes of writing at Bloomsburg University could help the advisory committee find points of leverage in the network where a small change or intervention could have a large ripple effect throughout the network.

As we noted in the previous section, a proven strategy for creating interconnectivity for a WAC program is an advisory board or committee. Oleksiak emphasizes the value of the WID advisory committee that included well-connected members such as a university council chair, three directors, two assistant vice presidents, and an associate dean. This administrator-heavy committee was effective at Bloomsburg University, but, on other campuses, a committee with representation from faculty or even entirely made up of faculty may be more effective, as it would be perceived as less top down.

A WAC committee's positioning also affects interconnectivity. A WAC committee that connects to an academic senate is more likely to have leverage within the system than an advisory board that is only connected to the WAC program but not to the rest of the network. Contrast Oleksiak's experience at Bloomsburg University with that of Morris at GSU. As depicted in her vignette, Morris encountered resistance from the faculty senate to the formation of a WAC program and advisory board, and part of the problem, according to Morris, was that she "did not have a title." As she said, "I was just an English professor, hired to do a job but not officially tasked to do it." Unlike Oleksiak, whose WID initiative connected to a hub from its inception, Morris began as a node, making it difficult to have the WAC innovation adopted by the actors in the network until she was able to connect to the network hub of general education. The sudden success Morris experienced once she connected to a hub speaks to the importance of these higher-level connections. In her vignette, Hyder speaks to the challenge of being an adjunct faculty member tasked with starting a WAC program. She found success by attaching WAC to "other movements" on campus, but her path might have been significantly easier if she was positioned from the start within a hub or cluster of hubs. A common mistake that many institutions make is locating WAC in an English department. It's uncommon for English departments to have strong ties to other departments across the curriculum, to the administration, and to other campus faculty development or assessment units. English departments are most often institutional nodes, not hubs.

Locating WAC in an English department has other pitfalls as well. As Art Young and Toby Fulwiler (1990) have posited, traditional English departments may fear that their literary mission is diluted by WAC, and they may not look favorably on administration and scholarship in WAC when it is time for the WAC director's promotion and tenure reviews. Dan experienced such issues when he took a position coordinating a new WAC program that the administration decided to locate in the English department. Although Dan felt that this decision wasn't ideal for the reasons mentioned in this chapter, the position did provide many positive structural features that created an ability to connect with and successfully intervene in the system. Dan was given the title "university reading and writing coordinator" and became the chair of a long-standing and very active subcommittee of the curriculum policies committee of the faculty senate focused on reading and writing. This subcommittee gave Dan a direct link to the central hub of the campus, the faculty senate. A significant course release, tenure-track status, and a solid operating budget allowed Dan to work at all scales of the system, from small workshops to semester-long learning groups, to department meetings and retreats, to organizing regional WAC conferences.

At first, the program thrived, and the English department faculty's response to WAC ranged from supportive to indifferent. However, as the composition faculty became more visible on campus, due to a series of major campus writing reforms, and as, at the same time, a wave of budget cuts hit the state university system, the literature faculty in the English department began to circle the wagons. Despite recent losses to writing program tenure-line faculty, leaving only two remaining, the English department elected to hire more literature faculty, and concurrently the major was changed from an English studies model to a traditional literary coverage model. Reforms that began with the WAC program and the faculty senate writing subcommittee were stalled or blocked by the English department, and a last ditch move by the writing faculty to create an independent writing department caused the literature faculty to take even more drastic measures to ensure WAC and the writing program were given the lowest priority for meager department resources. The situation deteriorated to the point where Dan left the institution, with the WAC program folding in his absence.

If the WAC program and the WAC director had been placed in the institution's center for teaching and learning from the start, it's likely that Dan would still be at the institution and the program still thriving. In retrospect, he should have made a stronger effort from the start to disconnect from the node of the English department and connect both himself and the WAC program to a more central hub. By the time he and his colleagues in composition did attempt to form their own hub—an independent writing program—it was already too late. In Dan's current institution, an independent writing program that serves as a hub for writing on campus, the WAC program is far more secure.

A WAC director located in a hub like an independent writing program, a writing center, or a center for teaching and learning will benefit not only from being in a hub, but also from the phenomenon of "preferential attachment," described by social network theory as the tendency of actors in a network being more likely to link to nodes that are already popular. The vignettes by Hyder and Morris speak to the struggles of WAC directors given little status within the network and not connected to hubs, and to the ways that interventions can more quickly reach a threshold of acceptance when WAC directors do connect to hubs—a QEP that led to a partnership with the institutional effectiveness, planning, and research team in Hyder's case, and membership on a general education task force in Morris's case. If Hyder and Morris had been given more network prestige and connectivity from the start—for example, through administrative titles that reflected their university-wide responsibilities, appropriate release time, a staff and sizeable budget, and an office within a network hub—they would have had a much easier time making sustainable interventions within the complex networks of their institutions.

Working toward Positioning the WAC Program for Greater Interconnectivity and Leverage in the Institution: Questions to Consider

1. Which units and programs act as hubs in the institutional network? Are there clusters of hubs?

2. Which location for WAC will give it the most interconnectivity within the institutional network?

3. With which units or programs can WAC partner? How can these partnerships become more formal and sustainable?

4. Which units or programs are most popular with faculty? Which are least popular with faculty?

5. Of which units or programs are the administration most supportive? Of which are the administration least supportive?

6. Is the WAC program moving toward a threshold of growth, or does it comprise the same small group of faculty who participate in WAC year in and year out?

7. What kind of advisory board or committee can be created to support WAC? How can this advisory board be connected to policymaking units? How can it be given clout and teeth?

8. Is the WAC program connected to the campus policymaking body?

Strategy 6: Consider the Impact of WAC on Faculty and Student Equity

A whole systems approach recognizes that disparities of power exist in all human systems, that changes to a system can affect different groups within the system differently, and that, when introducing change to a system, as WAC programs do, we need to be particularly cognizant of those groups with less power, less of a voice, and less visibility in the system. The whole systems principle of *equity* works to minimize disparities in current and future generations of those impacted by WAC. In other sections of this chapter, we draw from the opening vignettes to discuss the strategy; in this case, we did not receive any related vignettes, so we turn instead to the literature. In the WAC literature, two groups of marginalized faculty and students have emerged as a focus: (1) contingent labor and (2) multilingual student writers.

WAC and Contingent Labor

According to WAC lore, we know that WAC programs can unintentionally add to the ballooning of adjunct faculty on campuses, for one of two reasons. First, WAC programs may create new requirements for faculty to teach with writing but then not offer faculty development that shows them how to streamline writing instruction or integrate writing into their curriculum. Faculty with the power to select the courses they teach would then not choose these labor-intensive WI courses, leaving them for faculty with less departmental power—adjuncts. Second, WAC programs can create a situation like the one Michelle observed at Bridgewater State University: to entice faculty to teach WI, first- and second-year seminars would replace the large introductory courses with ones capped at twenty. Thus, instead of needing a single instructor to teach a 100-student lecture, five instructors were needed. Commensurate boosting of faculty hires in the departments did not take place, so departments hired adjuncts to teach these WI courses.

Despite the increasing role of contingent faculty in WAC programs, we found only one article that focused on this topic: Michelle LaFrance's (2015) "Making Visible Labor Issues in Writing Across the Curriculum." When LaFrance moved from directing a first-year writing program to directing a WAC program, she was surprised by the lack of conversation in WAC on contingent labor (p. A13). At George Mason University, where LaFrance directs a WAC program, a study by Allison, Lynn, and Hoverman (2015) revealed that 71 percent of faculty were contingent, and an unpublished report indicated that 30 percent of faculty teaching general education courses (such as WI courses) were adjunct (p. A14). LaFrance (2015) pointed out that the material conditions of contingent faculty, such as lack of office space and university-provided computers, as well as lack of access to curricular guidelines, sample syllabi, and faculty development programs, may impact the ability of adjunct faculty to support WAC pedagogies and practices, potentially impacting the program's effectiveness and sustainability. LaFrance called for more research to "uncover the complexities and contexts of contingency both nationally and in specific sites" (p. A15), and laid out questions that may also help WAC directors take into consideration the material realities of the faculty, as follows:

> How do different institutional contexts influence faculty as they design and implement their courses? How might faculty off the tenure-track be better enabled to partake in community building, collaboration, and professional development? And how might our pedagogical ideals recognize the issues that arise via contingency? (p. A15)

LaFrance's surprise at this gap in the WAC literature stems in part from her previous experience as a first-year WPA, an area where this area of scholarship is particularly rich. NCTE has published a policy statement supporting the rights of contingent faculty (National Council of Teachers of English, 2010), CCCC publishes a journal focused on this topic (*FORUM: Issues about Part-Time and Contingent Faculty*), and CWPA regularly features scholarship on contingent faculty through its annual conference and its journal *WPA: Writing Program Administration*. In WAC literature, however, adjunct faculty are hardly mentioned. McLeod and Shirley's (1988) 1987 survey did not include questions about contingent labor. Thaiss and Porter's (2010) survey did include a question about the status of the WAC program director (finding that 9 of the 482 surveyed directors were contingent) (p. 543), but did not include similar questions about those teaching WAC courses. Hyder's vignette is one of the few published voices by contingent faculty on WAC. This is an area deserving of more research, as well as more consideration when planning WAC programs. It also represents an important SI to be tracked for sustainability. The more WAC programs rely on contingent labor, the less likely they will be sustainable in the long run.

Multilingual Writers and WAC

In comparison to that for contingent faculty, the WAC literature on multilingual students has been growing quickly. It emerged as an area of focus with the publication of a special issue of *Across the Disciplines* and an edited collection on the topic (Cox & Zawacki, 2011; Zawacki & Cox, 2014). This research was spurred by the growing visibility of multilingual students on campuses, as universities, still recovering from the economic crisis of 2008, sought to increase enrollment by focusing recruiting efforts on international students, many of whom are multilingual. At the same time, immigration trends have led to increases in the numbers of a less visible but significant student population of US-educated multilingual student writers (Roberge, 2009). This line of scholarship was also spurred by research emerging from applied linguistics and L2 writing. The literature has focused on faculty responses to and assessment of L2 writing as well as the lived experiences of L2 writers in courses across the curriculum. Ilona Leki's work has been pivotal in this area. In her case study research on L2 undergraduates writing across the curriculum, which spans from 1995 to 2007, Leki documented the many ways in which a focus on writing in US undergraduate education has created an uneven playing field for multilingual students (1995, 1999, 2001, 2003a, 2003b, 2007). In "A Challenge to Second Language Writing Professionals: Is Writing Overrated?," Leki (2003a) asked, "What are the consequences, particularly for L2 English students, of placing such a high value on writing?" (p. 315).

What are the consequences? From the research, we can see that, in some cases, multilingual writers receive the same benefits as do their English-as-first-language peers from pedagogies endorsed by WAC: engaging in writing-to-learn activities (Fishman & McCarthy, 2001), participating in peer review groups (Berg, 1999; Tsui & Ng, 2000; Zhu, 2001), conferencing with the instructor (Ewert, 2009), seeing samples of student writing for an assignment (Leki, 1999), and receiving both holistic and local feedback on drafts (Goldstein, 2005; Hyland, 1998; Truscott, 1999). We know that they often develop coping strategies that allow them to either skirt or adapt writing assignments that are US-centric or otherwise out of reach (Leki, 1995), to draw on first-language literacies (Leki, 1995; Phillips, 2014), or to create networks of support for their writing (Phillips, 2014). But we also know that increased emphasis on writing can sometimes create a glass ceiling for multilingual writers, particularly if a WAC program is tied to a writing proficiency exam (Janopoulos, 1995; Johns, 1991), if instructors privilege standard written English (Fishman & McCarthy, 2001), if instructors shy away from engaging with multilingual texts (Leki, 1999; Matsuda & Cox, 2009), and if English-as-first-language peers refrain from engaging with multilingual writers in peer review groups (Leki, 2001). (For a more complete review of this literature, see Cox, 2011.)

Recent research in WAC and L2 writing has focused less on writing pedagogy and more on systematic support for these student writers. In "Mapping the Gaps in Services for L2 Writers," Martha Davis Patton (2011) described a needs assessment she conducted at the University of Missouri that included a survey of international students, interviews with administrators, faculty and international students, and a discourse analysis of international student papers. Her study revealed gaps across the institution: a lack of training in L2 writing among writing center tutors, first-year composition instructors, and WI course instructors; a lack of communication between different units that worked with L2 writers; and a lack of educational resources tailored for multilingual writers. But her analysis also initiated connections between nodes in the system, an important first step for strengthening the network of support. In "Campus Internationalization: A Center-Based Model for ESL-Ready Programs," Karyn Mallett and Ghania Zgheib (2014) described a program in which provisionally accepted international students take first-year composition courses and introductory content courses that are team-taught by applied linguistics faculty. This program led not only to stronger success rates for the students, but also to faculty development in L2 writing as a result of the collaboration between first-year composition and content faculty, who reported using insights from the experience to transform their courses across the curriculum. In "Writing Intensively: An Examination of the Performance of L2 Writers Across the Curriculum at an Urban Community College," Linda Hirsh (2014) compared the success rates of L2 writers in non-WI and WI versions of the same courses and found that L2 writers passed WI courses at higher rates, due to the pedagogical strategies used for scaffolding writing and student learning. Meghan Siczek and Shawna Shapiro (2014), in "Developing Writing-Intensive Courses for a Globalized Curriculum through WAC–TESOL Collaborations," described WI courses developed at Middlebury College and George Washington University by applied linguists that are designed to draw on L2 students' linguistic resources and lived experiences. In "In Response to Today's 'Felt Need': WAC, Faculty Development, and Second Language Writers," Cox (2014) laid out an approach to faculty development that could be used by WAC directors without a background in applied linguistics to systematically shift faculty from a *difference as deficit* stance toward what A. Suresh Canagarajah (2002) has called a *difference as resource* stance. Together, these studies point the way for WAC directors seeking to map out current support for L2 writers, create program structures and courses that support them, and create faculty development focused on inclusive pedagogy.

This line of research also highlights important gaps in the WAC literature. While much work needs to be done to fully understand how to best structure WAC programs and provide faculty development in relation to multilingual writers, even more needs to be done in relation to other student populations. To return to Leki's questions, what are the consequences of increased emphasis on WAC for first-generation college students, students of color, students from minority ethnic groups, students with disabilities, and other marginalized groups? One way to keep such questions in focus within a WAC program that serves significant numbers of these students is to identify and track SIs that measure program impacts on these populations. Usage statistics of support services, pass rates for classes among members of these student populations, and numbers of faculty participating in related faculty development are all examples of possible SIs.

Despite the lack of WAC literature in these areas, it is critical that WAC leaders think seriously about how changes introduced to a curricular ecology by the program impact all actors—instructors and students—and particularly those actors with less power, less of a voice, and less visibility in the university system. The following set of questions is meant as a starting point.

Considering the Impact of WAC on Faculty and Student Equity: Questions to Consider

1. On your campus, what percentage of courses is taught by tenure-track faculty, non-tenure-track faculty, and teaching assistants? How do these percentages break out per college or school? How do they break out for certain types of courses (e.g., general education courses, upper-level courses in the majors, courses that are connected to the WAC program)?

2. What are the material conditions of contingent faculty and/or teaching assistants on your campus? Do these instructors have access to office space, a computer, or copying services?

3. How are contingent faculty and/or teaching assistants supported as teachers on your campus? Do they have access to faculty development programs? Do they receive information about this programming through a faculty listserv or other venue? Do they have access to curricular guidelines or sample syllabi?

4. If you plan to introduce curricular change, how will these changes impact labor needs? For instance, will course caps be lowered? Who will teach the newly created sections? Or will new writing requirements be added to existing courses? If so, who currently teaches these courses and how will these changes impact them?

5. Under the current curriculum, which groups of students are succeeding and which are struggling, according to institutional markers of success and distress (e.g., GPAs, academic integrity charges, time to degree, incomplete/withdraw/fail rates)?

6. How is the current writing curriculum impacting specific groups of students (e.g., students with disabilities, first-generation college students, multilingual students, students from ethnic or racial minority groups, etc.)? (This may be a question on which writing center tutors can provide insight.) How would changes to the writing curriculum impact these groups? What faculty development currently exists for teaching specific groups of students?

7. If there are separate sections of courses for multilingual students, what does the writing pedagogy look like in these courses? How does this pedagogy relate to pedagogies endorsed by the WAC program?

8. In what ways can the WAC program work to reduce disparity for adjunct and other contingent faculty? For instance, how can the WAC program provide contingent labor with access to information about pedagogy, community around teaching, a voice in the program, and visibility in the wider campus community?

9. In what ways can the WAC program work to reduce disparity for diverse student writers? For instance, how can the WAC program partner with others on campus to offer faculty development related to specific student groups, make visible the achievements of diverse student writers, and promote fair and equitable writing assessment practices?

10. What changes in the faculty and student body do you anticipate? (For instance, is your university forming alliances with universities abroad that will bring groups of international students to campus? Is your university promoting early retirements and replacing tenure-track positions with non-tenure-track lines?) How will these anticipated trends impact the goals and development of the WAC program?

Strategy 7: Set Mission, Goals, and SIs

WAC programs often grow organically from an initial workshop and then develop in fits and starts as a director experiments with different projects or connects with diverse campus units. However, in keeping with the principle of *systematic development*, the programs that take the time to establish a mission and goals at the outset with a focus on long-term viability have a much greater chance of building sustainable projects and programs. Typically, a mission statement lays out the broad scope of what stakeholders hope to accomplish through a WAC program and clarifies its purpose. Such a focus enables the stakeholder group to formulate the parameters within which the program should function optimally by articulating SIs with their bands of equilibrium to track longevity at the time of establishing the mission, goals, and expected outcomes of the program and, subsequently, each project (e.g., WI initiative, faculty training, writing fellows program, etc.). This set of conversations typically leads to open discussion, engaged participation, and eventual ownership of the outcomes—all benefits of seeking *broad participation* while forming the mission and goals.

To our knowledge, there has not been discussion in WAC literature of mission statements and how central they are to the formation of WAC programs. While the development of a mission statement is often perceived as an exercise in common sense to represent the purpose of a WAC program, we present here a deliberative methodology for using the mission discussion to build stakeholder consensus and a comprehensive program vision. In this section, we first discuss the formation of mission and goals and then move to SIs. As the methodology for SI development was discussed in Chapter 3, here we focus on guiding the participatory process for SI development.

Formulating Mission and Goals

One way to start, as discussed by Oleksiak above, is to have the stakeholder group brainstorm key terms from the university mission statement, current strategic plan, assessment documents, high-impact practices terms, or other terms that have currency across campus. A strong WAC mission is tied to the nature of the local program (e.g., WI, CAC, faculty support, or assessment focused), distinguishes itself from other initiatives, and identifies how it will serve students, faculty, and the institution as a whole. It is also concise and supported by specific, measurable, attainable, realistic, and time-delimited goals.

Take, for example, the mission statement of the University of Missouri's campus writing program. A short version appears on their home page: "Our mission is to support faculty as the primary agents in educating students to reason critically, solve complex problems, and communicate with clear, effective language in discipline-specific ways." This version is focused, clear, concise, and learning specific, but is not really tied to WAC per se or the local program. The extended version on the mission page (University of Missouri, 2016a) is less concise but more program specific:

> Our mission is to support faculty as the primary agents of Writing Across the Curriculum (WAC) theories and practices in educating students through principles of "writing-to-learn" and "learning-to-write." We believe that teaching by these principles will enhance students' critical thinking abilities and better engage them in complex problem solving while they learn to communicate with clear, effective language in discipline-specific ways.

The focus on faculty is important here. It implies training, support, engagement, and broad impact. The terms "WAC," "writing to learn," and "learning to write" are clearly grounded in the field, but they are not program specific. The skills listed are important. Interestingly, they could apply to most curriculum or accreditation organizations for a wide range of fields. But a clear picture of the program only emerges in the annual report, which identifies faculty objectives of the campus writing program as:

- ◆ programs and instruction that promote critical thinking and meaningful learning;
- ◆ writing as a process that includes revision;
- ◆ collaborative opportunities for faculty to share their work and their questions.

These faculty goals are clear, focused, measurable, attainable, realistic, concise, and define what the mission seeks to achieve for faculty within this specific program at this institution. They are not yet, however, time delimited.

Students who are completing WI courses at the University of Missouri are expected to:

♦ pose worthwhile questions by . . .

♦ evaluate and know types of arguments by . . .

♦ give feedback and know how to use feedback on pieces of writing through . . .

♦ distinguish among fact, inference, and opinion by . . .

♦ articulate complex ideas clearly by . . .

♦ deal with problems that have no simple solutions by . . .

♦ consider purpose and audience by . . .

♦ understand ways of communicating effectively in the given discipline as shown through . . . [with each requirement in this list completed as appropriate for particular course objectives]

These goals meet the criteria of being specific, measurable, attainable, and realistic, while also leaving room for disciplinary differences. Like those for faculty, the student goals are not time delimited, but they could easily become so by noting at which point in a student's program the goals should be met. An advantage of thinking in terms of time-delimited goals is that it encourages us to think about the development of a vertical writing curriculum across a student's academic career, from the first year through graduation.

Missouri's mission page is an excellent case for new programs to consider. It provides an example of how a mission statement can change over time to become more effective. Rather than focusing primarily on the WID program, the revised mission and goals better represent the WAC program overall.

We noted, in the opening lines of this section, that WAC programs often grow organically as directors and committees experiment with program projects. As a result, most programs, if they have mission statements and goals, outgrow them over time, and need to revise them. Another important lesson is that mission and goals should consider long-term goals of the WAC program that extend beyond a specific project like a WI program.

The mission will be determined by the range of goals, which are in turn determined by the explicit outcomes anticipated from a WAC program.

Developing SIs and Bands of Equilibrium

A focused mission and goals allow stakeholders to develop a reasonable number of SIs that can be assessed and reconsidered as the WAC program develops. Although Oleksiak and the WID advisory committee he describes did not engage in a formal process of developing SIs and their bands of equilibrium for WID sustainability at Bloomsburg, in the committee's creation of a mission and goals we can see the seeds of a possible SI development process. For example, one of the charges of the WID advisory committee is to seek funding to meet the needs of the emerging WID program. As an SI, sustainable funding of the WID program connects to the "support system" level of the system levels model we introduced in Chapter 3 (see Figure 3.4). Once the WID advisory committee has considered the scope of the program, its members could collaboratively consider the different aspects of the SI "sustainable funding of WID" and come up with concrete, measurable parameters. As we pointed out in Chapter 3, SIs must be clearly defined, reproducible, unambiguous, understandable, and practical (the more tangible and measurable, the better). Programmatic indicators of success are specific types of program outcomes, but they also add a new dimension to the lore on developing outcomes for WAC programs since they force WAC leaders to develop outcomes (indicators of success) that are concrete and measurable.

The WID advisory committee might define the components of sustainable funding per year as "release time for director" ($10,000 for two classes a year), "operating budget for supplies" ($2,000), "funding for faculty development stipends" ($8,000), "funding for advertising" ($1,000), and "funding for a part-time staff member for clerical support" ($15,000), for a total of $36,000.

Once these aspects of the funding SI for WID are defined in a concrete and measurable way, a band of equilibrium can be developed. The *band of equilibrium* defines the upper and lower thresholds of sustainability for an SI. In this case, $36,000 is the actual amount needed to run the program for a given year. In a tight budget year, it could probably get away with training a few less faculty, halving the supplies budget, and eliminating advertising funding, but the remainder would be necessary. So the minimal level of funding to enable the program to function would be something like $32,000. The upper band might start at the base of $36,000 and add a few additional faculty to be trained ($2,000), funds for an assessment process with twenty normed raters ($10,000), and perhaps a departmental WAC grant ($5,000), for a total of $53,000. Without additional staff or support, the program would not likely be able to manage beyond these additional functions. On a scale of 1 to 5, with 1 marking the lower band at $32,000 and 5 marking the upper at $53,000, 3 would mark $42,500. Once the limits are set and financial ranges translated to the five-point scale, the band of equilibrium is set for that SI, and the WAC director can review and track the university's financial support of WAC over time.

After formulating the program's mission, vision, and goals, and operationalizing its first SI, the next step for Bloomsburg's WID advisory committee would be to identify the remaining program SIs, each time marking the upper and lower bands of equilibrium. Each of Bloomsburg's WID advisory committee charges—best practices, faculty resources, sharing information on teaching, offering recommendations on teaching at all levels, assessment of program effectiveness, and securing and sustaining internal and external funding—should be considered when devising SIs. Notice that this list touches on all three major systems of the university anthrosphere: human (social), support (economic), and natural (institutional) (again, see Figure 3.4). The first four charges address individual faculty development and workshops. The fifth, on assessment, is too general by itself to warrant a single SI, but could be addressed across several SIs that track individual student and faculty development and support, as well as program longevity. The sixth connects directly to economic support systems and infrastructure, the existing curricular ecology of departments and university programs, and program outcomes. It could easily inform a few SIs. To see what SI development might look like for Bloomsburg, we offer the following representative list for overall program tracking. Focusing on the human system, SIs might include:

- ◆ *Individual development* and *Social system*
  - ◊ range and quality of faculty support, discussions, workshops, and resource materials
  - ◊ preparedness of students for writing in the majors
- ◆ *Governance system*
  - ◊ level of engagement of WID advisory committee members
- ◆ *Economic system*
  - ◊ support for WAC director (including general respect, salary, and release time)
  - ◊ sufficiency of program funding
- ◆ *Infrastructure system*
  - ◊ office space and support services for WAC program
- ◆ *Curricular ecology and resource system*
  - ◊ impacts of WAC program on departmental curriculum
  - ◊ preparation level of graduating students for workplace or higher degrees
  - ◊ willingness of programs and faculty to participate
  - ◊ sufficiency of writing support services for students on campus.

This list does not, however, include specific SIs for each project: faculty fellows program and departmental WEC initiatives. The WID advisory committee would need to create sets for each and establish the bands of equilibrium.

We cannot emphasize enough the importance of the participatory process for forming SIs. There is a big difference between a program, project, mission, or even assessment process that is defined and delegated from above and one that emerges from a participatory stakeholder group approach. The latter introduces a range of complexities that a top-down initiative avoids; however, a top-down initiative is much less likely to succeed as it does not typically engage stakeholders across the system in decision making and program development. Ison (1993, pp. 47–48) noted that the principles of participatory projects include the following realizations: participatory outcomes are more mutually satisfying, experience and knowledge are context based, enthusiasm is triggered and heightened at the individual level, knowledge is both individually and socially constructed and impacts learning networks, and diversity of experience, knowledge, research, and action are assets to the complex system as a whole.

Targeted interventions in the normal feedback loops of WAC systems can, in fact, shift an indicator of distress into an indicator of success. For example, a program like the one that Juli Parrish and Eliana Schonberg describe in Chapter 6 (following) could be realigned within existing or revised WAC initiatives that were more definitively project based and managed. Such shifts could enable them to show improved faculty perceptions of WAC.

It is important to note also that some SIs will continue to be used for the life of the project, while others may be added or dropped as the program changes and grows. For example, a WID program will always want to keep track of the number of syllabi in compliance each year, and would therefore warrant an SI that is tracked from the inception of the program onward. In contrast, there are some SIs that may be more important when a program is just getting going, such as the number of tenure-track faculty newly trained in WID pedagogy. As the program grows over the years, those numbers may drop but stabilize. As long as there is a steady flow, it may not be necessary to track this SI after the first few years.

The discussions above on SI development help us see that, of the four vignettes that opened this chapter, Oleksiak's description of Bloomsburg's WAC program formation is the one that suggests the greatest potential for long-term viability at the outset. Oleksiak was hired as the WID coordinator, and was able to form a stakeholder group within his first term at Bloomsburg. His instincts to have the group establish the mission and charge for the WID advisory committee enabled its members to begin thinking more broadly about a mission for the WID program itself. Collecting key terms from across campus provided a context for discussion and led to the formation of Bloomsburg's WID program mission: the development of a "series of programs for faculty and students

designed to make writing an integral part of university education."
This broad charge sets an institutional context that is favorable
to WAC program development as an important curricular hub
university-wide. However, there is still more work necessary to
build a sustainable program. The next steps for the advisory committee at Bloomsburg could be to identify the specific goals of each
project and build the policies, support systems, and assessment
mechanisms to manage each one. Developing and tracking SIs
as a subsequent step would ensure that program parameters are
set and clear bands of equilibrium are identified for the program
and each of its major initiatives.

Setting a Program Mission, Goals, and SIs: Questions to Consider

1. Does your WAC program have a mission statement, and, if so,
   what are its explicit goals? To what extent is the mission statement tied to the nature of the local program (e.g., WI, CAC,
   faculty support, etc.)? To what extent is it tied to the university
   mission statement and other key university documents? How well
   does it distinguish the program from others on campus? How
   well does it articulate how the program will serve faculty, students, and the institution as a whole? Is it concise and supported
   by specific, measurable, attainable, realistic, and time-delimited
   goals?

2. Has your mission statement been revised since it was first developed? Most WAC programs grow and change over time. How
   well does your mission statement reflect its current implementation? If necessary, whom might you bring together to revise and
   update it?

3. To what extent does your mission statement reach beyond a
   single focus or project within the program? For example, if a WI
   initiative is central to the WAC program, what other projects are
   acknowledged (e.g., writing fellows program, faculty training,
   writing center, assessment process, etc.)? How might the mission
   statement be broadened to accommodate these broader aspects
   of the program, but still meet the stated standards in question 1
   of this list?

4. Has a set of SIs been identified, defined, and operationalized
   within your current program? If not, how might you start that
   process? If so, have they been identified for all important concerns

(e.g., director's support, stakeholder committee, financial support, curricular approvals, sufficient courses available to students, faculty support, course syllabus recertification process, etc.)?

5. Has the process of developing SIs been participatory? What stakeholder group has developed them? How should the group be expanded to be better representative of institutional goals?

6. Is it possible to deduce the viability and sustainability of current developments compared with alternative developments? In other words, is the range and scope of indicators sufficient to recognize the points at which the program is viable/functional at the lower end and the point at which it cannot be sustained at the high end (think of the band of equilibrium)?

7. Is there a clear process in place for finding an adequate set of indicators for program sustainability? And does that process provide ways to use this information for assessing program viability at different levels/scales of the institution?

CHAPTER SIX

Stage Three of the Whole Systems Methodology: Developing Projects and Making Reforms

In Chapters 4 and 5, we explored the first stages of the whole systems methodology, which focus on strategies associated with understanding and planning. The following four vignettes discuss particular projects and reforms that illustrate the *developing* stage of the whole systems methodology, which focuses on building WAC initiatives strategically and sustainably. Juli Parrish and Eliana Schonberg, University of Denver, describe collaborations between a writing center director and new WAC director that led to regularly offered faculty development workshops and institutes. Maggie Cecil and Carol Haviland, both at California State University, San Bernardino, discuss the importance of WAC directors positioning themselves as listeners when interacting with faculty across the curriculum in a narrative that highlights rewarding micro-level work with individual faculty. Zak Lancaster, a new WAC director at Wake Forest University, discusses the systematic approach he used to develop a WID-based faculty development seminar. Vi Dutcher, at Eastern Mennonite University, describes how she resuscitated a problematic WI requirement by planning for slow and gradual change.

Following these vignettes, we discuss four strategies that are key to the *developing* stage of the whole systems methodology: Strategy 8, maximize program sustainability through project-based program development; Strategy 9, make reforms at both the micro and system levels; Strategy 10, plan for gradual rather than rapid reforms to the system; and Strategy 11, deal with obstacles to program or project development systematically.

Stealth and Sustainability:
Writing Center Workshops as WAC

Juli Parrish and Eliana Schonberg
University of Denver

Whether this story is about starting or sustaining a WAC program depends on where one begins. When, as part of a freestanding writing program at the University of Denver—with the mission to "develop a robust culture of writing" on campus—we began thinking of ways to publicize our new writing center, our initial motivation was to make public the intellectual-order teaching work of that space. WAC was not yet our explicit goal.

Knowing that faculty are usually receptive to offers for help for their students, we advertised our willingness to create individually tailored classroom workshops. Of course, to discover what those needs were, we had to meet with faculty to discuss the class and the assignments, and soon, without us quite realizing it, a "stealth WAC" model was born.

Our workshops are a version of what Rebecca Moore Howard (1988) described as "in situ" workshops, aimed at helping faculty help their students. Perhaps not surprisingly, these workshops caught on much faster than other writing program WAC efforts designed to target faculty more explicitly, growing from twenty-one in our first year to more than ninety in our seventh. The story of starting this WAC initiative is a successful one by any measure.

But, when it comes to sustaining it, the waters muddy substantially. We remain confident in the value of these workshops for students across campus; for the writing program faculty who gain opportunities to team teach and to learn about the teaching of writing in other disciplines, and for the more than thirty-five departments and programs with whom we work. However, we have begun to question the sustainability of this workshop model, both in terms of potential burnout on the part of the writing program faculty who facilitate so many workshops each year, and also in terms of a problematic perception that we are only offering a service to faculty, not collaborating with them to develop their teaching abilities independent of us.

It was this questioning that prompted us to assess our workshop model by collecting electronic survey data after each workshop over the course of a year. In some ways, we have been pleased with the results: cross-campus faculty report valuing the concrete strategies we offer and the fact that we introduce our writing center to their students. However, less than half of the respondents reported as valuable other regular features of our workshops, such as offering students time in class to draft or revise, for example, and giving them a chance to ask their instructors questions about writing. What these items have in common is that they highlight the work that *students* do in our workshops, as opposed to the work that *we* do.

Perhaps most important, only about a third of our respondents reported finding valuable the work that they do with us: discussing their course materials and participating in the workshop planning. What does this mean? Perhaps that faculty value this work less than some of the other options. Our concern is that these faculty responses highlight the flaw in the stealth approach: for the sake of working with faculty, we subtly encourage a perception of ourselves as service providers, not collaborative teachers. This begs the question of whether our stealth model is too stealthy to be sustainable.

It may be true that relatively few faculty with whom we work seem to become dependent on us, and that the majority of them seem to be gaining rhetorical knowledge. It may be true, too, that these faculty implement ideas they learned with us and from us in future assignments or classes, or that, when they invite us back, it is because they value having another person in the room to espouse writing principles, which would signify a certain kind of success. But, this is also true: on one recent evaluation form, a faculty member reported that she hoped to "use" us or the peer review handout we'd offered her again. This, in a nutshell, is the problem: we risk being seen as the tool and not the craftsperson.

When we consider revisions to our workshops, we are left with more questions than answers: Is there a way to engage cross-campus faculty more actively in workshop facilitation? If we make more transparent the underlying WAC focus of our work, will that lead to better outcomes or just fewer contacts? As we struggle to balance success with sustainability, all while preserving our disciplinary identity and self-respect, we wonder most of all how we can work *with* faculty across campus and not *for* them.

Rhetorical Listening/Listening to Learn Rather Than to Correct

Maggie Cecil and Carol Peterson Haviland
California State University, San Bernardino

As we exited a faculty meeting in which our provost had summarized the Western Association of Schools and Colleges accreditation report and recommendations, a colleague whispered, "I know that she's right—that all of us need to incorporate more writing in our courses—but I just hate grading the papers my students turn in. I don't know what they do in those English classes, but, even by the time they are juniors, our majors still string together barely relevant quotes from scholars they don't understand, they still don't use APA properly, and their grammar is awful. How can I keep assigning writing when this is what I have to wade through?"

This being the 1007th time we had heard this question, a generous impulse was to tell him what he should be assigning in place of the "pick a topic that interests you and write a 2,000-word paper with at least eight scholarly citations"-type coursework, and a jaded response might have been, "Of course you hate to read what they see no reason to be writing."

A more useful response, for him and for us, however, was the one we chose: "Tell us more about your experiences; we hear that comment from others too and are really interested in understanding it better."

This truly interested "tell me more; I'm curious about what writing means in kinesiology" led to his description of the writing genres and processes kinesiologists use and to the habits of mind that shape their communications. We learned that they write all sorts of things in all sorts of ways: they write patient evaluations and treatment plans and grant proposals, they often collaborate with other health professionals such as dieticians and occupational therapists, they apply for high school coaching jobs, and they usually have to navigate websites to discover the organization and citation patterns peculiar to widely varying local requirements. Usually a "print record" remains, whether on paper, email, text, or "chart to cloud notes," and it may be used in court.

As he continued, we resisted the impulse to blurt out, "So what would happen if you asked them to write. . . ," and he ventured, "You know, if my students were writing some of these things, their writing might not be so horrible to read. In fact, I'll bet I might even learn something myself from their ideas about sending and storing data electronically. Right now, we are mostly stuck with generic platforms that we have to adapt, but we need to be developing our own that embody the ways we collect, transmit, and use data."

Our walk back through the commons stretched into forty-five minutes, Carol was late for an appointment with her chair, and Maggie missed the coffee she was counting on to fuel the next four hours of teaching . . . but we learned a lot . . . about kinesiology and about how to be WAC colleagues rather than WAC pests. Over the quarter, we met several additional times to draft some projects for his students as well as some ways that writing center tutors might interact as students develop these projects, Maggie revised one of her first-year writing projects, and Carol expanded a WAC seminar session to include what he'd taught her.

But the results of listening to learn rather than fixing or correcting didn't stop with just this one kinesiologist. The following term, he joined Carol's quarter-long faculty WAC seminar, at which he initiated a very thoughtful discussion of the writing of non-native English speakers. Rather than a generic lament about yet another category of "them," he began by saying that it was important for his MA program to include international students because they could bring up questions about culture and ethics that wouldn't occur to domestic students. So his question was constructive: "How can we best work with the MA theses of these students who want to study in the USA and who greatly expand the thoughtfulness of our seminars?" which is a question several other participants were wrestling with in their own department meetings. Then, at the end of the WAC seminar, he asked whether we would be interested in sitting in on one of his department meetings. "A couple of my colleagues were intrigued with that project we worked out and want to see if they can help their students write papers that are less hideous to read. Also, our chair keeps pestering us to do more of that writing the dean was talking about, so I thought that, as a group, we might think about how writing works in our discipline and maybe even coordinate some projects across some of our classes."

So we did attend their next department meeting, enthusiastic about how well this collaboration with our colleague was turning out, but the meeting was not quite as rosy. Some of his colleagues began to offer parallels between teaching healthy eating or strength training and teaching writing and were indeed interested in course designs that might incorporate writing. Others, however, were not.

Several were wary about taking on additional work, noting that adjuncts were teaching most of their lower division courses, so tenure-track faculty already had to serve on more committees and take on more thesis projects each year. One was downright hostile, reporting that a colleague in finance had learned the hard way that incorporating writing made "everyone hate you." He said that students avoided his colleague's courses because of the writing involved, which resulted in the colleague having low enrollments and her peers having over-enrolled courses. Also, he said that she became known as the chair's and the dean's toady because she was on the "writing bandwagon." He concluded by noting that, when his students completed his anatomy course, they "really knew anatomy" and didn't need future faculty to keep teaching it, so why couldn't English faculty deliver the same results?

The department visit was a mixed success, and we, of course, focused on the failures—until we remembered our initial colleague's comment about our coming to their meeting: "Who knows," he said, "We might even get better at talking about student writing rather than griping about it."

Yes, who knows? They did become more comfortable talking about student writing, and they revisited their teaching healthy eating/weight training/writing analogy. Their arguments also helped them bring their own writing experiences to their teaching discussions. We don't know what next they or we will learn, but we are certain that this approach of listening–engaging–learning, even though it is slow and not flashy, will lead to richer and more sustainable WAC/WID programs.

Challenges and Breakthroughs in a WID-Based Faculty Development Seminar: Reflections from a New WAC Director

Zak Lancaster

Wake Forest University

When I was hired as an assistant professor of English at Wake Forest University three years ago, I was charged with the daunting task of building a WAC program. I soon learned that earnest attempts had been made over the years to do this. Effort had been put into organizing workshops and inviting writing scholars to campus for panels and consultation. These endeavors, however, while useful, did not culminate in a durable WAC initiative, and I learned that no one person or group was to blame; rather, it appeared the parties and structures that needed to be connecting weren't connecting.

After a year of surveying the land, meeting staff and faculty, and offering brown-bag workshops, I concluded that there needed to be in place an annually recurring, incentivized seminar program for faculty across college divisions to come together, engage with writing theory and research, and be supported to design writing-enhanced courses in their fields. I learned that, while students were writing a lot across the curriculum, there was little visible writing instruction taking place on campus, apart from a one-semester first-year writing course that approximately a third of our students place out of. The purpose therefore of the "writing associates seminar" (WAS), as it came to be called, was to assist faculty to weave into their courses instruction and support for student writing. As I saw it, the WAS should take place in a nonhierarchical setting. It should be recurring, to ensure spread of effect, and it should inspire faculty to take on leadership roles in their home departments.

The WAS grew legs once our interdisciplinary writing minor was approved, just last year. WAS graduates can now be encouraged to submit their courses as electives for the minor, contributing toward a culture of writing on campus in which writing instruction is decoupled from the English department. Thanks to a supportive dean, a two-year pilot for the WAS was funded. We are now in the middle of the second iteration of the seminar. We meet as a group every two weeks from January to April with two summer retreats for reflection and course design.

So far there have been unforeseen challenges as well as pleasant surprises and breakthroughs. An early pleasant surprise was that, while funding for ten faculty participants was budgeted for the first year, we received twenty-four applications from faculty in every college division. In light of this robust response—one that showed unanticipated investment and needs across the university—we were able to fund eighteen participants during the first year. Another pleasant personal surprise is that I would end up learning as much as I have about teaching writing from my non-writing colleagues. Many of the participants brought to the table years of experience and expertise about everything from developing motivating and challenging writing assignments to offering feedback to students. As a newly appointed WAC administrator, I learned to listen closely to my colleagues' practices and concerns and to open myself up to learning from them—chemists, biologists, philosophers, sociologists, historians, and many others—about writing instruction in the disciplines.

In terms of challenges, I did expect that some faculty would be more "on board" than others; however, I didn't expect that engagement levels would fall as squarely as they have along status lines in this particular group. With clear exceptions, in this group, it was the pre-tenure faculty participants who expressed more openness to learning from writing research and to revisiting their teaching practices. I also see in their materials more radical overhauling of their writing assignments, in terms both of sequencing and uptake of rhetorical concepts like audience, purpose, and genre. These participants have allowed more room for process work, for using peer review, and for making assignment and genre expectations visible. In contrast, among several of the more senior colleagues, *rubric* seems to remain a taboo word, and there appears to be reluctance to reserve class time for explicit talk about writing, incorporating peer review, or developing assignments calling for alternatives to "domesticated" school genres.

As idiosyncratic as it may be to my experience, I mention this division because of the limitations and opportunities it has created for spread of effect. The senior participants have not engaged in the kinds of department outreach I had envisioned (at least that I can see yet—efforts may be happening behind the scenes). The junior participants, meanwhile, while more engaged, are concerned about ruffling feathers in their departments by proposing their courses for the minor, due to uncertainty about their colleagues' perceptions and effects on enrollment. Several junior participants were also concerned about assessment—specifically, that, by building in more writing support for their students, their grade distributions would move upward and this wouldn't bode well in tenure reviews. These concerns strike me now as valuable for my continued planning and reflecting as a WAC administrator.

These trends may be influenced by the particular emphases I chose in the WAS, such as practices like peer review and varied, process-based assignments, and there are also exceptions. I've heard through the grapevine, for example, that several senior participants have spoken up in department meetings about the need to revisit goals and assessment practices for student writing. Several junior participants have been organizing cross-disciplinary initiatives on their own, which appear to have been successful. For instance, five of them have organized a peer observation group, seeking opportunities for feedback from colleagues on their attempts to make writing more visible in their courses. Two colleagues invited me to co-facilitate writing workshops in their departments. Others from the 2014 cohort have visited this year's meetings in order to talk about strategies they've begun using in their teaching. Finally, much to my surprise, the 2014 group has remained unified as the inaugural cohort of writing associates, organizing happy hours and a "teaching circle" to follow up on their efforts during the seminar.

These latter initiatives reflect continued commitment among graduates of the seminar, most visibly so far among the pre-tenure participants. This type of commitment was initially supported by an incentivized, semester-long seminar, of course. But it appears also to be sustained by the participants' identification as writing associates, as knowledgeable teachers of writing. In addition to bonding as a cohort, they are seeking out further opportunities to hone their uses of student writing and to reach out to their department colleagues. Because of these early signs, I see the WAS as a key ingredient for launching a more durable WAC initiative at my institution. I am hopeful that it will find administrative support to continue running on an annual basis, involving more colleagues, and, more importantly, that it will continue to spark creative ideas from seminar graduates, who eventually will take up leadership positions in their departments and thereby contribute to an interdisciplinary WAC program.

Building a Campus Writing Culture:
It Takes a Village

Violet ("Vi") A. Dutcher
Eastern Mennonite University

Nine years ago, I was hired by a small liberal arts university to "fix" their writing problems. My compensation was one course release for my first semester. Clearly, they thought this fixing would take only one semester. As I investigated, with the support of the provost, I found a WAC initiative that required two WI courses beyond the required first-year writing course for all majors. Departments, however, were not offering enough WI courses for their majors; consequently, many students took upper-level WI courses in other departments, often unrelated to their majors, just to meet the requirements for graduation. Students appealed the requirement. Faculty resisted offering WI, citing over-enrollment and overwhelming labor. The general education director asked me to recommend canceling the requirement.

I was baffled. Why would faculty turn away from teaching their own majors their disciplines' writing practices? This attitude seemed counterintuitive. At my former institution, a large state university, I had been a member of the undergraduate university-wide writing program committee, and I reported back to my department; however, I had no experience leading a writing program, much less knowing how to build one.

I began reading everything I could find about writing programs. I consulted with experts in the field. I found the WPA listserv. I began meeting with departments in their regular meetings, listening to their complaints and, in some cases, demands that we get rid of this WI requirement. I began to realize that some of this pushback was directed toward the administration, but I did not know the cause.

As I listened and asked questions, I learned that, some years prior, during a survey of faculty and students, my new institution had learned that most students weren't writing long papers. In fact, they weren't writing much at all. Administration and some faculty were horrified, and they put in place the WI requirement that included an eight- to ten-page paper for all majors in their upper-level courses. This requirement came to the faculty from the provost's office.

I compiled a proposal to the provost that primarily stated that, while the initiatives were good ones, they had been sent from the top down, from administration to faculty; instead, the primary stakeholders, the faculty, needed to be the holders of this requirement. I did not recommend striking the requirement; rather, I recommended that we take steps to revive the initiative at the grassroots level. I also made the case that we needed a writing program to make our writing requirements cohesive and to build a writing culture unique for our needs.

I received a two-sentence response from the provost: "We did it wrong. Help us get it right." Since I was new and didn't know faculty well, she pulled together a writing committee, adding a representation from the graduate division. She increased my course release to one course release each semester of the academic year. She made me accountable to the provost, not a division dean, so that the writing program would be university-wide from the beginning.

I met with faculty in their departments, sharing my proposal. I emphasized that the purpose of the WI requirement was to teach their students their own discipline's writing style. I shared my goals, my dreams of our writing culture. The writing committee wrote a mission statement together. We designed and built a writing program website for our faculty and students. We chose a writing handbook required for all first-year students. Administration approved a nationally recognized cap on WI course enrollments. Our writing committee changed the WAC policy from requiring eight- to ten-page papers to a number of written pages students needed to write, thus supporting those departments that found a lengthy paper unrelated to their discipline for undergraduate students. I began to hold faculty workshops on grading, the writing process, and writing to learn.

Faculty started owning the requirement, offering more WI courses and collaborating with other departments regarding appropriate WI courses for their students. They began inviting me into their writing classrooms. I took writing tutors with me, writing tutors who had come through my tutoring practicum and were now trained to tutor their peers. We began to see a decrease in student appeals to waive the requirement.

Over the years, slowly, surely, we started to turn around the attitude toward WI courses. We began, together, to recognize what we valued in our writing and that of our students. This led to working together on writing assessment. The graduate programs have joined this effort, and I meet with them regularly, walking alongside. I work with the undergraduate and graduate deans and report to the provost.

Three years after I arrived on this campus, I initiated a weeklong writing retreat for faculty, staff, and graduate students. We schedule it for May, after our contracts are finished and before our children are out of school for the summer. We work on our writing together, and we discover that we share many writing anxieties with our students. We embrace our writing culture that is uniquely ours.

Strategy 8: Maximize Program Sustainability through Project-Based Development

The notion of identifying each component of a WAC program as a project that has its own cycles of understanding, planning, developing, and leading comes from sustainable development theory and builds from all ten of the whole systems principles. As we noted in Chapter 3, focusing on program components as projects enables directors to manage program growth and complexity. This focus also suggests that each project of the larger program is defined by its own set of activities that are initiated to achieve specific outcomes. Furthermore, each project has time and resource constraints and comes with its own mindsets and assumptions. Taken together, a set of projects is used systematically to fulfill the WAC program mission and goals. Using a project-based approach enables the WAC director or committee to prioritize which programs should be developed, in what order, and on what timeline to most impact the system, all of which maximizes WAC program sustainability.

The project approach for WAC program development confirms why Parrish and Schonberg sense that their "stealth" workshop program at the University of Denver is not sustainable. While their in situ workshops are generous and appealing to faculty, Parish and Schonberg's approach, as outlined in their vignette, does not work as an effective intervention to address a specific problem. Rather, they are providing services to address the broad mission of developing "a robust culture of writing" on campus. In fact, they note that the writing center workshops were not originally intended to serve as a WAC intervention, nor were they ever charged with a mandate. As faculty heard more about them, however, demand increased significantly. The program's developers saw a potential opportunity to raise visibility of writing on campus and leverage their presence in classrooms, but, without a clear and specific mission and charge that was agreed upon by faculty as stakeholders, it became clear that faculty had different goals for including the workshops in their classes than the writing center staff. Furthermore, faculty had little incentive to continue this kind of work after the workshop facilitators left.

Vi Dutcher, in her vignette, offers a counterexample that demonstrates how an unsustainable program can shift to become more sustainable and project based. She was hired to "fix" a WID program at a small liberal arts university. Similar to Cripps in his vignette in Chapter 4, Dutcher began her work by figuring out why the WI program was not working by gathering information from across campus and directly from faculty. She found that there were not enough sections being offered and that the WI requirements were not practical, in part because they had been determined by a top-down mandate. In response to her report, the provost gave Dutcher release time to rework the WI program, convened a WAC committee of stakeholders, and shifted her direct supervisor from a division dean to the provost. Each of these steps helped lead to a project-based intervention, with a clear set of problems, a clear set of targeted solutions, transparent lines of WAC leadership, and a grassroots approach to change. When Dutcher was invited into faculty classes with tutors, it was in service of the revised WI initiative. Over time, a student assessment process was started and a weeklong faculty retreat initiated. Each new program component was developed as a project, with its own cycle of understanding, planning, developing, and leading.

Still, as is the case with most WAC programs, Dutcher's initiative only measures student success and not program sustainability. For each initiative, the WAC committee should consider defining SIs that help to determine the band of equilibrium for each and anticipate issues that may impact project resilience. Bell and Morse (2008) noted that understanding sustainable development initiatives as projects means that SIs are a necessary part of the development process. Tracking these indicators through the entire project cycle ensures that program goals remain in clear focus and that shifts in purpose or practices may lead to additional SI development. While WAC directors should create the SIs in the planning stage, they should begin tracking individual projects in the *developing* stage of the whole systems methodology.

A tactic for tracking all SIs at one time involves using the AMOEBA approach (Laane & Peters, 1993; ten Brink, 1991; ten Brink, Hosper, & Colijn, 1991). "AMOEBA" is a Dutch acronym that, in full, refers to a "general method for ecosystem description and assessment" (Bell & Morse, 2008, p. 62). AMOEBA graphs are radar charts that can measure the upper and lower bands of equilibrium for all SIs of a program or given project in one snapshot. Figures 6.1 and 6.2 illustrate how all SIs for an individual project such as a WI program can be mapped together as an AMOEBA graph. Figure 6.1 represents a point in time when the (hypothetical) WI program was sustainable. The "doughnut" in the middle of the spider graph marks the lower and upper thresholds of the band of equilibrium. Each SI is measured on a five-point scale, with the inner band set at 1 and the outer band at 5. An example SI for assessing the sustainability of a WI requirement might be the capacity of the WAC director for maintaining this initiative in terms of how many hours per month the director can dedicate. The director may determine that the maximum monthly hours would be thirty (level 5), and the minimum hours would be ten (level 1), thus setting the middle level (3) at twenty. Once the program's stakeholder group sets the ranges for each of a project's SIs, an AMOEBA graph can be charted.

Creating these graphs regularly offers a negative feedback loop mechanism (described in Chapter 2) that enables interventions when conditions warrant change. If an SI moves above or below the band of equilibrium boundaries, the WAC director should take note. If the problem persists over time, action should

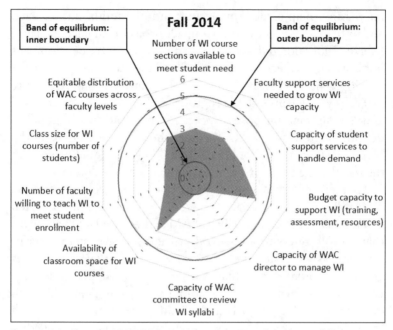

FIGURE **6.1**. *Sample AMOEBA map for eight SIs of a sustainable WI requirement within a WAC program.*

be taken to adjust the system. Figure 6.2 demonstrates the same WI program two years later, during which the program grew and shifted indicators to unsustainable levels. Notice that there are three SIs that are below the inner boundary and two at the inner boundary. While the availability of classroom space may be only a temporary problem, it could also be a result of more courses reducing class size to meet WI requirements as the number of WI sections grows. Combined with a lack of sufficient sections to meet student enrollment needs, the marginal capacity of additional faculty to teach more sections, lack of equitable teaching loads across faculty levels, and want of a budget sufficient to support and train faculty, it is clear that this program is in trouble. As noted earlier, an AMOEBA graph offers a snapshot of a program at a moment in time, so creating multiple graphs using the same SIs across a program's development allows for quick clear comparisons, providing longitudinal insights into a program's viability. As Figure 6.2 demonstrates, however, it is

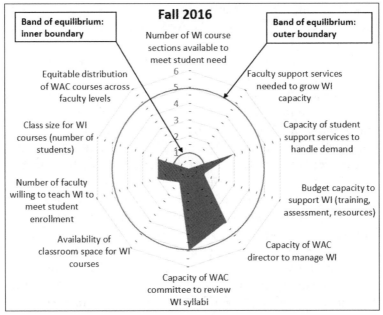

FIGURE **6.2.** *Sample AMOEBA map for eight SIs of an unsustainable WI requirement within a WAC program.*

important to understand which factors have led to shifting SI values. If, for example, additional support for faculty stipends could be provided and class size could be reduced slightly, it is possible that more faculty would be willing to teach WI courses, which would increase the availability of sections for students and make available additional classrooms with smaller capacities. Although the space problem may not be solved immediately, it might be further alleviated by shifting university schedules. A program with one marginal SI is much more likely to be sustainable in the short term than one with five problematic indicators.

Because SIs are chosen for their impact, predictive qualities, and ease of measurement, it should not be laborious to collect the data for these graphs. The more difficult it is to assess a given SI, the more it complicates the overall assessment. In such cases, the stakeholder group should justify the need for the particular SI (e.g., portfolio scores for capstone writing courses requested by the provost) or identify alternative SIs or other means of assessing it. Once the data are collected, creating these graphs as radar charts is easy in Excel (see Appendix A, where we provide a step-by-step process for Windows software).

Depending on a project's complexity, it might be necessary to use more than one AMOEBA graph to accommodate the desired SIs. Typically, however, one should suffice for each significant project in addition to the WAC program as a whole. It is important to note that SIs may need to change over time as projects and programs shift and grow. Additionally, there may be outcomes that a program director or stakeholder group wishes to track that do not offer clear benefits for understanding sustainability. For example, the graphs above do not include an SI for student success or writing quality. This absence does not suggest that writing outcomes are not important for sustainability, as program funding may be tied to student performance. However, program visibility, impacts on faculty and curriculum, and continued growth and innovation tend to drive sustainability more directly. Notwithstanding this fact, this hypothetical example would be strengthened by adding student success measures such as writing outcomes from departments with WEC programs or senior portfolio review results. Less direct measures, such as faculty perceptions of student writing, numbers of students publishing work as undergraduates, or numbers of students getting into graduate programs, are also useful but not easily correlated to WAC programs or program sustainability. We discuss assessment further in Strategy 14 (see Chapter 7).

A project-based approach to WAC program development acknowledges the complexity of the system and its curricular ecology and establishes a deliberate approach to program development. Programs that take a deliberate project approach are predictably more viable over time. The project focus also means that assessment is integrated into every WAC project. While some results will be made visible in public ways, such as student outcomes, faculty successes, and noteworthy program accomplishments, other indicators will serve only the WAC committee or director to ensure program continuity and integrity. In all cases, assessment provides feedback, sometimes at lower scales (e.g., faculty syllabi in a WI program) and other times at higher scales (e.g., a university-wide assessment of student writing). Finally, closing the loop in any assessment process enables growth and change, sometimes leading to significant transformation of individual projects or university-wide initiatives.

Maximizing Program Sustainability through Project-Based Program Development: Questions to Consider

1. What are the primary projects of your WAC program? Which aspects of the WAC program mission and goals are they fulfilling? Are there other projects your program needs to develop to fulfill the WAC mission and goals? If so, what are they and what timeline can you develop for their implementation?

2. What SIs have already been identified for each project (these may be visible in the annual report or in proposals for new program elements)? How do these SIs relate to the six major systems identified in Chapter 3 (see Figure 3.4)? What additional SIs should be developed in relation to each system?

3. Have a sufficient number of SIs been identified to represent the important aspects of the program? How can you tell?

4. Are your SIs worded in such a way that they can easily be used in an AMOEBA map? If not, how might you edit them?

5. How can you create a rating system (a scale from 1 to 5) for each SI so that you can establish a band of equilibrium, create a spider graph, and determine the sustainability of each project?

6. What does your analysis of the SIs reveal about challenges specific projects within your WAC program are facing? What interventions can be undertaken to solve these challenges? How can you use SIs and the bands of equilibrium to see if these interventions are effective?

7. How can these challenges and interventions be publicized in a way that ensures action, intervention, and change rather than a simple reporting of results?

Strategy 9: Make Reforms at Both the Micro and the System Levels

It's common for directors to focus on the micro level when building a WAC program. As many of the vignettes in this book demonstrate, new WAC directors often focus their efforts on developing projects that will help them begin to build a group of WAC enthusiasts: projects such as the annual faculty development seminar that Lancaster began at Wake Forest (described above) and the workshops that Weisser and Ryan created to support WI faculty at Penn State Berks, described in Chapter 5. Working at the micro level is not only personally satisfying, but also can help directors lay the groundwork for more substantial and transformative change further down the road, as illustrated by Cecil and Haviland's vignette above. Cecil and Haviland relayed how a conversation on writing instruction with a faculty member at a university-wide meeting led to multiple consultations on this instructor's writing assignments, the instructor joining a semester-long WAC seminar, and Cecil and Haviland's participation in department discussions on writing support. The focus on the micro level is also well documented in the WAC literature. As Weisser and Ryan noted in their vignette, experienced WAC scholars such as Susan McLeod and Elaine Maimon (2000) have argued that the faculty development workshop is a "starting point" for transforming writing pedagogy (p. 580). Toby Fulwiler (2006) described the faculty workshop as key to the success of his WAC program at Michigan Technological University. Micro-level projects such as these can be the best way to begin to build a grassroots network of faculty who are discussing and implementing WAC pedagogy and who are supportive of WAC policies and initiatives.

However, a WAC program that never moves beyond micro-level work is difficult to sustain, and may never get to the tipping point where it has a transformative effect on the campus culture of writing. In the WAC lore, a common tale is that of the WAC director who becomes burned out from being overwhelmed by ever-expanding micro-level demands on her time: a snowballing amount of requests for a popular workshop, multiple individual consultations scheduled after a visit to a department meeting, multiple faculty knocking on the WAC director's door to collaborate on research after implementing WAC pedagogies learned in a seminar. This impact can lead to a program that does not introduce institutional change at higher scales or identify points of leverage that could transform the entire system. WAC directors need to work at both the micro and macro levels to address the whole systems principles of *wholeness* (the WAC program as a significant intervention in a complex system), *broad participation* (engaging stakeholders from all levels of the system), and *transformational change* (introducing change not just to small groups of faculty but to the entire system and the ideologies that inform the system).

The value of moving up the scale from the micro to the macro is illustrated by Lancaster, who explains, in his vignette, that the Writing Associates Seminar (WAS) at Wake Forest University didn't fully take off until an interdisciplinary writing minor was approved: "WAS graduates can now be encouraged to submit their courses as electives for the minor, contributing toward a culture of writing on campus in which writing instruction is decoupled from the English department." Even this move up the scale may not be enough to have a campus-wide impact, however, and moving further up the scale might mean systematically integrating WAS across the university. One way to think of the relationship between micro and macro in this context is in terms of building connections and support systems that reach higher up the scales of the system. A micro-level seminar can connect further up the scale to an interdisciplinary writing minor, and an interdisciplinary writing minor could connect even further up the scale to a campus-wide writing requirement. These moves would require work at the higher scales of departments, colleges, academic senate, institutional assessment, etc. WAC directors can also aim to work at the very highest scales and make connections between their local institutional roles and WAC as a national and international movement by participating in national and international WAC organizations and conferences (a strategy detailed in Chapter 7).

WAC projects that operate at the macro levels typically require the support of actors within the network who spend most of their time at the macro level, and this speaks to the importance of WAC programs being located in network hubs (e.g., academic affairs, centers for teaching and learning, writing centers). It also speaks to the value of WAC directors reporting to an actor or actors that work at the macro level of the system (e.g., provost, academic senate, academic affairs dean), as opposed to a reporting line that ends at the siloed departmental level. Dutcher's vignette exemplifies this point, as she emphasized the importance of reporting directly to the provost, and "not a division dean, so that the writing program would be university-wide from the beginning."

It is important to see the connections between thinking about a WAC program as a group of projects (Strategy 8) and working at both the micro and macro levels (Strategy 9). After stakeholders have gauged the campus mood, mapped the network, and located points of leverage, they are well positioned not only to begin developing projects, but also to think about whether or not these projects work at multiple scales of the system and connect to institutional points of leverage for making change—goals that should be considered when developing SIs. What the WAC lore might lead a director to believe is an indicator of program success—a popular annual seminar and a director whose phone is always ringing with requests for workshops and one-on-one consultations—could actually be an indicator of program distress if the director burns out or the WAC network of participants never moves beyond a dedicated but small group of faculty. SIs should capture the importance of working at both the micro and macro level for program sustainability—measuring not just who is participating in WAC but at what scales of the system actors who are involved operate (e.g., only faculty, or also department chairs and deans and directors of other campus programs), whether WAC is affecting not just pedagogy but university policy, how many departments and not just individual faculty have formed relationships with WAC, the extent to which WAC is collaborating with other programs that are considered hubs in the campus network, and so on. The whole systems approach encourages us to think of projects not just as faculty development activities, but also as strategic interventions into complex systems, with the goal of transforming these systems across scales.

Making Reforms at Both the Micro and the System Levels: Questions to Consider

1. How much time and how many resources are the WAC director devoting to micro-level work, such as consultations and workshops, and how much are they devoting to macro-level work, such as campus writing requirements, campus writing assessment, campus writing policy, etc.?

2. To what extent does the WAC program involve actors at higher scales of the institution, such as provosts, deans, academic senate chairs, etc.?

3. At what scale of the institution is the person or people to whom the WAC director reports?

4. How can WAC connect projects at micro scales to projects at macro scales? How can WAC transform micro-scale projects into macro-scale projects? (Mapping relationships among systems on campus may help; refer to Chapter 4 for mapping tactics.)

5. What macro-scale changes to campus writing structures could help support WAC's micro-scale work (e.g., the formation of an independent writing department, the creation of a writing major or minor, an expansion of the campus writing center, the creation of an academic senate writing committee)?

6. What capacity does the WAC program have for growth? What will the program need in terms of release time, budget, staff, space, and leadership in order to be sustainable?

Strategy 10: Plan for Gradual Rather Than Rapid Reforms to the System

The principle of *systematic development* is key for the *developing* stage of the whole systems methodology. It emphasizes the connection between sustainability and building a WAC program incrementally. Systems theorists like Bela Banathy (1973) have argued that being aware that "all systems have constraints can make you more realistic about the nature of change" (p. 2). Campus writing programs are simply too complex, and—in the parlance of systems theory—their boundaries too open, to change rapidly. The constraints of complex systems should not just make WAC directors more realistic about change, but should also give us pause when we are considering any rapid and high-scale intervention. Often, in dealing with complex systems, "faster is slower," as Peter Senge (1990, p. 62) observed.

A common example of the need for patience and incremental change in the developing stage of WAC program building comes from Dutcher's vignette. Dutcher was hired with the expectation that she would "fix" the campus writing problem in one semester, and she was given just one semester of release time. This notion that a single person can be hired to provide a quick fix to a perceived writing problem is common in the WAC lore, and it is a situation the authors of this book have encountered numerous times when consulting with institutions starting WAC programs. Rather than try to rush and find a quick fix to the WI program—a move that would have most likely wound up failing, given the complexities of the problem—Dutcher took a more gradual and strategic approach. She first visited with departments to learn more about their concerns about the WI requirement. Then she put together a proposal for reforming the requirement and convinced the provost she would need more time, resources, and the support of a writing committee. She shared the proposal with departments and designed projects to support the changes to the WI requirement in order to make it sustainable. Administrators and faculty charged with creating WAC programs should think backwards from the ultimate goal of transformational change to the institution. This means seeing WAC as a long-term investment of time and resources. This also means providing the director with adequate release time, support staff, budget, space, etc. Furthermore, this means engaging in the systematic *understanding* and *planning* process we discussed in previous chapters: gauging the mood of the campus, mapping the system, gathering stakeholders, defining SIs, and finding points of connectivity and leverage.

One final example of the patience needed in planning projects and reforms, and of the value of incremental change, comes from the experiences of one of the authors of this book. After years of developing a WAC program and building allies at his previous institution where he was the WAC coordinator, the faculty senate writing committee that Dan chaired was charged with making a proposal for major reforms at the systems level to the campus writing program that would be voted on by the senate. Dan and the members of the writing committee would have liked to replace the upper-division timed writing test with a longitudinal portfolio and to eliminate the basic skills remedial courses that were being offered by a Learning Skills department that was separate from the English department's first-year composition program, both physically and pedagogically. From the moment these proposals were first discussed by the writing committee, however, there was a strong negative reaction from a variety of stakeholders across the system. The Learning Skills department, which had been a network hub for writing and "remediation" long before the WAC program was developed, used all of their leverage and connections within the network to try to prevent the proposal to replace remedial courses with a two-semester stretch composition model from ever making it to the senate floor. The many faculty from across disciplines who perceived of the upper-division timed writing test as a valid measure and the last bastion of ensuring writing standards, and who were also (inappropriately) using a passing score on the test as a prerequisite for some of the courses in their major, were both outraged that the test could simply vanish overnight and nervous about what they perceived as the workload burden of a portfolio system.

In the face of this institutional inertia—an inertia, according to systems thinking, that leads to stagnation in complex systems—the writing committee decided to aim for more gradual change. Rather than propose the elimination of the Learning Skills department and remedial courses, the committee proposed a small stretch course pilot. Rather than propose replacing the pass/fail exit exam with a portfolio, the committee proposed turning the test into a placement exam for WI courses. Not only was the proposal accepted by the senate, but, over the next five years, the committee also wound up achieving most of its original goals. The stretch course was a resounding success, and eventually the Learning Skills department was dissolved and the Learning Skills faculty were brought into the English department to teach both the stretch and the one-semester composition courses. This transition was not painless, but it was far easier than the battles that would have erupted if the writing committee had tried to force rapid change. In time, even the most skeptical faculty saw the wisdom in changing the upper-division timed writing test from an exit exam to a placement test, and since the test placed students into WI courses that often used portfolio assessment, it wasn't difficult to eventually make the argument that, in order for the placement to align with the curriculum, the test should be changed to a portfolio. At the time of this book's publication, Dan's former institution was piloting a portfolio version of the upper-division writing placement.

A key takeaway from Dan's experience is that interventions into systems are constrained not just by the complexity of systems or their tendency toward stagnation, but also by deeply embedded ideologies that become reinforced by the processes of the system. In the case of Dan's former institution, a deep-seated ideology that students are inherently "remedial" and need to be quarantined into "basic skills" classes and eventually removed from the institution altogether if they can't demonstrate correctness in "Standard English" was perpetually reinforced by students' poor performance in a sequence of non-credit-bearing remedial courses as well as on a timed writing test. Transforming both the curricular ecology and the ideologies that inform and are reinforced by the underlying system processes takes not months or years but decades of incremental work. That's not to say that rapid change to a complex system is never successful or beneficial, however. A budget cut to Dan's institution had the unintended but fortuitous consequence of making the provost decide to scale up the stretch courses twice as rapidly as planned, solely to save the university hundreds of thousands of dollars they were expending on the long series of remedial courses and on the budget for the Learning Skills department staff and release time. However, a proposal to make rapid and major changes to the campus writing program would have been met with a hailstorm of resistance, and Dan would have not only lost much of the political capital he'd built up over five years of doing WAC work, but also the changes probably would have never been approved by the senate—a body that by its nature is hesitant to make reforms that upset tradition if there is significant and vocal resistance to a proposal.

Systems theory teaches us that sustainable change requires a deep understanding of the system and the buy-in of stakeholders from across the system. It also teaches us that, because the parts and processes of systems form a web of connections, rapid changes in one part of a system can have unintended impacts on another part of the system, or can fail due to a lack of consideration of the constraints inherent in all complex systems. Systems theory provides a new way of looking at old wisdom from WAC lore: WAC is not a quick fix to a "problem" with student writing but a social movement for making transformational change to a campus culture of writing.

Planning for Gradual Rather Than Rapid Reforms to the System: Questions to Consider

1. What are the constraints to the reforms that WAC could make to the system?

2. Which WAC reforms will be perceived as most controversial? How do those reforms interact with the ideologies that underlie the system? What strategies for change would best foster the most buy-in across the institution?

3. Which parts of the system are actors most invested in, both in terms of emotional investment and with regard to investment of time and resources?

4. How will reform to the part of the system WAC is focused on impact other parts of the system?

5. Which WAC projects are at or near capacity due to their popularity or the amount of available resources?

6. What additional nodes could be connected to the current system as it grows over time?

7. If you have an immediate mandate with a short development timeline, how might you negotiate a more measured pace?

Strategy 11: Deal with Obstacles to Program or Project Development Systematically

All WAC program directors face challenges when launching and developing WAC programs and projects. In the opening vignettes for this chapter, Parrish and Schonberg discussed the challenges related to faculty viewing WAC as a service rather than a partner due to the project focus on classroom workshops, Lancaster shared the challenge of bringing senior faculty on board with the WAC pedagogies he endorses during faculty workshops, and Dutcher highlighted challenges related to reinvigorating a lapsed WI requirement. Other challenges include bottlenecked WI courses, rotating upper administration with changing agendas, budget cuts or budgets that need to be argued for piecemeal, campus attention turned to newer and sexier initiatives, lack of classroom space for small WI courses, and a lack of adequate compensation for the WAC director. Sometimes, challenges feel personal—as when an administrator chooses to shift some of the WAC program's budget to another program. Other times, challenges can seem as though they are etched into the structure of the university—as when a WAC director is told that the course-scheduling system simply can't handle the creation of course sections tagged as WI. Whether challenges such as these become obstacles depends on the *resilience* of the WAC program, how a WAC director anticipates challenges and approaches them when they arise, whether challenges are addressed through *broad participation* of stakeholders, and whether a WAC program is structured through *systematic development* to be flexible and dynamic while maintaining stability and identity (Walker & Salt, 2006).

A whole systems framework encourages us to take a systems approach to challenges, which includes not taking things personally, exercising patience, listening carefully, thinking logically, and using common sense when dealing with conflicts. A systems process for resolving conflicts necessitates a broader understanding of the challenge, which includes the collection of any necessary data, consideration of the scope of its reach, attention to primary stakeholders, a desire to balance the concerns that need to be considered, and a willingness to be flexible.

We can see this kind of approach in Dutcher's vignette. Her charge to address a problematic WI requirement in a single semester in itself reveals an ideology that views writing instruction as a simple issue rather than a complex and dynamic endeavor that reaches across an institution. One might imagine this charge in itself feeling like a personal attack—an attack against the richness and complexity of the field of writing studies. Indeed, we have witnessed writing scholars refusing to work with faculty and administrators who have such limited views of writing. Dutcher didn't have this reaction. In a sense, she treated the charge as a teachable moment. She used the semester to conduct research on the writing culture at the institution, uncovering an unsupported WI curriculum that both faculty and students skirted, distrust and even hostility between faculty and upper administration, and survey results from years back that revealed students were writing few long papers, a finding that spurred administration to create the WI requirements. Dutcher's research revealed problems with how the university thought about writing, administration's heavy-handed approach to increasing the amount of student writing, which they seemed to see as synonymous with fixing the campus writing problem, and a culture of faculty resistance to top-down curricular change. In short, Dutcher started to put together a picture of the systemic nature of the challenges. She then used this information to write a proposal for a grassroots approach to build a campus culture of writing, which was approved and actively supported by upper administration and welcomed by faculty.

To structure a WAC program for resilience, we recommend leaning on the program mission and goals to determine whether a change to the program would mean a change to the program's central identity or an alternate approach to achieving the same goal. Resilience theory reminds us that the systems that persist in the face of challenges are those that are able to adapt to change and even become transformed while "remaining within critical thresholds" (Folke et al., 2010, para. 24). In WAC, those critical thresholds are anchored by the program mission and goals and the SIs developed to manage growth. Parrish and Schonberg's vignette is a case in point. They realized that the way in which they structured a writing center-based WAC project—classroom writing workshops—had led faculty to identify the program as a service unit rather than a campus partner. A survey revealed that faculty saw the workshops as useful for students, but not as useful for faculty in rethinking pedagogy. The sheer number of units requesting workshops showed that the project met one of their goals—to "publicize our new writing center"—but not the other goal—to publicize "the intellectual work" of the writing center. And, in its limited effect on faculty's writing pedagogy, this project was also not fulfilling the program mission: to "develop a robust culture of writing" at the University of Denver. What may be needed here is program transformation—an alternate way of meeting the same goal and working toward the same mission. They could transform this one project into another, such as a faculty development learning circle, which would position the writing center faculty more as having disciplinary expertise while still impacting classroom pedagogy. Or they could choose to use this experience to argue for a more sustained and systematic approach to faculty development, putting together a writing committee, and moving through the steps described in this book to plan and develop a full WAC program.

The challenges faced by Parrish and Schonberg could have been anticipated from the start of the project. As we discuss earlier, it's important to identify existing feedback loops and establish others in addition to SIs in order to assess whether a project is meeting its goals, whether the project will remain sustainable at different scales, and to determine paths for adapting the program once certain goals are met. In this case, the fact that thirty-five departments and programs are using this classroom workshop service means that the project successfully met the goal of spreading the word about the writing center. Nevertheless, one must ask how this goal fits into the larger mission of developing a campus culture of writing. How will the writing center use this visibility to influence the campus writing culture? How is this project seen as a step in reaching larger goals?

Lancaster tells us, in his vignette, that junior faculty have been embracing the writing pedagogies his program endorses more quickly and enthusiastically than senior faculty. This difference in ideology between the two generations of faculty has caused junior faculty to worry about the potential fallout in terms of relationships within their departments and effects on the tenure and promotion process. Lancaster is right to be concerned about this dynamic, as tenured faculty have influence not only on departmental decisions and tenure cases, but also on discussions about cross-campus curricular changes. Lancaster's next moves might be to further investigate past writing initiatives that may be affecting tenured professors' responses to his program, tension between junior and senior faculty (such as disparities in salary), and histories of different faculty development initiatives on campus to determine the approaches to which tenured faculty will most likely respond. He may also seek to introduce structural changes to the university, such as a collaboration with other faculty development program directors and administrators to craft a statement on the value of engaged teaching strategies for tenure review committees.

We should also acknowledge that there are circumstances in which challenges to WAC projects and reforms are warranted. At times, WAC directors may hold onto a project for personal reasons, even though the project is not the most effective way to reach program goals. Sometimes, WAC programs become in-groupy, without clear mechanisms for newcomers to join the program or become part of the community. Or the WAC director may feel threatened by a new faculty development initiative such as the creation of a learning and teaching center. In times of scarcity, other programs may wonder at the size of the WAC program budget and vie for its resources. Like any program director, a WAC director may become territorial, dogmatic, or inflexible. It's also possible that the WAC director could lose others' trust. If faculty or administrators perceive the WAC director as having a personal agenda, not one tied to the program's mission and the common good of students and faculty, people may mistrust the director's motives. If the WAC director is overcommitted and becomes disorganized, not returning emails, showing up to meetings late or not at all, or not accomplishing promised tasks, people may begin to doubt the director's ability to successfully launch and develop a particular project. It's important for WAC directors to use challenges to a project as an opportunity to reflect on their own ways of communicating with others, ways of presenting themselves and their programs, and their approaches to handling conflict. In fact, one difference between being simply a member of a department and a WAC program director is that the stage is larger, and WAC directors are on that stage wherever they are on campus—at other faculty development events, at committee meetings, at presidential forums. With this increased visibility comes increased responsibility for representing the program well.

Dealing with Obstacles to Program or Project Development Systematically: Questions to Consider

1. At what scale is the problem? Is the problem related to a particular stakeholder (e.g., a faculty member), a program (e.g., a first-year seminar program), a department, a school or college, the university, or entities outside of the university (e.g., an accrediting body)?

2. What is the nature of the problem? Is the problem related to ideology (e.g., understanding of writing/WAC)? Process (e.g., creating a registration process for WI courses)? Resources?

Competing priorities? Changes in university mission? Changes in upper administration?

3. What steps can you take to de-escalate concerns, avoid personality conflicts, and identify reasonable solutions?

4. Take an honest look at yourself. Did you do something that disrupted people's trust? For instance, did you present a WAC program or initiative as tied to personal goals rather than tied to student learning or the program's mission? Did you become overly domineering during a meeting? Did you appear disorganized?

5. What information is needed before addressing the problem? Do you understand the history of the tensions around this issue or other contributing factors?

6. What potential problems can be anticipated during the development stage of a project? What steps can be taken to either prevent a problem or deal with it when it arises?

7. When stumped on how to respond to a challenge, what resources can you draw on? Who can you turn to that you trust, either on campus or outside it (e.g., from the larger network of WAC program directors)?

CHAPTER SEVEN

Stage Four of the Whole Systems Methodology: Leading for Sustainability

In Chapters 4 to 6, we provided strategies for the whole systems methodology stages of *understanding*, *planning*, and *developing*, with a focus on how to develop sustainable WAC initiatives and projects. To truly be sustainable, however, a WAC program also needs to ensure that it remains visible and is continually assessing and revising its role in the institutional system. A WAC program should also guard against the leader(s) becoming overextended, as well as plan to ensure leadership succession. The four vignettes that open this chapter explore different aspects of WAC leadership, with a focus on leading for sustainability. Mary McMullen-Light, Metropolitan Community College–Longview, illustrates how a long-established program continues to keep itself visible, and thus relevant at a community college, as a result of moves made by the program leader. Chris Thaiss, University of California, Davis, discusses how planning for leadership succession and distributing its leadership in the WAC program is important to consider from the start of a WAC director's appointment. Terry Myers Zawacki, George Mason University (emeritus), discusses how a WAC leader can use institutional assessment to gain leverage and resources for a WAC program. Beth Daniell and Mary Lou Odom, Kennesaw State University, discuss how WAC program assessment can be used to plan for program sustainability.

Following these vignettes, we explore the fourth stage of the whole systems methodology, *leading*, and discuss four strategies key to effective and sustainable WAC leadership: Strategy 12, keeping the WAC program visible through different types of communication; Strategy 13, learning about and making connections to systems beyond the institution (such as WAC-related organizations, but also accrediting bodies for different fields); Strategy 14, using assessment to keep the WAC program positioned effectively within the university system; and Strategy 15, creating a plan for WAC leadership that is sustainable. At the end of this chapter, we reflect on the recursivity of the whole systems approach.

Sustaining a WAC Program through Reinvention

Mary McMullen-Light
Metropolitan Community College–Longview

For a WAC program to stay alive at a community college, it continually has to be reinvented. Emphasis on the word *continually*. Once established, even vibrant programs can peter out, blow up, or get absorbed by other campus entities. One way around such scenarios is through reinvention.

Reinvention is the fine art of keeping a finger on the pulse of the larger forces at play on any campus and adapting the WAC program accordingly. Whether it is new initiatives taking hold, a changing of the guard in the administrative ranks, faculty retirements coupled with new hirings, political winds buffeting agendas, governmental pressures coming to bear, or funding concerns, something is happening—always. WAC leaders should take note of these considerations and help guide the program around or through them in these ways:

- ◆ Scan the environment for new initiatives arising and think about how the WAC program can support these, or collaborate with the key players.

- ◆ Know where you are in the accreditation cycle; time, energy, and goodwill of faculty can get syphoned off of WAC work during peak periods when an institution is preparing for these kinds of large-scale endeavors.

- ◆ Read outside of WAC and composition; stay in touch with education issues, especially as they pertain to higher education, debated in *The Chronicle of Higher Education*, *Inside Education*, your state legislature, and the mailroom of your college.

- ◆ Pursue relevant and timely projects that advance the WAC program's mission and enhance the WAC experience for faculty.

- ◆ Let go of what doesn't work—ever or just anymore.

Several times in my twenty-one years as the WAC director at a community college, I consciously steered the program in directions according to shifts I was observing in the higher education landscape. Early in my time at the college, assessment became a critical and required element of our accreditation, and it was clear that the WAC program had much to offer by way of resources—knowledgeable and experienced WAC faculty in all disciplines who could step up and lead these efforts and help their colleagues understand fundamental concepts of evaluating student writing. Rapidly, the WAC program became well integrated into all of the writing assessment conducted at the college. That connection yielded a new crop of WAC participants who became involved because they wanted to contribute to accreditation. All of this served our accreditation very well. It was essentially one of the first reimaginings of our WAC program, and it highlighted how the program could serve the college more broadly. This significantly expanded its influence within the college culture and directly led to the creation of a WI graduation requirement.

Reinvention does not have to be large in scope to have impact. For the twenty-fifth anniversary of the WAC program, we devised ways to look forward instead of simply looking back—by pushing WAC out of the office and encouraging faculty into the pool of social media. We started a blog to use as a tool for asynchronous professional development. Because some faculty at that time had limited exposure to social media, we sponsored mini-workshop sessions on memes and texting and the discussion of a book that shed light on the behavioral shifts accompanying technology; all so faculty could better understand how student writing was now situated in a larger cultural context that was invisible to them. These small efforts overtly connected WAC to social media in ways that might not have been obvious to faculty and administrators otherwise.

Sometimes it's not about starting something new, but, rather, letting go of something that has worked really well. We ended a very successful writing fellows program after fifteen years because variables well beyond our control, like rising tuition and a sagging economy, made being a writing fellow a financially less attractive enterprise for eligible students than it had been in previous years. Once we faced down the worst-case scenario by putting it on indefinite hiatus, it freed us to consider new possibilities for the program to connect in direct ways with students. What emerged from this perceived loss was the creation of a highly successful, large-scale, student showcase that quickly became a signature event for the entire college.

Finally, when everybody on your campus has seemingly done everything they can do with WAC, what then? Reinvent yourself by helping others have WAC: become philanthropic. Our WAC program spent a year helping a local high school develop a WAC program. We also created a three-day professional development experience for novice WAC directors at two-year colleges across the country. These experiences were rich in reward and learning for everyone involved and brought new insights and perspectives to WAC program participants that we otherwise could not have had.

Whether a program is five or twenty-five years old, it can benefit from some degree of reinvention. This is particularly important at community colleges, where demographics and enrollments shift rapidly and sometimes dramatically in response to economic and other trends.

Preparing NOW for Your WAC/WID Future: Building Leadership Continuity into Program Structure

Chris Thaiss
University of California, Davis (emeritus)

One of the important messages to come out of the international WAC/WID mapping project research concerns sustainability of programs through transition of leadership to ensure continuity. Though some directors of long-running programs have been in charge more than ten years, average length of leadership in long-running programs is five years (Thaiss & Porter, 2010), meaning that director transitions almost always must occur if a program is to last. Well before this research came out, I was mindful of this principle at both George Mason (where I was until 2006) and at University of California, Davis, my most recent home. As early as the mid-1990s, Eric Miraglia and Sue McLeod (1997), reporting on their survey of WAC leaders, expressed directors' fears that their programs would fail once they could no longer serve. Because WAC programs, unlike academic departments, usually don't have defined terms for chairs/directors, insuring transition must be a goal of the current director. Unless a director wants to be in that position for life (a highly unrealistic ambition!), making plans for succession needs to be a priority.

Fortunately, I had, as WAC director at Mason since 1991 (as well as director of composition since 1989), been able to secure some support for an assistant director, a position held over several years by colleagues Ruth Fischer and Terry Myers Zawacki. We also had a formal faculty senate committee, chaired by mathematician Stanley Zoltek, to provide continuity. Because both Ruth and Terry were able administrators, and played key roles in developing the WI curriculum that the faculty senate had passed in 1993, they could take on leadership of the program when I would at some point step aside.

Indeed, that happened sooner than I anticipated. In 1998, I accepted the position of chair of the English department—which I felt comfortable doing because I knew that the WAC and composition programs would be in good hands. Ruth became director of composition, and

Terry became director of WAC and director of the writing center. Terry, of course, went on to direct WAC at GMU for more than fifteen years.

At University of California, Davis, where I went in 2006, I was fortunate to inherit a model of continuity admirably established some years before. Our entire university writing program (an independent unit) of lower- and upper-division courses is set up on a WID and writing in professions model; we have numerous administrative roles that ensure flexibility and continuity through committed WAC-oriented faculty.

Specifically in regard to outreach with other departments, we have a five-member "WAC team," each member receiving some reassigned time. Each person, including the assistant director for WAC workshops (the team leader), serves a roughly three-year term, and the team structure ensures that newer members will become able to step into the leadership role at some point. Again, our entire curriculum is on a WID/writing in professions model; this means that, when we bring on new faculty, one expectation is that they will learn to teach several WID or writing in professions courses (e.g., writing in science, writing in business, writing in health professions, journalism, etc.), and therefore learn a multidisciplinary perspective that will help prepare them for service on the WAC team, if they wish.

Though it may seem premature for new WAC initiators—excited by beginnings—to project to a time when they will give over leadership to someone else, such projection is realistic. It need not take away from their excitement in order to nurture the seeds of continuity by cultivating a small team of potential leaders. Partnering with the writing center or the teaching excellence center can be one way to build this team, but, in the first participants in a workshop for cross-departmental instructors, there may be the future leaders of the program, and the new director can look for them. In negotiating for resources from administrators, new leaders might consider asking for reassigned time for more than one person, even if this means less reassigned time for one. Above all, planning for succession means keeping in mind that the program doesn't belong to the director, but to all those who take part in and benefit from it.

Friends in High Places: Institutional Assessment as Powerful Ally in Achieving WAC Goals

Terry Myers Zawacki
George Mason University (emeritus)

As Mason's long-time WAC director, I'd learned early on that the assessment office is one of the best friends a program can have when it comes to supplying data to bolster funding requests, developing questions for the senior survey around the effectiveness of the WI requirement, or using assessment mandates as a stick to accomplish programmatic faculty development goals when other new (and usually better funded) initiatives take the focus off WAC and eat up the little time faculty may have to pay attention to undergraduate writers. Which gets me to the point of this short vignette—how a mandate from our State Council of Higher Education requiring each institution to assess students' writing competence (among other competencies) led to the development of a discipline-embedded, faculty-led assessment process that was subsequently named as a model program by CWPA (see http://wpacouncil. org/assessment-gallery).

One of the most important lessons I'd learned from Mason's associate provost for institutional effectiveness is that the purpose of assessment is to improve teaching and learning, and that this can happen when faculty help to develop the plan, participate in the process, and have a vested interest in the results. Both process and results contribute in turn to their understanding of the effectiveness of their course and the curriculum of the major. When the state mandate arrived at Mason's door in 2001, allowing each institution to develop assessment plans compatible with its mission and culture, both the associate provost and I immediately began to strategize about how we could use the mandate to our advantage to sustain the strong WAC culture Mason is known for. In my case, that advantage involved the opportunity for ongoing faculty development around teaching with writing, while, for her, it was a way to foreground writing outcomes in departmental academic program reviews that include a requirement to map the courses where curricular outcomes are being addressed.

Prior to the state mandate, she had already convened and we were co-chairing a cross-disciplinary writing assessment group charged with designing a survey to help us understand, among other things, areas where faculty deemed student writers needed improvement (George Mason University, 2001). The survey results informed the subsequent assessment plan that we and the writing assessment group members, many of whom also served on the WAC committee, developed in response to the mandate. Our plan entailed a holistic scoring process using student papers written for an assignment given in an upper-division WI course in the major and assessed by faculty teaching in that major. While the process we designed is context sensitive and rhetorically based, in that we asked departmental assessment liaisons (appointed by the chair) to choose an assignment that best represented the kinds of writing valued in the major, we also recognized the limitations of using one paper in one course to generate a rubric that could be used to evaluate a random sample of student papers and, further, to report on students' competence as writers in the major. Had we the time, resources, and faculty commitment, our preference would have been to use portfolios to give us a richer, fuller picture; however, we knew from experience that such a plan would meet with intense faculty resistance.

In spite of these limitations, the process we used helped to accomplish a number of WAC goals—some unforeseen, such as, for example, the realization on the part of faculty participants that such systematic conversations with colleagues about student writing can be both fun and productive. And, while I knew that these departmental conversations would necessarily bring up questions around the role assignment design plays in students' difficulties or successes in fulfilling teachers' expectations and would also help to give faculty a language for talking about their expectations more clearly and with more specificity, I didn't anticipate that they would also lead to discussions around the appropriateness of the designated WI course for achieving writing outcomes for the major. Also unforeseen was the way in which a focus on a single piece of writing would lead to faculty questioning their values and writing advice to students in comparison to what their peers value and advise. All of this and more happened in most of the departmental assessment workshops I led. But I cannot overemphasize what I gained in return: a greater understanding of ways of knowing and doing in increasingly complex disciplinary and cross-disciplinary communities of practice, a better appreciation of the challenges faced by student writers and faculty who teach with writing across the curriculum, and a much more nuanced approach to the faculty development work I do.

WAC Assessment from Start to Finish

Beth Daniell and Mary Lou Odom
Kennesaw State University

Perhaps uncharacteristically for a brand new WAC program, our work with WAC on our campus began with an attempt at assessment. Our new dean had been on campus for only a month or so when he called us—Beth, the composition director, and Mary Lou, the writing center director—into his office because he had heard that we might know something about WAC. (We did, having worked respectively with standout programs and WAC leaders at Clemson and Wisconsin.) The dean explained that, at his previous university, he had attended a WAC workshop, and he thought the experience had made him a more effective teacher. Thus, he wanted to explore starting a WAC program at Kennesaw State University. But first, he asked us to write a report proving to him that such an effort was worth it. He wanted us to show that WAC worked.

We re-read articles and books we had read previously. We searched for articles and books specifically on assessing WAC. We read reports that discussed experiences such as how using writing in a psychology class had yielded higher final grades than in the previous term when no writing was assigned. We found analyses of the work of eighth graders in a geography class making higher scores than students who were not writing about what they were learning. We even read explanations of how certain characteristics of WAC make the kind of certainty our dean wanted unlikely to exist. For example, WAC programs vary widely and are designed purposely to speak to the local environment; some universities have a strictly voluntary program, while others have an institutional WI requirement. Such variety makes standard assessment practices difficult to discern. Additionally, directors are often so busy getting funding for startup activities such as workshops that they forget assessment. Even when WAC programs do begin, they often do so in an ad hoc sort of way with the means of assessment all over the place (e.g., differences in how many teachers attended the workshop from year to year, grades, writing samples from students, anecdotes from teachers, and so forth and so on).

Hence, when we concluded our report to the dean, we included in our list of recommendations for a WAC program on our campus that assessment be built into any plans for a WAC program. Ultimately, the dean decided that the "proof" we'd uncovered was sufficient, and we moved forward with a WAC initiative in our college. Our program, in fact, operates with three levels of assessment annually: (1) directly after our annual workshop featuring a prominent WAC scholar, we ask our faculty participants to fill out a survey; (2) students in our WAC-focused classes complete an end-of-term survey developed in concert with our WAC faculty fellows (those professors who work with us and one another as they develop one class to include WAC strategies); and (3) these WAC faculty fellows then incorporate their student survey data into their own reflective five-page narrative.

Initially planned to allow us to "prove" the effectiveness of our WAC program in the ways we understood our dean and other administrators to want, we now have come to see WAC assessment in a far different light. Certainly, we demonstrate the success of and need for the program by citing not only faculty and student comments, but also statistical data regarding engagement from student surveys. However, now in the seventh year of our WAC program, our assessment practices have turned out to be far more productive and meaningful—in some unexpected ways—than we could have expected.

We use our post-workshop assessment to direct our choice of the following year's workshop leader and to work with that leader in defining the focus of the session. From the faculty narratives, we have begun to understand how different disciplines use and perceive WAC. This knowledge has dramatically increased our effectiveness in working with the fellows, which has, in turn, helped with sustaining and growing the program. Our annual assessment of the fellows' experiences and the survey results from their students have proven a rich source of data resulting in numerous conference presentations and article and chapter publications for us but also for a number of our faculty fellows across the disciplines. In addition to the obvious benefits this scholarship has for the authors, upper administration found it particularly persuasive in term of the usefulness of WAC.

The only problem is that it has, so far, been difficult to step back from the yearly reports in order to look comprehensively at survey results and faculty narratives. At times, we feel a bit overwhelmed by how much we have collected, yet, at the same time, we are eager to discover the surprises we are sure to find as we continue our examination of the data.

Strategy 12: Communicate Regularly and at All Levels of the System to Keep the Program Visible

The whole systems principle of *visibility* means that program development, assessment, and change are transparent, regular, and public. This principle also refers to the idea of promoting program events and successes through multiple means of reporting. Visibility is a principle that informs all aspects of the whole systems process, but, in sustainable development theory, it is a key component of the final stage. In their Imagine approach, Bell and Morse (2008) contended that understanding and planning are of little value if stakeholders don't get the message out and influence policy (p. 189). They suggested making communication and publicity the job of all stakeholders, which speaks to the value in WAC of having a cross-disciplinary committee or advisory board and of nurturing teacher-leaders who will spread WAC pedagogy and help promote WAC policies, projects, and events. It is also helpful to keep in mind lessons from network theory. More energy should be spent connecting and publicizing through hubs—or clusters of hubs—than individual nodes. One goal of communication should be reaching the threshold point, where visibility begins to grow exponentially. In the case of publicizing a WAC program, the threshold point would be the point at which awareness of WAC goes beyond the core group of WAC enthusiasts, so that administrators, faculty, and staff at all scales of the institution are aware of WAC. Programs that remain constantly below this threshold will have a difficult time getting their message out in "competitive systems in which nodes fight for links" (Barabási, 2002, p. 106). Mark Granovetter's (1973) conception of "strong ties" and "weak ties" also helps in thinking through WAC program visibility. If WAC directors communicate and publicize program events and successes only to "strong ties"—allies of the WAC program—the message will never reach a threshold and connect to "weak ties"—those on campus who are not yet familiar with WAC but could be linked.

Throughout this book, we have talked about the importance of WAC programs becoming integrated with campus networks, but one unintended consequence of a program becoming part of the fabric of an institution is that it could be in danger of becoming less visible. As McMullen-Light points out in her vignette, WAC programs can be in danger of becoming "absorbed," and thus their visibility needs to be regularly assessed. When program stakeholders develop SIs, indicators of visibility should be considered, such as the number of times WAC is mentioned at university-wide meetings or events, the number of times WAC appears in campus publications and events calendars, the number of new members joining a WAC listserv or email contact list, and how often WAC is asked to collaborate with other campus units. WAC program visibility can be promoted in multiple ways. In this section, we discuss tactics for increasing program visibility on campus and off.

Increasing WAC Program Visibility on Campus

In the WAC lore, the advice on increasing program visibility often centers on holding workshops, inviting outside speakers to lead WAC events, and publishing brochures on the program. While these tactics are certainly valuable, there are many other tactics available for making programs more visible. Essentially, all communication from the program that goes out to the university should be considered part of program visibility.

WEBSITES AND SOCIAL MEDIA

Digital campus networks have become as critical as face-to-face campus networks in publicizing a WAC program. An extensive website can become a faculty development hub and can be used to link to external systems such as the WAC Clearinghouse. Social media outlets such as Facebook and Twitter embody the network theory concept of creating rich linking. McMullen-Light describes, in her vignette, the way a faculty development blog helped an established WAC program at Metropolitan Community College–Longview reach more faculty, and how this move led to workshops on teaching with social media. An example of a program that takes full advantage of digital media is that at George Mason University (2016), which publishes a faculty development blog and maintains an extensive website with links to the Mason WAC presence on Twitter and Facebook.

Newsletters

Many WAC programs distribute newsletters, either through print or email distribution sites such as MailChimp or Constant Contact. Newsletters can include information about upcoming events, faculty development advice, and profiles of faculty who make effective use of WAC pedagogy. Stakeholders from across campus can be invited to contribute to the newsletter, making it a tool for increasing network connections. Example newsletters can be found on the WAC websites of Southern Connecticut State University (2016) and Plymouth State University (2016).

Faculty Meetings and Governance Bodies

Most institutions of higher education have formal governance bodies that meet regularly, typically in the form of an academic or faculty senate. Senate meetings have stakeholders from across the institution, often at different scales of the institution, making these meetings ideal for publicizing WAC from a network and sustainability perspective. Often, open forums are held at the beginning of these meetings, but it may also be possible to connect the WAC program more formally to these governance bodies through, for example, a senate writing, campus curriculum, or assessment committee. WAC directors seeking to gain support for a new program could also request time on the agenda of meetings led by deans and department chairs.

Annual Reports

An effective tactic from the WAC lore is to prepare an annual report, even if no one asks for one, and to distribute the report strategically. In a whole systems approach, this strategy would involve distributing the report to macro levels in the institution, such as to upper administration, as well as to distribute it widely to promote visibility, such as through a program website. When preparing reports, be especially aware that administrators receive many reports from campus units and programs, and so consider putting critical information in formats common to the report genre, such as bulleted lists, tables, and infographics. One particularly impactful graphic is a map of program relationships in the form of a mind map or network web. Such maps can demonstrate how each component of the program is woven into the fabric of the university culture and curriculum. They also often offer perspectives that most administrators don't typically consider. One WAC program's process of designing a report is described in the vignette by Daniell and Odom. Examples of program reports can also be found on the writing program websites of the University of Missouri (2016b), the University of Central Florida (n.d.), and the University of Vermont (2016).

Assessment

WAC programs should be engaging in several forms of assessment, as we discuss below in Strategy 14. It is important to note here that assessment may be used as a tactic to increase program visibility. University-wide emails to announce assessment procedures or departmental notification of participation keep both the purpose and outcome goals of student writing in the public eye. Regular syllabus review procedures remind faculty of WAC criteria syllabus compliance and reinforce practices introduced at workshops. Since assessment is such an integral part of annual reporting and assessment results are often shared on WAC websites, it should be a priority to highlight how these results are used not only to reflect current goals, but also to change and improve programs and curriculum.

LISTSERVS AND DISTRIBUTION LISTS

One way to build a communication network is to build a listserv for WAC event participants. These lists may be used to advertise events, continue conversations begun at WAC workshops, engage faculty in ongoing discussions on pedagogy, and share calls for papers, conference announcements, and new publications. The least impactful type of listserv activity may seem to be workshop announcements, but even these notifications help to keep WAC visible and present and to encourage conversation on student writing across campus. For instance, after Michelle offered a workshop on working with multilingual writers at Bridgewater State University, faculty who hadn't attended the workshop approached her for advice for working with these students, simply due to the announcement. These lists may also expand to connect to external systems related to the WAC program. For example, if the WAC program hosts a regional conference or provides faculty development to local secondary schools, as described by McMullen-Light, attendees can be added to the listserv.

CAMPUS-WIDE PUBLICATIONS

Publications such as a student journal, a campus writing handbook, or a faculty development guide for teaching writing reach multiple nodes of a campus network, and also create the perception that WAC is a fundamental part of the system. These types of publications are a natural way, too, to gather stakeholders from across the institution. For instance, faculty across disciplines could serve as reviewers for a student journal, the library or writing center might be invited to co-sponsor a writing handbook, and faculty who have participated in WAC programming could contribute advice to a faculty development guide.

Campus publications can be easily found on university websites. Examples of student writing in journals may be found on the writing program websites of American University (2016) and Northeastern University (2011). Examples of discipline-specific writing handbooks can be found at the Oregon State's (2016) WI curriculum program website, which provides links to numerous writing guides, such as "Writing in Ecology," by the Department of Botany and Plant Pathology, and "Taking an HDFS View of the World," by the Department of Human Development and Family Sciences. Examples of pedagogy guides can be found on the WAC websites of Salisbury University (2015) and Eastern Illinois University (2016).

STUDENT CELEBRATIONS OF WRITING

Showcasing student writing is a way to work against the deficit model of WAC as a program to "fix" student writing problems, and an excellent way to communicate the WAC message to students and faculty across disciplines. Some WAC programs in the United States have connected student writing showcases with the National Day on Writing. McMullen-Light created a "large-scale student showcase" at Metropolitan Community College–Longview "that quickly became a signature event for the entire college" (see her vignette). Some universities have undergraduate research centers or initiatives that can be valuable collaborators for student writing showcases. Florida Atlantic University combines the efforts of the WAC program and the office of undergraduate research and inquiry by hosting a student publication ceremony to celebrate students whose work has been published.

Increasing WAC Program Visibility off Campus

Systems theory compels us to consider the benefits of connecting to broader networks. In higher education, these networks include national organizations, conferences, and publishers. Publicizing a WAC program beyond the campus can bring the kind of national recognition that is especially valued by upper administration. Many of the WAC programs with a national profile, such as those at George Mason University, Washington State University, North Carolina State University, and the University of Missouri–Columbia are well known in part from the many conference presentations, articles, and books about the program that have been published by the WAC leaders. In the following sections, we discuss some ways to publicize the WAC program beyond the campus.

WAC Organizations

WAC directors can post descriptions of their programs on the WAC Clearinghouse, become involved in organizations such as the Northeast Writing Across the Curriculum Consortium (NEWACC), and attend the WAC Standing Group meetings at the CCCC. Increased visibility is just one benefit of connecting to systems beyond the university; additional benefits are discussed below in relation to Strategy 13.

Presenting and Publishing Research

Some conferences have an explicit WAC theme, such as the International Writing Across the Curriculum (IWAC) conference, Writing Research Across Borders (WRAB), and International Writing Centers Association conferences. Others are focused more broadly on writing but include WAC-focused presentations, such as the CCCC, NCTE, and CWPA conferences. The following journals that focus on publishing WAC research can be found on the WAC Clearinghouse website: *The WAC Journal*, *Across the Disciplines*, and *Double Helix: A Journal of Critical Thinking and Writing*. Most disciplines have journals focused on pedagogy, which can be an excellent target for research done collaboratively with faculty outside of writing studies.

Public Events and Outreach

A relatively simple way to extend the reach of the program beyond the campus is to open some WAC events to others in the region or even across the country. McMullen-Light counsels, in her vignette, that when "everybody on your campus has seemingly done everything they can do with WAC," it may be time to "help others have WAC." The WAC program at Metropolitan Community College–Longview did this by helping local high schools develop WAC programs and creating a three-day professional development experience for novice WAC directors at two-year colleges. Additional examples include a regional WAC conference, a regional faculty writing support program, or a public forum on student writing, such as was held at Bridgewater State University (see Cox & Gimbel, 2012, 2016).

It is important to note that no WAC program engages in all of the visibility activities listed above, but this wide range of tactics offers WAC directors ideas that might complement or build upon practices already in place and helps demonstrate that regular elements of program communications do more than provide information. Conscious attention to program visibility can also lead to highly valued student and faculty recognition.

Communicating Regularly and at All Levels of the System to Keep the Program Visible: Questions to Consider

1. What would be the most effective digital venues for publicizing the WAC program? A website? Blog? A Facebook page? A combination of media?

2. What formal meetings of governing bodies act as hubs for campus communications? A faculty or academic senate? Meetings of deans? Meetings of department chairs?

3. Who would be the most appropriate audiences for an annual report? Given the audiences for the report, what would be the most appropriate content and document design? How can the report be made visible and accessible to the greatest number of actors in the campus network?

4. What types of campus-wide publications and events would be most effective for expanding the reach of the WAC program (e.g., a student writing journal or conference, a student writing handbook, a faculty development guide or retreat or conference)? Which campus units could be invited to help edit/organize/facilitate the publications or events? Which publications or events are most likely to be sustainable?

5. What routine communications, public activities, or advertised opportunities can you adapt to raise campus awareness of WAC on campus?

6. How can WAC leaders publicize the program beyond the campus? What national and regional institutions, organizations,

conferences, and publications can the WAC program connect with?

7. Which avenues of promotion will provide the most visibility for the effort put forth? Consider the institutional mission and context in prioritizing WAC promotional efforts.

8. What indicators can be used to assess the visibility of the WAC program? Which metrics would be important to pay attention to on your campus? (See Chapter 6 for information on determining effective SIs.)

Strategy 13: Be Aware of Systems beyond Your Institution and Connect to Those That Are Beneficial to the WAC Program

In her vignette, McMullen-Light encourages WAC directors to look beyond the borders of the WAC program and pay attention to the accreditation cycles on campus as well as conversations about higher education as they play out in *The Chronicle of Higher Education, Inside Education*, and state legislatures. Her advice echoes the whole systems principles of *wholeness, integration, leadership*, and *transformative change*, which encourage us to look beyond the borders of the system within which organizations operate to consider the many surrounding, overlapping, and intersecting systems, as these systems all connect and thus impact one another. In higher education, these systems include the many regional organizations that accredit colleges and universities, as well as the disciplinary organizations that accredit specific degree programs. In the United States, these systems also include the Department of Education, as changes in K–12 education impact the writing knowledge, skills, and attitudes of incoming college students. These systems also include writing-related organizations such as NCTE and CWPA, which provide resources and networks useful to WAC directors. We urge WAC directors to pay attention to the systems beyond their campus border for two reasons: (1) to make use of resources, policies, and standards used within these systems as leverage, and (2) to note changes within these systems that may positively or negatively impact the WAC program or the campus culture of writing. Below, we discuss accrediting organizations and writing-related organizations.

REGIONAL, STATE, AND DISCIPLINARY ACCREDITING ORGANIZATIONS

Maggie Cecil and Carol Haviland's vignette, in Chapter 6, mentions one regional accrediting organization—the Western Association of Schools and Colleges. In total, there are six accrediting organizations that serve geographical regions of the United States, as follows:

1. the Middle States Association of Colleges and Schools

2. the New England Association of Schools and Colleges

3. the North Central Association of Colleges and Schools

4. the Northwest Commission on Colleges and Universities

5. the Southern Association of Colleges and Schools

6. the Western Association of Schools and Colleges

There are also state-level accrediting bodies, such as the State Council of Higher Education of Virginia, which is highlighted in Zawacki's vignette (see also Zawacki & Gentemann, 2009; Zawacki, Reid, Zhou, & Baker, 2009). While each state has a state-level office or organization focused on higher education, the extent to which the state-level organization plays a role in accreditation of colleges and universities varies widely. George Mason, the context for Zawacki's vignette, was required by the State Council of Higher Education of Virginia to develop a six-year plan and assessment plan (copies of which are available from the State Council of Higher Education of Virginia website). California State University, San Bernardino, Cecil and Haviland's institution, is accredited by the regional accrediting organization, and only the teacher education programs are accredited by state-level boards (California State University, San Bernardino, 2016). Disciplinary accrediting agencies also abound, with seventy-six such organizations listed on the State University System of Florida (2016) website. All regional and disciplinary accrediting bodies are subject to review by the Council for Higher Education Association, which compels these organizations to encourage institutions to develop student learning assessment plans and processes in relation to standards set by the organization (Whittlesey, 2005, p. 10), and encourages all accrediting bodies to include standards on written communication. For instance, recent standards for accreditation published by the New England Association of Schools and Colleges and the Commission on Institutions of Higher Education (2016) include a requirement that "graduates successfully completing an undergraduate program demonstrate competence in written and oral communication in English" (p. 9). As is typical of these types of statements, this standard is broad and vague. *Competence* is not defined, and approaches for supporting writing are not laid out. Further, these standards do not include written communication under the section "The Major or Concentration"—only information related to "mastery of the knowledge, information resources, methods, and theories pertinent to a particular area of inquiry" (p. 10). However, we know that a WAC program can also promote learning within the discipline.

For support in turning such broad requirements into a more defined set of standards, curricula, and faculty development offerings, upper administration may turn to a WAC director (as demonstrated in Zawacki's vignette). They may also ask a WAC director to gather data as evidence that the university is meeting written communication standards (as did the University of Minnesota—see their report to the Higher Learning Commission of the North Central Association of Colleges and Schools, which refers heavily to their WEC program led by Pamela Flash; University of Minnesota Twin Cities, 2015). In Zawacki's vignette, collaboration with the assessment office during the accreditation process led to opportunities for faculty development and more visibility for the WAC program. In McMullen-Light's case, the increased focus on writing assessment spurred by accreditation highlighted the important role of WAC for fostering writing assessment knowledge across campus. And, for Flash at University of Minnesota Twin Cities (2015), the emphasis on the WEC program in the North Central Association of Colleges and Schools self-study raised the profile of the WAC program, showing it as integral to the success of the university's educational goals, thus adding to the program's sustainability. Flash has also used disciplinary organizations as leverage. In "A Writing Program for Mechanical Engineering," Durfee, Adams, Appelsies, and Flash (2011) described how the Mechanical Engineering department at the University of Minnesota joined the WEC program and tied writing program evaluation into an Accreditation Board for Engineering and Technology review. WAC programs have long depended on such organizations for leverage. In his introduction to a special issue of *Language and Learning Across the Disciplines* that focused on the engineering curriculum, Earl H. Dowell (1999) referred to the Accreditation Board for Engineering and Technology as a "stick" that compels engineering departments to emphasize communication skills (p. 17).

If a WAC director is not contacted by upper administration in relation to institutional or degree program accreditation, the director would be wise to use proactive tactics. A first step would simply be to find out to which accrediting bodies the university reports, a list that is often included on university websites. For instance, the California State University, San Bernardino, website lists fourteen disciplinary organizations that serve to accredit its programs, from art to social work. A next step would be to locate past accreditation reports, which are required to be publicly available. A further step would be to become familiar with accreditation frameworks and standards, especially for institution accreditation, and for any degree program that the WAC program seeks to work with on curriculum development or assessment. Determining where the institution and different departments are in the accrediting cycle could also be useful, not only in order to be aware of when a WAC program's assistance might be valued, but also to know when campus energy may be otherwise consumed. As stated by McMullen-Light in her vignette: "Time, energy, and goodwill of faculty can get syphoned off of WAC work during peak periods when an institution is preparing for these kinds of large-scale endeavors."

WRITING-RELATED ORGANIZATIONS

Writing-related organizations provide resources that WAC directors can utilize in order to be more effective leaders, provide evidence for arguments made to administration and departments, and provide professional networks for the director to lean on—an important resource, given the many complexities of WAC program leadership.

One such set of resources is the different kinds of documents that writing-related organizations craft and endorse: statements, white papers, and frameworks. We have found the following particularly useful in WAC administration:

- ◆ "Statement of WAC Principles and Practices" (International Network of Writing-Across-the-Curriculum Programs, 2014);

- ◆ "Framework for Success in Postsecondary Writing" developed collaboratively by NCTE, CWPA, and the National Writing Project (National Council of Teachers of English, Council of Writing Program Administrators, & National Writing Project, 2011);

- ◆ "NCTE Framework for 21st Century Curriculum and Assessment" (National Council of Teachers of English, 2013);

- ◆ NCTE–WPA *White Paper on Writing Assessment in Colleges and Universities* (National Council of Teachers of English & Council of Writing Program Administrators, 2008);

- ◆ "CCCC Statement on Second Language Writing and Writers" (Conference on College Composition and Communication, 2001);

- ◆ "WPA Outcomes Statement for First-Year Composition 3.0" (Council of Writing Program Administrators, 2014);

- ◆ "Defining and Avoiding Plagiarism: The WPA Statement on Best Practices" (Council of Writing Program Administrators, 2003);

- ◆ "Framework for Information Literacy" (American Library Association, 2016); and

- ◆ the VALUE rubrics of the Association of American Colleges and Universities (2009) (see also Rhodes, 2009).

These kinds of documents can be shared with task forces, writing committees, departments, faculty, and administrators to educate them on best practices, provide summaries of large bodies of knowledge from writing studies, and demonstrate that the actions advocated for by the WAC director are backed by disciplinary organizations. For example, the "Statement of WAC Principles and Practices" (International Network of Writing-Across-the-Curriculum Programs, 2014), which the three of us helped craft, provides a snapshot of WAC, condensing forty years of WAC scholarship and lore into a twelve-page document designed to provide guidance to administrators and faculty as they develop WAC programs. The document also has an extensive bibliography, useful for introducing administrators and faculty to the field. Documents like the "CCCC Statement on Second Language Writing and Writers" have been used by WAC programs to argue for increased and campus-wide support for multilingual students. These kinds of statements carry with them a kind of weight that garners respect among administrators and faculty.

These writing-related organizations also host conferences and listservs that create access to professional networks and thus WAC lore. Important conferences for WAC include those listed above in the section on program visibility. Key listservs for WAC directors include WPA-L (a listserv maintained by CWPA that includes all writing-related programs) and WAC-L (an international listserv maintained by the University of Illinois at Urbana–Champaign's Center for Writing Studies). For more specialized writing-related listservs, see the comprehensive list maintained by the WAC Clearinghouse (another important resource for WAC directors).

Mentorship is another key reason for WAC directors to become involved with these organizations. At the CCCC Annual Convention, the WAC Standing Group offers an annual business meeting during which WAC directors and scholars meet in small groups for roundtable discussions on WAC-related topics. The recently organized WAC Graduate Organization (WAC–GO) is creating opportunities for graduate students to network with experienced WAC directors at the biennial IWAC conference and other venues. Those in easy reach of New England might also consider attending NEWACC meetings. As stated on its website, mentorship is woven into the organization's mission: "NEWACC . . . aims to foster collaboration among area WAC programs and provide opportunities for members to draw on each other's expertise and experience through conversations and workshops, at periodic meetings, and through a NEWACC listserv" (Northeast Writing Across the Curriculum Consortium, 2016). To our knowledge, NEWACC is currently the only regional WAC organization in the United States, but those in other areas could seek out regional writing centers association conferences, which often have a strong WAC focus, or the newly organized summer CCCC conferences.

An additional potential source of mentorship is outside speakers, invited to campus to present a WAC workshop or talk. These speakers can be identified through the WPA listserv or through local networks. Often, such consultants will take the time to speak with the WAC director several times before arriving on campus, in order to learn more about the program and campus writing culture. During these conversations, the consultant may give advice on how to best use his or her time on campus, such as arranging meetings between the consultant and administration or writing committee. One such meeting might also be with the WAC director, to talk through the program's history and potential next steps. Relationships with consultants can continue past the initial consultation. In fact, it may be useful to think of a consultation not as a one-time event, but as part of a series of consultations that can be used to develop a certain trajectory for a WAC program. For example, Michelle has made annual visits to universities to mentor their writing programs in developing comprehensive support for multilingual writers. Jeff has recently consulted for a community college and a university in launching new WAC programs using our whole systems approach through a series of Skype meetings, phone calls, and campus visits (see Chapter 8 for more details on these WAC programs). Such systems of support beyond an individual institution provide a larger context within which institution stakeholders can situate their WAC programs. While each program is different and context specific, too often they are imagined only as isolated curricular interventions, a perception that may lead to a loss of support, visibility, and credibility over time.

Being Aware of Systems beyond Your Institution and Connecting to Those That Are Beneficial to the WAC Program: Questions to Consider

1. To which regional and state accrediting bodies does your institution report? Where is your institution in the accrediting cycle? How is your institution currently assessing the written communication standards for accreditation? Who is leading this part of the assessment? Which models are they drawing on for writing assessment? What do past accreditation reports say about student writing?

2. To which disciplinary accrediting bodies do departments at your institution report? Of these, which include standards for written communication? For those departments with which WAC is seeking to collaborate (e.g., to develop a WEC initiative), where is the department in the accreditation cycle? What models have been used for writing assessment? What do past accreditation reports say about student writing?

3. Have there been any recent changes in the standards for written communication or assessment requirements by any of the accrediting bodies important to your campus? How might these changes impact the campus culture of writing, WAC's prospects for becoming further integrated into campus, or WAC's opportunities to introduce and foster change in how the campus supports and assesses writing?

4. Which organization-endorsed statements, frameworks, and white papers might be used as leverage to forward WAC program goals and/or inform current campus conversations about student writing?

5. To what extent is access to mentorship for the WAC program director built into the WAC budget (e.g., for organization membership fees, travel to conferences and institutes, travel to regional meetings, hiring WAC consultants)?

6. If a WAC consultant is scheduled to come to campus, how might the WAC director most effectively use the consultation as an opportunity for mentorship? Would multiple interactions be possible (e.g., a series of phone meetings, Skype meetings, or visits), so that the WAC director can seek ongoing feedback as the program develops and the consultant's advice is implemented?

7. How might you tap into new WAC initiatives or play a role in representing your WAC program through such initiatives?

Strategy 14: Assess and Revise the WAC Program

Just as programs can lose their support if they are not connected to networks beyond their own institutions, they can also tend toward segregation and stagnation if assessment feedback loops are not built into program development. The principles of *systematic development*, *broad participation*, and *feedback* are all implicated in the assessment of WAC programs and the revision cycles that can lead to *transformative change*. In Chapter 4, in which we described the *understanding* stage, we talked about developing state SIs as part of understanding the context before introducing change. In Chapter 5, focused on the *planning* stage, we discussed the development of a program mission, goals, and state and impact SIs through a participatory process. In Chapter 6, covering the *developing* stage, we discussed the implementation of projects designed to collectively meet the program mission and goals and the use of AMOEBA graphs to track project sustainability. In the *leading* stage, the program mission and goals are revisited, project assessment data are gathered, and additional data related to program SIs are tracked in order to assess the WAC program as a whole. WAC directors can use this information to manage program growth, reconsider the program mission and goals, and revisit WAC's position within the wider university system.

It is important to note that a whole systems approach to assessment builds on the strong tradition of WAC assessment literature, but also focuses assessment in ways that previous scholarship has not considered. The landmark works on WAC assessment—Kathleen Blake Yancey and Brian Huot's (1997) edited collection *Assessing Writing Across the Curriculum* and Yancey et al.'s (2009) special issue of *Across the Disciplines*—have offered approaches to developing assessment practices and examples of assessment used to support various goals within different institutional contexts for diverse types of WAC initiatives. Many of these examples show WAC assessment as extrinsically motivated, prompted by campus administrators, governing agencies, and granting agencies that are seeking confirmation of a program's effectiveness. For instance, Yancey and Huot (1997), in their introduction, described the purposes of assessment as identifying "what the program is doing well," learning "how the program can improve," and demonstrating "why the program should continue or should be funded" (p. 7). We can see this same kind of motivation in two of the vignettes that opened this chapter. In Zawacki's case, assessment was motivated by the State Council of Higher Education of Virginia who began requiring that each institution assess students' writing competence. In Daniell and Odom's case, an administrator asked for evidence of WAC's effectiveness before the program was even launched.

Because WAC assessment is often driven by outside groups, the goals of the assessment are often aligned with those groups' goals, which are often focused on student learning and writing outcomes. For example, in laying out the assumptions that should guide WAC assessment, Yancey and Huot (1997) stated that assessment should begin with an explicit understanding about the nature of writing and focus on learning and teaching and their interactions with the goal of enhancing them. We can see this focus on student writing outcomes and teaching in Zawacki's vignette, in which assessment centered on departmental discussions of student writing from a particular assignment. In these cases, theories of writing and learning guide assessment, rather than theories on program development.

The fact that WAC assessment is also often driven by theories of writing and learning influences the kinds of data typically collected during the assessment process. Because writing improvement and changes in writing pedagogy are difficult to capture, programs often take a scattershot approach to data collection, collecting data from students, such as papers, portfolios, and survey data, as well as data from faculty, such as syllabi, assignments, and narratives from faculty involved in faculty development, all of which may be seen in the vignettes that open this chapter. In the WAC literature, we also see the collection of benchmarking information, observations, program artifacts, and evidence of faculty participation in faculty development such as workshop attendance numbers and seminar satisfaction surveys (see, e.g., Selfe, 1997). Although Edward White (1990b) advised "measure everything possible—something may work out" (p. 195), this approach can lead to more data than can be used, interpreted, or analyzed, the situation in which Daniell and Odom find themselves: "At times, we feel a bit overwhelmed by how much we have collected."

The differences between the assessment approaches that WAC directors typically use from those advocated by a whole systems approach are significant. The former, while regular, direct, systematic, and coherent, focus primarily on outcomes (learning and teaching). The whole systems approach includes all of these facets (typically as one or two of many SIs) but also emphasizes systematic review of program mission, goals, and the projects designed to meet the mission and goal—all of which are intrinsic to program sustainability. Further, a whole systems approach reviews the WAC program's position in the wider network, as changes in the university system can move WAC from a hub to a node, a loss of leverage that could jeopardize the program. The literature on assessment in WAC is virtually silent about the fact that nearly half of the programs that are started disappear within ten to twenty years (Thaiss & Porter, 2010). In the whole systems approach, program sustainability is a key concern, integrated across the program's development.

Such an approach might have enhanced Daniell and Odom's assessment process. They end their vignette by saying, "the only problem is that it has, so far, been difficult to step back from the yearly reports in order to look comprehensively at survey results and faculty narratives." Their current process only focuses on program components—projects—without a clear process for stepping back to look at the program as a whole or examining assessment data collected over time. We advised, in Chapter 3, that assessing for sustainability requires a different mindset from typical assessment practices. Bell and Morse (2008) have noted that only the parameters of sustainability can be measured, not sustainability itself. Furthermore, because an individual's vision of sustainability determines the approach to measurement, this approach can be changed by shifting the measurement mindset (Bell & Morse, 2008, pp. xvii–xviii), which is a primary aim of Strategy 14. Bell and Morse suggested further that a participatory stakeholder process has the greatest chance of impacting the assessment mindset when it is inclusive, concrete, transparent, and practical to implement. Thus, a whole systems approach to assessment addresses the issues faced by Daniell and Odom, as well as program sustainability, by focusing on several key approaches:

1. Tracking indications of success and distress related to the program mission, goals, and outcomes and whether they are still the appropriate SIs, as these will shift over time as the program develops. This tracking can include both direct and indirect measures.

2. Tracking, through the use of AMOEBA graphs, whether SIs for each project remain collectively within their bands of equilibrium and thus sustainable.

3. Ensuring that SIs for the program as a whole remain collectively within their bands of equilibrium by aggregating project SI data as well as tracking SIs related to the program as a whole with AMOEBA graphs.

4. Tracking wider changes in the university system to ensure that the WAC program remains visible and is positioned for leverage.

To address the first goal, Daniell and Odom could look at the broader mission, goals, and outcomes of the Kennesaw State University WAC program, and, if these are not clearly articulated, they might be reshaped using tactics we have discussed in Chapter 5. To address the second goal, they could examine how effectively the current projects (a faculty development workshop and a faculty fellows program) are meeting the program mission, goals, and outcomes. This would mean not looking solely at teaching and learning outcomes, but also at indirect measures of program sustainability, and thus they might engage in the process of determining project SIs and then creating AMOEBA graphs, as discussed in Chapter 6. To address the third goal, they might develop and assess program SIs, as described in Chapter 5, as well as look across the project AMOEBA graphs to determine the sustainability of the program as a whole. To address the fourth goal, they might develop and assess program SIs, as described in Chapter 5, as well as look across the project AMOEBA graphs to determine the sustainability of the program as a whole. They might also use the mapping approaches we described in Chapter

4 to consider how their WAC program is positioned at their own institution and in the wider Kennesaw State University system, and then revisit this map a couple times a year to see how the university may have changed and consider whether these changes could either jeopardize the WAC program or create possibilities for a shift in the program's position that would increase visibility and leverage.

The whole systems approach to WAC assessment allows a WAC director to have a clearer understanding of how the different program components are working together to meet the program's goals, how the program is operating within the systems of the university, and, by engaging in assessment cyclically, how the impact of the WAC program on the curricular ecology is changing over time. Such an approach would not only provide the data needed to prove program effectiveness to stakeholders—data that are manageable, targeted, and easily evaluated—but also provide the WAC director with necessary information for revising the program's role in the system, thus promoting program sustainability.

Assessing and Revising the WAC Program's Role within the System: Questions to Consider

1. What writing assessment practices currently exist at your institution and to what extent do they align with WAC program mission and goals?

2. How would you characterize the purpose of the assessments in your WAC program and the kinds of assessment data collected? To what extent do your assessment practices focus on teaching and learning outcomes, and to what extent do they focus on program sustainability?

3. In developing and assessing program SIs, have you considered the human, support, and natural systems of your institution (see Chapter 3, Figure 3.4)?

4. How effectively are the program SIs capturing the data needed to assess the program's outcomes? Do they need to be adjusted? What are these data telling you about the impact of the WAC program on the curricular ecology and about the program's sustainability? What adjustments need to be made to the program as a whole?

5. Look across data collected in relation to each project. How effectively are these projects working in concert to meet the program mission, goals, and outcomes? How sustainable are these projects as a set? Do any projects need to be adjusted or new projects initiated?

6. Look at data collected across time in relation to the program. What do these data tell you about the ways the program has changed and grown? Has the program turned any indicator of distress into indicators of success? What could be adjusted to keep the program resilient?

7. Revisit the systems maps created during the *planning* stage of the whole systems methodology. What in the university system has changed since this map was first made? How might these changes impact WAC? How might the WAC program be repositioned for more leverage?

Strategy 15: Create a Plan for Sustainable Leadership

The whole systems principle of *leadership* involves identifying an individual or team that can serve as the hub for the program, with the authority on campus to lead a cohesive effort of planning, launching, developing, and assessing WAC. In the WAC literature, effective leadership is often seen as central to the success of a WAC program. For example, in "Whither WAC?," Miraglia and McLeod (1997) concluded that "an enduring program . . . is very much the product of a pioneering, persevering, and creative leader" (p. 55). Leadership advice in the literature on starting and developing WAC programs includes being respectful of disciplinary differences, avoiding the missionary approach, being a good listener, being supportive and empathetic to different faculty needs and concerns, being open to collaboration, and remaining diplomatic in negotiating complex campus politics while at the same time advocating for WAC (see, e.g., McLeod, 1988b). This advice is helpful and is based on the experiences of savvy, long-time WAC directors; however, it is limited by its primary focus on the traits and leadership styles of individual WAC directors, and it has yet to fully engage with the vast literature on leadership, particularly educational leadership. Although there are certain styles and personality traits that lend themselves to success in

WAC director positions, theories of leadership have evolved from a focus on individual personality and influence to the social construction and distribution of leadership (Hazy, Goldstein, & Lichtenstein, 2007; Northouse, 2001). We believe it is time for concepts of WAC leadership to evolve as well.

Leadership theories—much like WAC lore on leadership—originally focused on personality traits within individuals (trait theories of leadership). Scholars studied individuals who were considered great leaders to derive a set of inherent qualities that could be used to separate the born leaders from the followers. Even when context was considered, the emphasis was on which individual behaviors or styles were appropriate for the situation (situated, contingent, and path–goal leadership theories). Leadership theory evolved away from this trait- and behavior-based approach to focus on the process of negotiation between leaders and followers, but this scholarship is often focused on leader and "subordinate" dyads (leader–member exchange theories of leadership). More recently, leadership theory has focused on the ways that leaders can empower the individuals and groups they serve (transformational leadership and servant leadership theories) (Hazy et al., 2007; Northouse, 2001). All of these approaches, from trait theory to transformational leadership, focus on an individual's ability to exert influence on others, and Hazy and colleagues (2007) argued that they are derived from "traditional bureaucratic notions of organizations in which the world is knowable, social systems are predictable, and organizational outcomes are deterministic of leader actions and follower responses" (p. 9). Systems theorist Peter Senge (1990) criticized traditional leadership theories for being too focused on short-term events and charismatic heroes, rather than on systematic forces and collective learning (p. 340). Theories of leadership currently emerging from systems and network theories describe a more socially constructed perspective according to which leadership is distributed in group interactions in complex environments. The framework for whole systems leadership is referred to in the literature as *complex systems leadership theory* (CSLT) as discussed in Chapter 3.

CSLT argues that leadership is a system function and should have the goal of changing and improving the way actors in the system interact, primarily through transforming the structures and processes of the system. According to CSLT, leadership is not within individuals but emerges through interactions among actors (Hazy et al., 2007). A map of the network of a university might reveal, for example, that, despite the hierarchical structure of president, provost, and deans, it's actually an assessment office or a writing center that has the most influence on the curriculum and the most connections with which to make transformational change. According to CSLT, effective leadership involves changes in interactions and structures that lead to more sustainability and equity, always in relation to organizational contexts; it is "the context of organizational interactions that determines the potential and quality of members' contributions" (Goldstein, Hazy, & Lichtenstein, 2010, p. 15), not solely an individual leader's influence or vision. This focus on interactions, structures, and contexts means that the role of a WAC director is less about being a visionary individual acting boldly and decisively, but, rather, a facilitator who "construct[s] the right kind of networks of exchange" (Goldstein et al., 2010, p. 39), thus creating richer connections within the network. Effective leaders working in complex networks are skilled at coalition building, mentoring, and acting as brokers between nodes (Balkundi & Kilduff, 2006, p. 423). Goldstein and colleagues (2010) explained that complexity science has taught us how the traditional emphasis on a heroic leader may stifle innovation, since this singular focus may decrease connectivity and ground-up adaptations (p. 2). Ultimately, the role of the leader is to optimize "a system's capacity for learning, creativity, and adaptability" (Uhl-Bien, Marion, & McKelvey, 2007, p. 301) by building coalitions and generating interest across campus.

Although the ability to motivate and engage faculty across disciplines is certainly a helpful quality in a WAC director, as the "Statement of WAC Principles and Practices" (International Network of WAC Programs, 2014) posited, the success and sustainability of a WAC program should not "hang on the personality and charisma of the director" (p. 3). A WAC director working solo who attempts an intervention aimed at making transformative change to a complex system will lack the connections across scales and hubs of the system of a more distributed leadership team such as a WAC advisory board or a group of cross-disciplinary teacher-leaders. Distribution of leadership will also help a WAC director avoid burnout from being overwhelmed with projects, and will create a better chance for a leadership succession since there will be others prepared to take on the director role or argue for the hiring of a new director. There are many tales from WAC lore of dynamic WAC leaders whose programs crumbled when the leader stepped down or left for another institution. Distributed leadership models can help guard against this reliance on a single individual's energy or career choices.

Distributed leadership may take different forms. It could be a WAC director advised by a university writing committee or WAC advisory board that has representation from administration, faculty from different schools or colleges, leaders from different curricular and faculty development programs and initiatives, and even students. Or a WAC director may be supported by an assistant or associate directors who focus on different pieces of the program, such as a writing fellows program or a WEC initiative. On campuses where it is not possible to assemble a writing committee, advisory board, or group of assistant directors, a WAC director could pull together an informal group to serve in an advising capacity, as Michelle did at Bridgewater State University with the creation of the "WAC Network" (see Chapter 5, Strategy 4). In addition, a WAC director should not be a voting member of the governing WAC committee if she is the primary manager, motivator, trainer, and facilitator of WAC projects. Consolidating too much control in one person provides openings for people or units across the institution to challenge or dismiss program decisions as the agenda of a single individual.

Thaiss emphasizes two approaches to distributed leadership in his vignette at the start of this chapter, both of which proved successful when it was time for the director to transition out of the leadership role. At the George Mason WAC program, Thaiss was able to secure an assistant director position. When he later took a position at another institution, the WAC program was able to make a successful transition as the assistant director, Zawacki, took on the role of director. WAC program leadership was even more distributed at Thaiss's next institution, University of California, Davis, where there is a WAC director who works with a team of three to five writing specialists (who serve three-year terms), and these specialists are connected to the central hub for writing at the university—an independent writing program focused on campus-wide writing. Most WAC programs are on a smaller scale than the programs described by Thaiss, which can make sustainable, distributed leadership difficult. A common story from the WAC lore is an original group of dedicated WAC advocates who work hard as a committee or advisory board for a number of years, but then lose energy through attrition, retirements, and burnout. It is critical for WAC leadership roles to be revitalized by recruiting new members and making fresh connections to other campus units.

This model of leaders with WAC expertise, given substantial release time, positioned within a campus hub, with support from a committee or advisory board, and a stable source of funding for the creation of extensive projects is a common thread of vignettes from the most sustained and extensive WAC programs. Chris Anson and Deanna Dannels's vignette from Chapter 1 describes a program that did a national search for a tenure-line director and assistant director with expertise in CAC and positioned them within a centrally funded campus hub (the campus writing and speaking program) that is advised by an interdisciplinary campus writing and speaking board. Timothy Oleksiak's vignette from Chapter 5 also describes a national search for a program leader with expertise in WAC and the support of an interdisciplinary WID advisory committee. In the present chapter, Thaiss references one of the longest-standing WAC programs, the program at George Mason, which has a tenure-line WAC director and assistant director with WAC expertise, a substantial budget for faculty development projects, and an ex officio membership for the WAC director on the interdisciplinary writing committee that oversees WI courses. Contrast the possibilities for sustainable leadership of these programs with other vignettes of WAC leadership from our book that reveal issues all too common in the WAC lore—an adjunct English instructor asked to lead WAC part time (Marla Hyder's vignette in Chapter 5), a faculty member given a course release for one semester to design a WAC initiative that would "fix" the student writing problem (Vi Dutcher's vignette in Chapter 6), and a writing center creating a stealth WAC initiative that has quickly become difficult to manage (Juli Parrish and Eliana Schonberg's vignette in Chapter 6). To help avoid putting WAC leaders in difficult situations, institutions developing WAC programs should look to model programs at peer institutions and consider how leadership is structured and what resources leaders are given at those institutions. One resource for finding model programs is the WAC Clearinghouse. Through hard work and skillful diplomacy, someone without prior WAC expertise and without institutional clout or resources can build a WAC program, but sustainable programs that have a transformational effect on the campus culture of writing usually position a leader and leadership team in ways that make WAC an ongoing and central focus of the institution.

Although current leadership theories have turned away from traits and styles of individual leaders, the concept of expertise is still critical for WAC leadership and program sustainability, as evidenced by recent job ads for WAC leadership positions. Most institutions that conduct national searches for a WAC leader now require a PhD in writing studies with a focus on WAC, as well as experience in writing program administration. Typical wording from recent job ads for WAC positions also emphasizes innovation: "identify emerging trends, best practices, and research results related to student success issues," "innovate, advocate for, and administer campus-wide efforts to improve writing," and "innovate with technology." WAC leaders that do not bring a deep knowledge of the field to the position or do not gain knowledge of the field by keeping up with recent research and programmatic innovations (e.g., by taking advantage of some of the resources mentioned in Strategy 13 of this chapter) may put their programs and the culture of writing on campus at risk of stagnation.

The advantages of hiring a leader with a PhD in writing studies, knowledge of WAC, and experience with writing program administration suggest the appointment of a midcareer professional at the rank of associate or full professor who reports to central administration, such as the vice provost of academic affairs, a positioning that lends itself to institutional clout. We acknowledge that not all institutions will have the resources to hire at this rank. Furthermore, reporting lines and rank of WAC leadership positions will be context specific. However, hiring a designated program leader who has the release time, expertise, budget, connection to a central hub, and rank that carries credibility will lead to a WAC program that has more impact on the curricular ecology and is more sustainable.

Creating a Plan for Sustainable Leadership of the WAC Program: Questions to Consider

1. What are the leadership structures of WAC programs that can serve as models for your campus?

2. What types of expertise does the leader/leadership team need?

3. Should the leadership position(s) be faculty, staff, or administrative, and at what rank? Within your context, which type of positioning will be most sustainable and provide the leader(s) with the ability to work successfully across disciplines and at all scales of the system?

4. How can leadership be distributed across the system?

5. To whom does or will the leader report? To what scale in the system does the person or group leader report?

6. What kinds of resources are needed for the WAC leader(s) to build sustainable projects? How much release time is designated for the leader(s)? What size budget is needed? How sustainable is the funding source?

7. What might the leadership succession look like?

On the Recursivity of the Whole Systems Approach

Before moving on to the final chapter of our book, we would like to pause and reflect on how the fifteen strategies delineated above come together. The fact that they are numbered and are set in what may appear to be a lockstep order may lead to the impression that they are meant to be used one by one, with Strategy 15 representing the end of the road, resulting in a polished (and finalized) WAC program, much like a piece of writing at the end of a long writing process. However, as the truism goes, pieces of writing are never finished, only abandoned. In WAC program development, if the program is seen as "finalized," attention will move away from the many SIs that give a sense of the program's vitality and endurance.

Perpetual change and revision is an inherent part of a whole systems approach. McMullen-Light's vignette provides an example of a WAC program that continued as a vibrant dynamic program over the program's long history through a process of "reinvention." McMullen-Light describes how she continually monitored the WAC program as well as "pulse of the larger forces at play" on campus, in accrediting organizations, and in the literature and public discourse on higher education. Throughout her program's development, she continually returned to the strategies we've identified as part of the *planning* stage—determining the campus mood, understanding the system in order to focus on points of interactivity and leverage, and understanding the ideologies that inform the campus culture of writing. This recursive cycle led to new opportunities for becoming more integrated into the university, reevaluating the effectiveness of WAC projects (and, at one point, letting go of a writing fellows program that was no longer effective), and reaching beyond the borders of her campus to collaborate with local high schools and community colleges.

When it appears that a WAC program is meeting its stated goals on an ongoing basis, it is time to revisit the mission, identify new goals, and develop new projects. The cycle of energy that drives sustainable WAC programs will naturally wax and wane over the life of the program, but, if it is inactive for too long, the visibility of the program will diminish. WAC directors need to gather stakeholders to review the program as a whole—evaluate SIs, create new maps of the system, identify which projects and initiatives are languishing, locate emerging points of leverage and new centers of gravity, re-engage with intersecting and overlapping systems, and reassess the WAC program.

The Recursivity of the Whole Systems Approach: Questions to Consider

1. How stable are the pieces of the program that have been developed?

2. What is the next move for the WAC program—vertical growth (up the scales)? Lateral growth? And how would this move affect the sustainability of the WAC program?

3. How should the mission change when a former project is retired or a new project takes hold?

4. How has your institution's network map grown or shifted over time? What do those changes suggest about the WAC program?

5. Which SIs demonstrate patterns of change over time and which are most predictive for signs of distress?

6. How often can you reasonably create AMOEBA graphs for each project to assess level of functioning within bands of equilibrium, and how do those bands shift over time?

7. What additional resources are needed each year or with the introduction of new projects? How might you ensure that new projects are not built without recurring resources to support them?

8. What problems seem to recur year after year? What can be done to address them?

9. As the program grows, how can assessment practices be consolidated to reduce duplication of effort across multiple scales of reporting?

10. If the program has contracted, what information do you need to gather from around the university to start the cycle again?

CHAPTER EIGHT

The Potential for Transformational Change: Implications of the Whole Systems Approach for WAC at Every Scale

WAC pedagogy has been theorized for decades, and an extensive scholarship on writing-to-learn and learning-to-write pedagogy has been developed by the field, but WAC scholarship has yet to offer an adequate theoretical framework and methodology for building, revising, and revitalizing WAC programs in ways that can address and confront the challenge of WAC program sustainability. In this book, we have begun to address this gap by drawing on theories of complexity to offer a set of principles for building sustainable WAC programs, a methodology to put those principles into praxis, and a connected set of strategies that relate to the stages of our methodology. Our whole systems approach also provides a theoretical and methodological framework for important areas of WAC program building that have been undertheorized, such as leadership, equity, and assessment.

As a powerful lens for re-seeing WAC programs, this framework can help those wanting to start a WAC program better understand the kind of energy, commitment, and time involved in getting WAC off the ground, providing an argument for slowing down the timeline of the launch so that a program has real impact and endurance. This framework can help those developing a young WAC program to build the program systematically and prioritize among multiple pressures, making decisions that do not endanger the program's future nor further disempower those already marginalized on campus. Our approach can help those leading a well-established program determine what steps to take for it to become visible and vibrant again, seen not only as part of the fabric of the institution, but also an important part of the institution's future. It may also be applied to other kinds of programs that seek to shift the curricular ecology of a university, such as graduate communication support programs, undergraduate research programs, or quantitative literacy programs. Any academic unit, program, initiative, or intervention can draw on the whole systems approach to make systemic and transformational change to institutions of higher education.

While the previous chapters sought to flesh out the theory, methodology, strategies, and tactics in the context of existing WAC program vignettes, this final chapter uses the whole systems lens to look forward, in several ways. First, we discuss two WAC programs that are currently using whole systems strategies to begin programs, thus exploring how different types of institutions put our theories to use. We then identify limitations of our work that we hope will be addressed as institutions and scholars extend the work we have begun here. The implications of this approach extend to research as well, so we also pose new research questions in our field. Finally, we move our lens onto the field of WAC itself, considering how transformational change and sustainability could be examined at the highest scales to envision a national WAC organization.

Programs in Process

Throughout this book, we have emphasized that the whole systems approach is not a lockstep process but a theorized methodology with recommended strategies for developing sustainable WAC programs from the time a program is conceived. Our own collective experiences and those represented in the vignettes have helped us to propose this model, but it was not until Jeff started consulting for two very different institutions that were building WAC programs from the ground up that we had a chance to begin testing what we have been presenting. The results from both institutions so far seem to confirm that the steps of the methodology cycle are instructive.

Jeff was contacted first by the newly appointed WAC director at Texas A&M University–San Antonio to help her and the cross-disciplinary WAC committee consider strategies for starting their WAC program. Texas A&M University–San Antonio is a branch campus with about 5,500 students. Approximately 60 percent of its population are first-generation college students; 70 percent are Hispanic or Latinx, and 64 percent of their students are first generation (Texas A&M University–San Antonio, 2016). At the time Jeff met the director in January of 2016, Texas A&M University–San Antonio was making plans to transition from an upper-division two-year college to a four-year institution for fall 2016. Prior to starting these changes, the institution established a four-semester set of mandatory one-hour student support courses. A university-wide portfolio was also instituted, and a WAC program was being proposed. Jeff was asked to lead two Skype conversations with the nascent WAC committee in February and March to help them explore how they might implement a WI program.

The second institution, Valencia College, is the third largest community college in Florida, with more than 60,000 credit-seeking students enrolled across five campuses, and about 32.0 percent Hispanic, 32.5 percent Caucasian, and 18.0 percent African American students (Valencia College Institutional Research, 2015, p. 2.1). All faculty participate in a five-week professional development program for four hours a day. The associate provost of communications was tasked with initiating a WAC program, which she was imagining as the development of a WI requirement that would serve all campuses. She asked Jeff to visit campus and help them consider possible models, as well as get them started laying out their goals.

These two institutions could not be much more different in terms of size, scale, and program contexts. When Jeff first began working with them, however, they shared three basic objectives: (1) to implement the program over the summer in preparation for the upcoming fall semester, (2) to provide substantial faculty support, and (3) to develop a set of writing-based courses.

The implementation time frame for both was geared for a straightforward curricular initiative that could be instituted within about four to six months. In his first discussions with program initiators, Jeff shared the fifteen strategies of the whole systems approach to encourage them to think beyond the scope of a single curricular initiative. It was clear to him that both institutions needed to slow down their development time frames in order to gain more stakeholder support, understand existing support for writing on campus and how it tied to the WI initiative, and to deal with campus complexities.

In his first meeting with the six-member Texas A&M University–San Antonio committee, Jeff introduced what amounted to the understanding stage of the whole systems methodology by offering four key points about WAC program development: (1) the need for mapping out visually how the program they were imagining would tie into existing initiatives on campus; (2) the need to establish a clear mission statement and goals; (3) understanding the band of equilibrium within which a specific WAC program or project can function productively; and (4) developing a set of SIs to track the emergence, growth, and sustainability of a nascent WAC program. In preparation for the follow-up meeting, the committee mapped out their program relationships on campus in advance and spent time with Jeff talking about mission and goals and discussing strategies. A decision was made to scale back the project and establish pilot courses to test out strategies, develop WI criteria, and formulate an assessment plan. An interim provost established a six-week training workshop to prepare all faculty for the significant university-wide changes underway. When the new provost arrived mid summer, he supported the committee's desire to slow down the implementation process from that fall 2016 to the fall of 2021, a decision the committee had made that spring. He also supported the committee's recommendation to shift to "writing-intentional" courses from WI and enabled one class to be piloted. Additional workshops were planned for October and December. At the time of writing, a small group of instructors are planning to pilot WI courses in fall 2017 after participating in required training and working with the WAC director. By 2021, all entering students will be required to take four WI courses. As the downward expansion of the institution evolves, so will the WAC program.

At Valencia, the dean of communications for the West campus had brought together a mix of fifteen or so faculty and administrators from across several campuses. There was not yet a WAC director nor a WAC committee. Here, Jeff presented the full whole systems approach and then walked the group through mapping exercises, mission statement drafting, and goal setting. At one moment during the discussion, a faculty member said he thought the group needed to spend more time understanding before they proceeded to planning a program. Others agreed.

In follow-up conversations after the visit, Jeff was informed that a WAC director had been selected, and a small WAC committee recommended. A second, even larger stakeholders' meeting was scheduled for late September. Concerns that the main campus was highly interested and satellite campuses only marginally so prompted the larger stakeholder meeting, at which they discussed institutional leverage points, including the summer training program, action research, critical thinking, assessment, and a planning team. Afterwards, the partner campuses seemed more on board. The dean of communications had shifted her perception of WAC from a quick initiative to a much broader focus on who and what is involved.

The whole systems approach helps us understand why each institution really needed to slow down and how doing so has enabled both to think of WAC differently. It would have been a mistake for either institution to jump headfirst into a WI initiative without broadening their perspectives and considering sustainability.

Limitations of This Theoretical Framework and Book

We recognize that, as programs make use of our whole systems approach, they may discover that the principles can be further streamlined or that the strategies may be further elucidated. We look forward to seeing this theoretical framework put into action more widely, and to the inevitable refining of the methods, principles, strategies, and tactics that we've laid out. Further, the theories we drew from in developing the whole systems approach to WAC—complexity, systems, social network, resilience, and sustainable development theories—are all large and dynamic areas of scholarship from which more concepts and methods useful to the development of sustainable and transformative WAC programs may be drawn. We drew from these theories the pieces that seemed most relevant to the goals and contexts of WAC programs while attempting not to distort or undervalue the original theories, but there may be nuances that we overlooked or newer developments that we missed. This work is not intended to be used as a way to critique existing programs or previous WAC program-building strategies. Rather, it works to understand why so many WAC programs that have been previously active stagnate or go dormant. No doubt there are programs that have been built and sustained that have not followed the methodology we propose. We do not claim that our four-stage process is the only way to build a successful and sustainable program. We look forward to witnessing the ways in which WAC scholars continue to draw from these theories as they refine this theoretical framework for WAC and apply it to their programs.

Finally, it is the nature of a book such as this to be somewhat overwhelming, as we are introducing a theoretical framework and a large number of principles, strategies, and tactics. This book has many moving parts, and the theoretical frames may be wholly unfamiliar to the readers. We would advise those feeling overwhelmed to return to the four-stage methodology we present in Chapter 3, as this is the core of the process from which the principles and strategies were distilled.

Implications of This Book for WAC Scholarship

Throughout the book, we have talked about whole systems praxis, connecting our theory and principles to WAC practice through a methodology, strategies, and tactics. However, this approach offers not just implications for WAC practice, but WAC research as well, and may lead WAC scholars to reframe existing research questions or develop new ones. In the following section, we discuss the ways that the whole systems approach may reframe existing research questions as well as introduce new areas of research in relation to WAC program sustainability, program effectiveness, student writing within complex systems, and program leadership.

Investigations of What Makes for a Sustainable WAC Program

There is WAC research that is concerned with how to ensure that programs endure and with the qualities of long-standing programs, but the research has not applied sustainability theory to WAC programs or made the study of sustainability of central importance. The whole systems framework encourages researchers to consider whether programs that appear to be thriving may not be sustainable, which could reveal that a popular WAC initiative is growing too rapidly without considering the inevitable constraints of the complex institutional system, or that a WAC program has become so integrated into the institution that it is no longer visible and no longer assessing and revising its role in the system. SIs represent another area that merits further research, not least because they force us to reconsider the goals and processes of assessing writing programs. If common indicators can be tracked across programs, the field will have empirical evidence for the conditions that promote and impede program longevity, conditions that are now bound in lore. The whole systems approach also encourages researchers to consider transformational change as a part of sustainability, and to measure not just the survival of a WAC program but whether it has succeeded in changing the campus culture of writing.

Research questions focused on what makes for a sustainable WAC program could include:

- What are the most sustainable locations for WAC programs?
- Are there common leverage points for making sustainable change at institutions of higher education, and how can WAC directors best use those leverage points?
- What types of WAC projects and initiatives are most sustainable?
- What are the strongest indicators of WAC program sustainability and distress?
- What SIs might be identified across institutions and programs?
- Are there sets of SIs that would be particularly useful for WAC programs at different points in their development?

- ◆ Are there SIs that serve specific kinds of programs, such as WI and WEC, or individual WAC projects like fellows programs or faculty workshops?

- ◆ What will analysis based on the whole systems approach reveal about why some WAC programs fail and others are sustained over time?

Investigations of the Effectiveness of WAC Programs

The whole systems approach forces us to rethink how we define effective WAC programs. Some programs may appear effective but are not sustainable, and some programs that do not seem to be having an effect may be making incremental changes that will eventually reach a threshold point and transform the institution. Some programs may be successful by the standards of the administration or tenure-line faculty but might be creating inequities for multilingual students or contingent faculty. WAC programs that are working primarily at the micro level could have success at the lowest scales of the system but never reach the higher scales needed for transformational change to the campus culture of writing. A possible example is represented by "stealth WAC" (see, e.g., Parrish and Schonberg's vignette in Chapter 6), which may have small effects on an institution, but is unlikely to have the network leverage and visibility needed to make transformational change. The whole systems approach also encourages researchers to consider location within nodes and hubs of the network when thinking about what makes for a successful WAC program. Programs that appear effective but are housed in a campus node (such as an English department) or run by a contingent faculty member who lacks leverage in the system will most likely not be sustainable. Programs that rely solely on strong ties (a small group of WAC true believers) will most likely never connect to the weak ties that would help bring WAC initiatives to a threshold of transformational change. Finally, researchers should measure effectiveness of WAC programs not only according to how WAC affects the pedagogy of individual instructors, but also in respect to the ways WAC transforms structures and ideologies. The whole systems approach raises the stakes for what is considered an effective WAC program because of its focus on sustainability and transformational change.

Research questions focused on what makes for an effective WAC program might include:

- What are the most effective approaches and tools to help WAC directors map and model campus systems?

- What WAC projects are scalable, and what are the best approaches for moving projects up institutional scales from micro to macro?

- How far up the scale should change be fostered in university curricular ecology to achieve desired impacts without its leadership networks losing control of that change?

- What are the relationships between WAC initiatives and faculty and student equity? What kinds of WAC projects increase faculty and student equity, and which might unintentionally create inequities?

- Which theoretical frameworks help us understand and improve WAC program development and administration?

- How can we deal with obstacles to program or project development systematically?

Investigations of Writing in the Context of Institutions as Complex Systems

In a whole systems framework, WAC scholars would focus more of their research at higher scales of institutional systems. They would ask how campus programs and units (departments, academic senates, teaching and learning centers, writing centers, etc.) act as nodes and hubs within campus networks, how the structures and processes of campus networks affect WAC programs, and how campus structures shape the ideologies and behaviors of actors within campus systems. The concept that systems shape behaviors would lead researchers to focus less on individual personality or pedagogy and more on how university systems, as well as broader systems beyond the university, affect writing. WAC longitudinal research that has provided some of the richest and most contextualized perspectives on students writing across the curriculum, such as Lee Ann Caroll's (2002) *Rehearsing New Roles*, Anne Herrington and Marcia Curtis's (2000) *Persons in Process*, Barbara Walvoord and Lucille Parkinson McCarthy's (1990) *Thinking and Writing in College*, and Marilyn Sternglass's (1997) *Time to Know Them*, all mention how institutional structures and social and economic influences play a role in shaping the writing of the students in their case studies. But these longitudinal WAC studies focus primarily on students and teachers as the unit of analysis, and, with the exception of a chapter in Sternglass (1997) on institutional testing, the structures and processes of the system and how the system shapes the institutional culture of writing are not as prominent as individual actors within the system. A whole systems approach foregrounds how system structures and processes influence the actors in the system.

Research focused on WAC assessment could also be reconsidered from a whole systems approach. Assessment research projects that fail to consider the ways complex institutional systems are shaping student writing and the teaching of writing may not capture the full scale of the assessment scene. Researchers focusing on SIs may be especially interested in investigating assessment across departments and programs, and even across institutions. This focus could lead to a consideration of SIs that are common across WAC program types and contexts, or perhaps provide sets of indicators that new WAC directors might consider as they develop or grow new projects. Such studies would challenge the notion that outcomes assessment is only useful within local departments and should be focused primarily on student writing outcomes.

Research questions focused on writing in the context of complex systems might include:

♦ How do systems structure behaviors regarding writing at institutions of higher education? For example, how do institutional writing assessment processes, physical locations of writing programs and resources, and state and national writing policies and position statements structure the attitudes and behaviors of students, faculty, and administrators?

- How are the conceptions of writing within the larger regional and national systems shaping WAC at local institutions?

- What are the implications of the whole systems approach for the place of student writing in program assessment?

- What institutional structures and processes shape the way we collect and analyze data for writing assessment?

Investigations of Effective WAC Leadership

Very little research has been devoted to WAC program leadership, and there are almost no studies that place WAC program leadership within the broader context of leadership theory, and especially educational leadership theories. Complex systems leadership theory (CSLT) (discussed in Chapters 3 and 7) reframes research questions on WAC leadership, focusing less on the role of individual leaders and more on how leadership is distributed. It thus encourages us to focus our research on processes and structures that foster richer and more sustained connections across institutions. CSLT also complicates researchers' interpretations of the growth of the field of WAC, which has traditionally focused on individual leaders making heroic changes in the face of uninformed provosts or calls from the public to "fix" student writing. The story of individual leaders developing WAC programs from scratch and working together as "close ties" in informal networks was a necessary first stage in WAC's leadership development, parallel in many ways to the leadership stories of other writing studies disciplines such as basic writing and writing centers. But the whole systems approach invites us to explore more sustainable leadership models for WAC, especially as the founding members of the field retire. Just as basic writing and writing centers now rely on formal institutional structures more than individual leaders, this approach can be used to consider more distributed leadership models. Research should focus on leadership at the national level, the ways that rich connections nationally and internationally are being formed by leaders, the structures and processes that WAC leaders are putting in place to ensure succession of leadership, and the ways that new leaders are mentored and welcomed into the field, including leaders from underrepresented groups.

Research questions focused on what makes for effective WAC leadership might include:

◆ Based on the study of how complex networks operate, where should WAC programs be positioned and how should leadership be distributed?

◆ How is WAC leadership distributed in institutions and across branch campuses?

◆ What roles do WAC leaders play to coordinate WAC efforts across branch campuses, state systems, local K–12 districts, or other higher education institutions in the region?

◆ What are the most effective processes and structures to ensure WAC program leadership succession?

◆ How do new WAC leaders gain support and find mentorship beyond their institutions?

◆ How can leadership across national WAC organizations be examined in light of a whole systems approach?

Implications of This Book for the Organization of WAC as a Field

In this section, we reflect more broadly on the implications of the whole systems approach for WAC as a field. What might this approach reveal to us about the ability of the field to remain vibrant, to be sustained, and to continue having a transformative effect on the field of writing studies?

Throughout the book, we have discussed how work across scales at an individual institution might look. In Chapter 2, where we define how transformational change can be facilitated at multiple scales, we connect such change to resilience, noting that forced transformational change from legislative acts, state funding, WAC organizations, or even best practice documents has more leverage to shift local culture than unforced change at the local institution. However, we note too that forced changes can also significantly impact the resilience of a local program by shifting the culture in undesirable directions or initiate changes over which local organizers can lose control. Thus, change at the highest scales needs to be made judiciously, with broad input, and with a clear understanding of its potential impact on individual programs and each of the supporting organizations governing the field. This caution is not meant to discourage change at the highest scales but to qualify what kinds of change might be most productive.

With this goal in mind, we lay out the different components that constitute the field of WAC in the United States, including its organizations, conferences, and journals, and then consider ways that the whole systems approach can help us reflect on the current organization of the field and to imagine possible futures. In Table 8.1, we provide a chronological summary of the field of WAC in order to understand the various components that comprise the field.

There is much to admire in the evolution of WAC as a field in the United States. Some components—INWAC, the WAC Clearinghouse, *The WAC Journal, ATD*—have long histories, providing the field with visibility and credibility. Within these organizations are strong leaders with decades of experience as WAC scholars, program leaders, and practitioners. The WAC Clearinghouse has become a widely recognized source of WAC information and scholarship, not just storing resources but initiating scholarship through its many publishing ventures and hosting websites of WAC organizations, such as NEWACC. And, as indicated by the many WAC organizations that have emerged in the last decade, it is clear that WAC remains a vibrant field, connecting with other higher education movements within the United States (such as the critical thinking movement) and internationally (through WRAB).

Less apparent from Table 8.1 is the fact that a national WAC organization that connects WAC organizations, journals, and conferences does not exist in the United States. While one may think that the WAC Clearinghouse, the IWAC conference, the WAC listserv, and WAC journals are structurally connected to one another, in reality, they are distinct efforts, led by separate (though often overlapping) leadership. The network map of the organizations, journals, and programs and their relationships

TABLE 8.1. Chronological Summary of WAC Field Components in the United States

Organization	Year launched	Host/leader	Role in WAC	Connections to other WAC organizations
INWAC	1981 (by Chris Thaiss)	Led by Thaiss until 2015; led by co-chairs Michelle Cox, Jeffrey Galin, Anne Ellen Geller, and Dan Melzer in 2016	Comprised of a group of loosely affiliated WAC programs and a board of consultants; maintains a directory of WAC programs; hosts an annual CCCC Special Interest Group meeting during which board members mentor novice WAC directors; developed the "Statement of WAC Principles and Practices" (International Network of Writing-Across-the-Curriculum Programs, 2014).	Website is hosted by the WAC Clearinghouse; annual meeting hosted by CCCC; INWAC was reconstituted as the CCCC WAC Standing Group in 2017.
WAC-L	1991 (by Gail Hawisher)	Hosted by University of Illinois at Urbana–Champaign's Center for Writing Studies and led by the program director (currently, Paul Prior)	Originally launched after the University of Illinois held its first WAC faculty seminar in order to "increas[e] the study, teaching, and visibility of writing studies across our large research institution and beyond" (Hawisher, personal correspondence, August 6, 2016); now serves as a platform for national and international conversations about developing WAC programs.	Used by WAC organizations to make announcements related to WAC events, calls for papers, and job ads; used by members of WAC organizations to discuss WAC-related matters.
IWAC conference	1993 (by Art Young, Clemson University)	Rotating hosts since 1999	This biennial conference, which started as the National WAC Conference and was renamed in 2004, brings together WAC directors, practitioners, and scholars.	Materials from IWAC conferences are archived on the WAC Clearinghouse.
Language and Learning Across the Disciplines	1994–2004 (by Sharon Quiroz and Michael Pemberton)	Not continued	This was the first peer-reviewed, academic journal focused on WAC.	In January 2004, *Language and Learning Across the Disciplines* merged with *Academic Writing* to form *Across the Disciplines*.

Continued on next page

Table 8.1 continued

WAC Clearinghouse	1997, morphed into *Academic. Writing* in 2000, then was relaunched in 2002	Launched by Mike Palmquist; currently led by Palmquist and an editorial team	Originating as a collection of resources for the WAC program at Colorado State University, this site now hosts WAC-affiliated websites, provides access to information about WAC programs and practices, publishes journals and book series related to WAC, and provides open access to WAC books.	Hosts the websites for NEWACC, INWAC, ATD, and *The WAC Journal*; publishes ATD, co-publishes *The WAC Journal* and a number of book series.
The WAC Journal	1999 (by editor Roy Andrews)	Hosted by Plymouth State University from 1989 to 2012, when Clemson University began hosting; edited since 1995 by Andrews	Founded in 1989 by Mary-Lou Hinman as a newsletter for the Plymouth State University WAC program, and became a national WAC journal 10 years into its history, under Andrews's leadership.	Currently copublished by the WAC Clearinghouse, which also makes the journal's archives available.
Academic. Writing: Interdisciplinary Perspectives on Communication Across the Curriculum	2000-2004 (by Mike Palmquist)	Not continued	This journal provided a venue for peer-review articles on WAC and was a repository for materials related to WAC program administration, pedagogy, and research.	The journal originated as an attempt to legitimize the WAC Clearinghouse as scholarly work, then became a journal on the WAC Clearinghouse website; it later merged with *Language and Learning Across the Disciplines* to become *Across the Disciplines*.

Continued on next page

Table 8.1 continued

Across the Disciplines: A Journal of Language, Learning, and Academic Writing	2004 (by Sharon Quiroz and Mike Palmquist)	ATD has been edited by Michael Pemberton since 2005.	From its inception, ATD has "share[d] the mission of the WAC Clearinghouse in making information about writing and writing instruction freely available to members of the CAC, WAC, and ECAC communities" (WAC Clearinghouse, n.d.a); this open-access peer-reviewed journal has served as an important venue for WAC scholarship.	Published on the WAC Clearinghouse.
Critical Thinking and Writing Conference	2006 (by Robert Smart)	Quinnipiac University	This biennial conference seeks to bring together the WAC and critical thinking movements.	Out of this conference came NEWACC and Double Helix.
International WRAB conference	2008 (by Charles Bazerman)	International Society for the Advancement of Writing Research	This conference grew out of a biennial conference at University of California, Santa Barbara; focuses on "writing development across the lifespan, including the early acquisition of writing, writing across grade levels (K–20), in the disciplines, as well as in the workplace and other community and institutional settings" (University of California, Santa Barbara, 2008) and seeks to foster exchange and collaboration among writing researchers around the world.	Has affiliations with academic writing organizations outside of the United States.
NEWACC	2009 (by Michelle Cox, chair, and Kati Pletsch de Garcia, associate chair)	Rotating leadership; currently led by Laurie Ann Brit-Smith (chair) and Katherine E. Tirabassi (associate chair)	This regional WAC association's mission is to "provide the local region with expertise in research-based Writing Across the Curriculum practices, program development" and to "foster collaboration among area WAC programs and provide opportunities for members to draw on each other's expertise and experience" (WAC Clearinghouse, n. d.).	Meetings hosted by the Critical Thinking and Writing Conference and the Northeast Writing Centers Association Conference.

Continued on next page

Table 8.1 continued

Double Helix: A Journal of Critical Thinking and Writing	2013 (by Glenda Pritchett)	Quimipiac University	This journal seeks to bring together the WAC and critical thinking movements.	Emerged from the Critical Thinking and Writing Conference, publishing papers culled from the conference and from open calls.
WAC–GO	2015 (by Michelle La-France, Brian Hendrickson, Alicia Russell, and Al Harahap)	Rotating leadership; currently led by Alicia Russell, (chair), Vicki Davis (coordinator), Justin Nicoles (research support chair), and an advisory board of experienced WAC scholars	Founded "to promote graduate student scholarship, seek out funding and support for graduate student research activities, and connect graduate students with cross-institutional research, administrative, and teaching mentors" (WAC Clearinghouse, n.d.b); modeled on WPA–GO (Writing Program Administrators–Graduate Organization), which is sponsored by CWPA.	Coordinates with WAC conferences and the CCCC WAC Standing Group to offer events that connect graduate students with experienced WAC directors and scholars.
CCCC WAC Standing Group	2017 (by Michelle Cox, Jeffrey Galin, Anne Ellen Geller, and Dan Melzer)	Rotating leadership; currently led by Dan Melzer (past chair), Michelle Cox (chair), and Jeffrey Galin (incoming chair)	Provides an annual meeting at CCCC for the WAC community; organizes an annual special topic CCCC panel or workshop on WAC.	Emerged from the INWAC Special Interest Group at CCCC; creates a formal connection between WAC and CCCC; coordinates with WAC–GO.

shown in Figure 8.1 demonstrates how loosely the nodes of the field are connected. In Figure 8.1, nine clusters are depicted: Quinnipiac University, Plymouth State University, Colorado State University, CCCC, University of California, Santa Barbara, University of Illinois at Urbana–Champaign, the IWAC conference, and the WAC–GO, as well as the WAC programs themselves (depicted by "WAC Programs" in the middle of the figure). Solid lines connect organizations with structural connections, showing, for example, that the *WAC Journal* emerged from Plymouth State University's WAC Program and is copublished by the WAC Clearinghouse. Dotted lines denote less formal connections, connecting, for example, WAC–GO to the IWAC conference and the WAC Network board of consultants, as WAC–GO has coordinated with both of these groups to organize mentoring opportunities for graduate students. Most striking in Figure 8.1 is that WAC programs themselves, while at the heart of the field of WAC, have no connections to any WAC organizations (unless that program houses or initiated a WAC journal, conference, or listserv), and no organization acts as a central hub connecting all of the different WAC organizations.

The lack of a central hub for WAC may be related to the histories of the different WAC organizations. Several of them started as projects within campus WAC programs. For instance, the WAC Clearinghouse was originally the Colorado State University's WAC website, WAC-L was originally a listserv for the University of Illinois Center for Writing Studies, and *The WAC Journal* was originally a newsletter for Plymouth State University's WAC program. Each of these organizations grew with the field, evolving to reach beyond campus borders.

The cluster of Quinnipiac University–affiliated WAC organizations (the biennial conference, journal, and regional organization NEWACC) all emerged from Quinnipiac University's WAC program, which was launched and further developed with two Educational Foundation Grants, funds used to initiate the Critical Thinking and Writing Conference and subsequently the *Double Helix* journal. As Smart (2013) explained, the regional consortium "grew from the need in tough economic climates to provide a clearinghouse of tools and ideas for greater New England area colleges and universities with an interest in WAC or with an

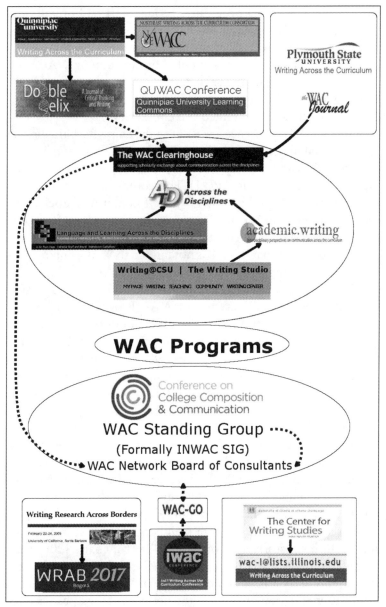

FIGURE 8.1. *Visual map of the field of WAC.*

existing WAC or WID program" (p. 1). Smart had organized a meeting of WAC program directors at the first conference in 2008, at the height of the recession, and many expressed dismay that the only venues for mentorship and collaboration among WAC leaders existed at the annual CCCC INWAC Special Interest Group meeting and biennial IWAC conference, both of which were out of reach for those with limited travel budgets.

The WRAB conference grew out of the Santa Barbara writing research conferences (held in 2002, 2005, and 2008), and became "Writing Research Across Borders" the year it was hosted by George Mason University (2011). This conference currently travels internationally and is hosted by the International Society for the Advancement of Writing Research, an organization that grew out of WRAB, but has a constitution, mission, and election cycle. It should be noted that WRAB is not limited to WAC, but includes in its focus writing research emerging around the world, across levels (primary, secondary, and tertiary), and in the workplace.

The International Network of WAC Programs, which may sound like a central hub, was actually "an informal community of teachers, researchers, and institutions" (WAC Clearinghouse, n.d.a). Led by Chris Thaiss from 1981 to 2016 (when it was reconstituted as the CCCC WAC Standing Group), INWAC met annually as a CCCC Special Interest Group for roundtable discussions led by the board of INWAC consultants, a group appointed by Thaiss based on their expertise in WAC and willingness to attend the Special Interest Group. The members of INWAC were loosely affiliated through their desire to have their program listed in the INWAC directory, a list published on the WAC Clearinghouse since 2006, and, from 1981–2005, in a paper directory, financially supported by the National Writing Project and contributions from members (WAC Clearinghouse, n.d.b). In his historical account of INWAC, Thaiss (2006) has speculated that the existence of INWAC may have played a role in preventing the formation of a national WAC organization: "I admit to wondering at times if the network, by its presence for more than twenty years, hasn't misleadingly given the appearance of being the national organization that WAC might need and so diminished the desire or incentive to others who might have built one" (p. 140).

The lack of a national WAC organization in the United States may also result from the fact that, for much of its history, WAC was conceived not as a field but as a curricular reform movement existing on college campuses. In "The Future of WAC," Walvoord (1996) explained that WAC "did not enlarge itself by becoming a national organization with a nationally articulated agenda and a media image, but by the springing up of campus WAC programs" (p. 61). WAC started on individual campuses, and then spread to other campuses through the originating WAC program directors. As described by Walvoord (1996):

> WAC in higher education was spread primarily through travel-ing workshop leaders such as Toby Fulwiler, Elaine Maimon, and me. WAC resembled independent congregations linked by itinerant preachers rather than a strongly organized central church with a central orthodoxy. (p. 61)

Walvoord suggested further that, because WAC was decentral-ized and focused more on the micro level (individual campuses), it did not concern itself with macro-level concerns. Rather than create a national organization with its attached conferences, journals, listservs, and literature, as did other types of writing programs (see, e.g., CWPA or the International Writing Centers Association), as Walvoord (1996) explained, "WAC's theory and research were folded into the journals and conventions that served writing faculty" (p. 61). She observed that this focus on the micro level may also explain why WAC literature tended to focus on campus-related concerns: the "strategies, organizational form, membership, and resources" of WAC programs (Walvoord, 1996, p. 62). Walvoord commented that membership in a cam-pus WAC program was often determined by who showed up at workshops. We can see the effects of this philosophy of decentral-ization on WAC scholarship and organizational structures today. For instance, the membership of INWAC's board of consultants was determined by who showed up at the CCCC Special Interest Group meeting, and membership in the INWAC Directory was determined by whether the director had logged into the WAC Clearinghouse in the past two years (International Network of Writing-Across-the-Curriculum Programs website).

Walvoord's insight that WAC does not have a "central orthodoxy" leads to another reason why WAC may have not established a central organization: fear of the development of a central orthodoxy. One effect of the decentralization of WAC has been, as Walvoord (1996) pointed out, "wide latitude for varying interpretations and theories" (p. 64). WAC was born within the heyday of the process movement and the spirit of the late sixties, a time of rebellion against the traditional constraints of academia and society at large. In "Writing Across and Against the Curriculum," Art Young (2003) noted that, in the early days, WAC "felt absolutely subversive to 'education as usual'" and the pedagogies introduced at WAC workshops "felt anti-establishment" (p. 473). WAC has been, at its heart, a grassroots movement, driven by committed volunteers and lofty ideals, and spread through faculty relations and informal networks across campuses. It is understandable why those who were part of this original generation of WAC scholars might recoil at the thought of a central national organization, something that smells of bureaucracy. But, as Walvoord (1996) argued in her prescient article, without a central organization, WAC has been unable to take part in national movements that impact writing (Walvoord named the four present in 1996; p. 68), individual campus WAC programs have been left vulnerable, losing faculty and funding without the backing of a larger organization (p. 70), and WAC has been unable to move past its focus on the local to work at the national level to achieve goals (p. 74). Further, as Thaiss (2006) has stated, without a formal national organization, WAC hasn't been able to "create an agenda to focus efforts, issue position statements, establish and publish standards, conduct statistical surveys of members, and, maybe most basic, ensure continuity through an orderly process of succeeding leadership" (p. 139).

We believe that the primary reason that WAC has been unable to work cohesively at the national level is that, from the lens of ONA, the field of WAC may be seen as a series of nodes, without a central hub, and those who developed these nodes have a vested interest in them. From the lens of sustainable development theory, the field of WAC may be seen as a loose collection of projects. Without a central hub connecting the many WAC organizations, there are no formal processes or structures for determining goals for WAC as a field, working together to develop projects, collaborating across nodes, or working to ensure the sustainability of the field. And, without this central hub, there are few points of leverage for making change across the field. Further, some of these organizations have had the same actors serving as leaders for many years. While these leaders have done admirable work with their many years of service, many of these organizations lack mechanisms for distributing leadership or bringing in new leadership, a situation that threatens sustainability.

What may also be less apparent from Table 8.1 is that many of the actors that have leadership roles in these organizations belong to a relatively small network. A quick purview of the editorial boards of the WAC Clearinghouse and *ATD*, the past INWAC board of consultants, and past chairs of the IWAC conference will reveal many names in common. This is not a criticism, as we three are also part of this network and serve on the WAC Clearinghouse editorial board, *ATD* editorial board, and, with Anne Ellen Geller, developed the CCCC WAC Standing Group. We are simply noting that these same groups do not have mechanisms for creating weak ties and thus for bringing in new leadership, alternative voices, and novel perspectives. These WAC organizations do not have built-in structures for sustainability. The WAC journals do not have term limits for their editors and rarely have calls for reviewers. The IWAC conference has no clear process for creating its biennial leadership team, maintaining a standing budget, or connecting to other WAC organizations.

As a field, WAC has few means of mentoring young scholars or novice program directors—of creating the weak ties necessary for expanding the network. The CCCC Standing Group plans to continue the tradition of creating opportunities for the mentorship of new WAC directors at CCCC meetings, and the newly established WAC–GO is creating events that bring together graduate students interested in WAC and seasoned WAC scholars and practitioners, but these mentorship opportunities are limited given the number of WAC programs starting annually across the United States. Even at the level of program, few mentorship opportunities exist, as few WAC programs appoint assistant or associate program directors and few PhD programs in writing studies offer coursework in WAC theory and practice or roles for graduate students in WAC program administration. Without the prospect of distributed leadership at the level of program and the level of field, sustainability is threatened.

Resilience as a field also relies on the creation of new knowledge. New scholarship in WAC is especially important given the changing landscape of higher education, with changes in faculty and student demographics, competing faculty development initiatives, and emphasis on assessment. While writing this book, we were struck again and again by our field's reliance on lore for many aspects of program development and leadership. At recent conferences, we have noticed that those presenting on WAC program development lean heavily on WAC scholarship from over twenty years ago.

CSLT also complicates researchers' interpretations of the growth of the field of WAC, which has traditionally focused on individual leaders making heroic changes in the face of uninformed provosts or calls from the public to "fix" student writing. The story of individual leaders developing WAC programs from scratch and working together as "close ties" in informal networks was a necessary first stage in WAC's leadership development, parallel in many ways to the leadership stories of other writing studies disciplines such as basic writing and writing centers. But it may now be time for a more sustainable leadership model for WAC, especially as the founding members of the field retire. Just as basic writing and writing centers now rely on formal institutional structures more than individual leaders, it may be time for WAC as a field to institutionalize and distribute leadership. Research on leadership for the field of WAC should consider the ways that WAC leadership is being distributed, the ways that rich connections nationally and internationally are being formed by leaders, the structures and processes that WAC leaders are putting in place to ensure succession of leadership, and the ways that new leaders are mentored and welcomed into the field, including leaders from underrepresented groups.

We should note that, during the three years of writing this book, a series of conversations began that may reshape the ways in which WAC as a field is organized. When Thaiss handed leadership of INWAC to Geller and the three of us in 2016, we began to engage the INWAC board of consultants and other

WAC stakeholders in discussions about the threats we perceived to the sustainability of the field of WAC from a whole systems perspective, including supporting more opportunities for WAC scholars to assume leadership roles at the national level, more mentorship opportunities for WAC administrators and scholars, and more national coordination of WAC resources. We moderated discussions on the future of WAC at CCCC 2016, IWAC 2016, and CCCC 2017, and conducted a related survey in January 2017, results of which were presented at CCCC 2017. From these conversations emerged three new initiatives.

First, as we note above, INWAC was reconstituted as the CCCC WAC Standing Group, a change that formalized the relationship between WAC and CCCC, creating two permanent spots on the CCCC program: an annual business meeting and WAC-related workshop or panel. Further, this reconstitution led to rotating leadership, which fosters greater sustainability and more leadership opportunities at the national level.

Second, conversations about the need for more mentorship opportunities in WAC had been circulating for some time. Michelle LaFrance initiated WAC–GO in 2015 along with then-graduate students Brian Hendrickson, Alicia Russell, and Al Harahap to create mentorship opportunities for graduate students, and had considered opening the group to junior faculty, but the needs for graduate mentorship in WAC are so great that the organization decided to focus on this population. INWAC had provided mentorship at the yearly Special Interest Group meetings through roundtable discussions led by members of the INWAC board of consultants. While this activity may continue during the WAC Standing Group business meetings, this short meeting has never provided enough time for true mentorship. This led to the second new initiative: a summer institute. When Terry Zawacki and Paul Anderson suggested the development of a summer institute on WAC program administration at the 2017 CCCC meeting on the future of WAC, we all agreed the idea was good and timely, particularly because it has been more than a decade since the last UNC Charlotte Wildacres' Annual WID retreat, which had been offered for twenty-two years (Bosley, 2003). The first three-day summer WAC institute will be held in June 2019. Its primary goal will be to assist new and prospective leaders of WAC/WID or similar initiatives in the United States and internationally at planning, developing, and sustaining their programs. The institute will also support experienced directors who face new challenges or wish to expand, update, or revitalize their programs.

Third, we came to the realization that the field of WAC was missing a central organization. When the three of us put together a timeline of WAC organizations (Table 8.1), we began to see the field as both organizationally fragmented and led by a small group of leaders with strong ties and with few entry points for new leadership. From this timeline, we pieced together the visual map of WAC as a field (Figure 8.1), which amplified our sense of a field without a center. Recognition of these threats to field sustainability led to the third initiative: the formation of the Association for Writing Across the Curriculum. A working group formed to develop this new association during the CCCC 2017 meeting, and has been composing a mission and values statement as well as bylaws and articles of incorporation for 501(c)(3) status. Among its goals, the Association for Writing Across the Curriculum seeks to formalize connections among the different WAC and other writing-related organizations to reach mutual goals; foster scholarly work on WAC; sponsor research on WAC issues; support communication among diverse stakeholders engaged in WAC research, teaching, and learning; support existing mentorship opportunities related to WAC practices, program development, and research; advocate for students, faculty, staff, and administrators through resolutions, statements, and studies on issues of importance to WAC programs; and promote the visibility and impact of WAC in the public sphere (Association for Writing Across the Curriculum, 2017). These discussions will continue over the next year.

With this context in mind, we pose the following questions:

◆ How has the national WAC movement impacted conceptions of literacy within the larger regional and national systems related to higher education?

◆ How is leadership distributed in the national WAC movement?

◆ What processes and structures have WAC leaders put in place to create richer networks?

◆ How are new leaders—and especially students and teachers from underrepresented groups—welcomed into the national WAC movement?

◆ What SIs may be developed to assess and track the sustainability of WAC as a field?

◆ What larger systems, structures, and processes can the national WAC movement put in place in order to shape the national conversation about writing, help make transformational changes to the cultures of literacy at institutions of higher education, and promote the sustainability of the field?

A Different Mindset for WAC

We have offered questions focused on sustainability and transformational change throughout this book, and, whether we are considering the impact of a single project, a formal WAC program, or the field of WAC itself, the whole systems approach encourages us to apply the lessons of complexity theories in order to launch, revitalize, and revise WAC. Our fifteen principles and methodology of *understanding*, *planning*, *developing*, and *leading* encourage WAC program leaders and the leaders of the field to aim for broad participation and rich connectivity, with slow and systematic development and a focus on equity. Our principles and methodology encourage distributed leadership within individual WAC programs and for WAC as a field, with an emphasis not just on small groups of strong ties, but also on visibility and outreach to weak ties. Developing SIs early in the process, and assessing those indicators and continuously revising, should be a goal of both WAC directors at individual institutions and the field of WAC. The lessons of complexity sciences teach us that WAC programs are more sustainable and have greater impact if they are located in hubs such as independent writing programs, writing centers, and centers for teaching and learning, rather than in nodes like English departments, and the field of WAC itself will have more impact if it shifted from loosely connected nodes to an organization that can serve as a central hub, with greater visibility, broad stakeholder input, a concern for equity, national integration, and greater leverage for making change.

We understand that the whole systems approach is challenging, as it asks WAC leaders, scholars, and the field itself to undertake a different mindset than has been applied to WAC previously. We believe that the complexity theories informing our approach address key gaps in our forty-five years of practice building WAC programs, and have significant implications for how we move forward as a field. It is our hope that the whole systems approach addresses the lack of resilience that has plagued so many WAC programs and may threaten the field itself. Finally, the whole systems approach will help WAC leaders make the kinds of sustainable and transformational changes that have long been the goal of the field.

APPENDIX A
Step-by-Step Process for Creating Radar Charts (AMOEBA Graphs) in Microsoft Excel 2013

The data are recorded in a standard spreadsheet with SIs listed down column A and program years across the top. Figure A.1 demonstrates the data layout (the odd spacing of items 4 to 6 are adjustments for label layout in accompanying charts).

	Fall 2014	Spring 2015	Summer 2015	Fall 2015	Spring 2016	Summer 2016	Fall 2016
Number of WI course sections available to meet student need	3	4	4	2	3	1	0
Faculty support services needed to grow WI capacity	3	3	3	2	1	1	0
Capacity of student support services to handle demand	3	3	2	2	3	3	3
Budget capacity to support WI (training, assessment, resources)	4	2	2	3	2	2	1
Capacity of WAC director to manage WI	1	4	3	4	4	4	4
Capacity of WAC committee to review WI syllabi	1	4	4	2	6	5	5
Availability of classroom space for WI courses	4	4	4	2	2	1	1
Number of faculty willing to teach WI to meet student enrollment	2	3	3	1	2	2	2
Class size for WI courses (number of students)	2	2	2	4	4	4	2
Equitable distribution of WAC courses across faculty levels	3	4	3	3	2	2	0

FIGURE A.1. *SI data for a WI initiative over seven academic terms.*

To create the charts in Excel on a Windows computer, select the full data. Select the INSERT tab, then the spiderweb icon in the menu ribbon, and then the desired radar chart option. Once the layered chart is created, size it proportionally so all of the labels are legible. Then right-click the chart area and choose Select Data. Uncheck all except the first data column. This step reveals only one data layer and sets up a template for all charts. Then select the INSERT tab, Shapes, and then Oval to add the inner and outer bands of equilibrium. Select No Fill under the paint bucket icon for each. Right-clicking on the chart axis brings up the Axis Options under which appears the graph icon that enables adjustments to Chart Bounds (in this case, 0 to 6) and the ability to add Tick Marks if you choose. Figure A.2 shows the values for Format Axis that result in the accompanying chart.

To change default line colors, select the paint bucket icon in the Format Axis options. We chose Solid Line under Line options. Once the master chart is created, we recommend copying and pasting this fully formatted chart into as many new Excel sheets in the workbook as there are data columns. Then right-click on the chart axis, choose Select Data, and check the appropriate data set for each sheet as well as unchecking the one that served as the template. **Don't forget to change the chart title.** These charts can then be pasted into Word files for reporting purposes. The trends they represent over time provide a representation of program change, resilience, and sustainability.

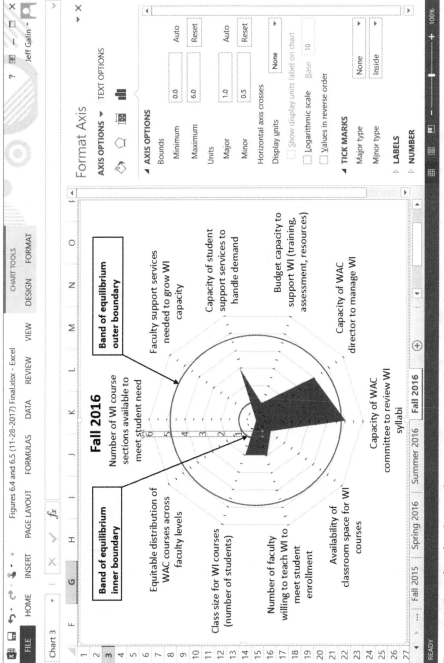

FIGURE A.2. *Sample radar chart with accompanying axis formatting options.*

REFERENCES

Adler-Kassner, L. (2008). *The activist WPA: Changing stories about writing and writers.* Logan, UT: Utah State University Press.

Allison, M., Lynn, R., & Hoverman, V. (2015). Indispensable, but invisible: A report on the working climate of non-tenure-track faculty at George Mason University. Department of Sociology and Anthropology, George Mason University. Retrieved from http://www .chronicle.com/items/biz/pdf/GMU-Contingent-Faculty-Study.pdf

American Library Association. (2016). *Framework for information literacy for higher education.* Retrieved from http://www.ala.org/ acrl/standards/ilframework

American University. (2016). *Atrium: Student Writing from American University's College Writing Program.* Retrieved from http://www .american.edu/cas/literature/wsp/atrium.cfm

Anson, C. M. (2006). Assessing writing in cross-curricular programs: Determining the locus of activity. *Assessing Writing, 11*(2), 1000–1112.

Anson, C. M., Carter, M., Dannels, D., & Rust, J. (2003). Mutual support: CAC programs and institutional improvement in undergraduate education. *Language and Learning Across the Disciplines, 6*(3), 26–38.

Anson, C. M., & Dannels, D. (Eds.). (2009). Profiling programs: Formative use of departmental consultations in the assessment of Communication Across the Curriculum. [Special issue: WAC and Assessment]. *Across the Disciplines, 6.* Retrieved from https://wac .colostate.edu/atd/assessment/anson_dannels.cfm

Association for Writing Across the Curriculum. (2017). *Mission, values, and activities (draft).* Retrieved from https://wac.colostate.edu/awac/

Association of American Colleges and Universities. (2009). *VALUE rubrics.* Retrieved from https://www.aacu.org/value-rubrics

Balkundi, P., & Kilduff, M. (2006). The ties that lead: A social network approach to leadership. *The Leadership Quarterly, 17*, 419–39.

Banathy, B. H. (1973). *Developing a systems view of education: The systems-model approach.* Seaside, CA: Intersystems.

Banathy, B. H. (1992). *A systems view of education: Concepts and principles for effective practice.* Englewood Cliffs, NJ: Educational Technology.

Barabási, A.-L. (2002). *Linked: The new science of networks.* Cambridge, MA: Perseus.

Bean, J. (2011). *Engaging ideas: The professor's guide to integrating writing, critical thinking, and active learning in the classroom.* San Francisco, CA: Jossey-Bass.

Bell, S., & Morse, S. (2008). *Sustainability indicators: Measuring the immeasurable?* (2nd ed.) [Adobe Digital Editions version]. Retrieved from https://www.u-cursos.cl/ciencias/2015/2/CS06067/1/material_docente/bajar?id_material=1210909

Benford, R. (1992). Social movements. In E. F. Borgatta & M. L. Borgatta (Eds.), *Encyclopedia of sociology* (vol. 4, pp. 1880-1887). New York: MacMillan.

Berg, C. E. (1999). The effects of trained peer response on ESL students' revision types and writing quality. *Journal of Second Language Writing, 8*(3), 215–41.

Bosley, D. S. (2003). Announcing the UNC Charlotte Wildacres' 2003 annual WID retreat. *Academic.Writing: Interdisciplinary Perspectives on Communications Across the Curriculum.* Retrieved from https://wac.colostate.edu/aw/connections/wildacres_2002_retreat.htm.

Bossel, H. (1999). *Indicators for sustainable development: Theory, method, applications.* Winnipeg, Manitoba, Canada: International Institute for Sustainable Development.

California State University, San Bernardino. (2016). *Accreditation.* Retrieved from http://bulletin.csusb.edu/accreditation/

Canagarajah, A. S. (2002). *Critical academic writing and multilingual students.* Ann Arbor, MI: University of Michigan Press.

Caplan, N. A., & Cox, M. (2016). The state of graduate communication support: Results of an international survey. In S. Simpson, N. A. Caplan, M. Cox, & T. Phillips (Eds.), *Supporting graduate student writers: Research, curriculum, and program design* (pp. 22–47). Ann Arbor, MI: University of Michigan Press.

Caroll, L. A. (2002). *Rehearsing new roles: How college students develop as writers.* Carbondale, IL: Southern Illinois University Press.

Carter, M. (2003). A process for establishing outcomes-based assessment plans for writing and speaking in the disciplines. *Language and Learning Across the Disciplines, 6*(1), 4–29.

Carter, M., Anson, C. M., & Miller, C. (2003). Assessing technical writing in institutional contexts: Using outcomes-based assessment for programmatic thinking. *Technical Communication Quarterly, 12*(1), 101–14.

Chamely-Wiik, D., Dunn, K., Heydet-Kirsch, P., Holman, M., Meeroff, D., & Peluso, J. (2014). Scaffolding the development of student research skills for capstone experiences: A multi-disciplinary approach. *Council on Undergraduate Research Quarterly, 34*(4), 18–25.

Checkland, P. (1981). *Systems thinking, systems practice.* New York, NY: John Wiley & Sons.

Condon, W., & Rutz, C. (2012). A taxonomy of writing across the curriculum programs: Evolving to serve broader agendas. *College Composition and Communication, 64*(2), 357–82.

Conference on College Composition and Communication. (2001). *CCCC statement on second language writing and writers* (rev. 2009). Retrieved from http://www.ncte.org/cccc/resources/positions/secondlangwriting

Cooper, M. (1986). The ecology of writing. *College English, 48*(4), 364–75.

Council of Writing Program Administrators. (2003). *Defining and avoiding plagiarism: The WPA statement on best practices.* Retrieved from http://wpacouncil.org/positions/WPAplagiarism.pdf

Council of Writing Program Administrators. (2014). *WPA outcomes statement for first-year composition (3.0).* Retrieved from http://wpacouncil.org/positions/outcomes.html

Cox, M. (Ed.). (2011). WAC: Closing doors or opening doors for second language writers? [Special issue: WAC and Second Language Writing]. *Across the Disciplines, 8*(4). Retrieved from https://wac.colostate.edu/atd/ell/cox.cfm

Cox, M. (2014). In response to today's "felt" need: WAC, faculty development, and second language writers. In T. M. Zawacki & M. Cox (Eds.), *WAC and second language writers: Research towards linguistically and culturally inclusive programs and practices* (pp. 299–326). Fort Collins, CO: The WAC Clearinghouse and Parlor Press. Retrieved from https://wac.colostate.edu/books/l2/chapter12.pdf

Cox, M., & Gimbel, P. (2012). Conversations among teachers on student writing: WAC/secondary education partnerships at BSU. *Across the Disciplines*, 9(3). Retrieved from https://wac.colostate.edu/atd/second_educ/cox_gimbel.cfm

Cox, M., & Gimbel, P. (2016). Talking about writing across the secondary and college community. In J. Blumner & P. Childers (Eds.), *WAC partnerships among secondary and post-secondary institutions* (pp. 19–36). Fort Collins, CO: WAC Clearinghouse and Parlor Press. Retrieved from http://wac.colostate.edu/books/partnerships/chapter2.pdf

Cox, M., & Zawacki, T. M. (Eds.). (2011). WAC and second language writing: Cross-field research, theory, and program development [Special issue: WAC and Second Language Writing]. *Across the Disciplines*, 8(4). Retrieved from https://wac.colostate.edu/ATD/ell/index.cfm

Cragun, R. T., & Cragun, D. (2006). *Introduction to sociology*. Edition 1.0. Wikibooks. Retrieved from https://issuu.com/milad.hd/docs/intro_to_sociology/82.

Cross, R. (2014). *What is ONA? Introduction to organizational network analysis*. Retrieved from http://www.robcross.org/research/what-is-ona/

Davis, A., & Cozza, V. (2014). WAC/WID campus concerns: "Growing pains" or perspectives from a small branch campus. *Across the Disciplines*, 11(3), 1.

Dowell, E. H. (1999). Introduction: Four carrots and a stick. *Language and Learning Across the Disciplines*, 3(2), 13–18.

Durfee, W. K., Adams, B., Appelsies, A. J., & Flash, P. (2011). *A writing program for mechanical engineering*. Paper presented at 2011 ASEE Annual Conference & Exposition, Vancouver, B.C. Retrieved from https://peer.asee.org/a-writing-program-for-mechanical-engineering

Eastern Illinois University. (2016). Writing across the curriculum. http://castle.eiu.edu/~writcurr/

References

Environment Canada. (2010). *Planning for a sustainable future: A federal sustainable development strategy for Canada*. Retrieved from http://www.ec.gc.ca/dd-sd/F93CD795-0035-4DAF-86D1-53099BD303F9/FSDS_v4_EN.pdf

Environment Canada. (2013). *Planning for a sustainable future: A federal sustainable development strategy for Canada 2013–2016*. Retrieved from http://publications.gc.ca/collections/collection_2016/eccc/En4-136-2013-eng.pdf

Ewert, D. E. (2009). L2 writing conferences: Investigating teacher talk. *Journal of Second Language Writing, 18*(4), 251–69.

Fishman, S. M., & McCarthy, L. (2001). An ESL writer and her discipline-based professor: Making progress even when goals do not match. *Written Communication, 18*(2), 180–228.

Flood, R. L. (1990). Liberating systems theory: Toward critical systems thinking. *Human Relations, 43*(1), 49–75.

Flood, R., & Romm, N. R. A. (Eds.). (1996). *Critical systems thinking: Current research and practice*. New York, NY: Plenum Press.

Folke, C., Carpenter, S. R., Walker, B., Scheffer, M., Chapin, T., & Rockström, J. (2010). Resilience thinking: Integrating resilience, adaptability, and transformability. *Ecology and Society, 15*(4), art. 20. Retrieved from http://www.ecologyandsociety.org/vol15/iss4/art20/

Fulwiler, T. (2006). Writing across the Michigan Tech curriculum. In S. H. McLeod & M. I. Soven (Eds.), *Composing a community: A history of writing across the curriculum* (pp. 157–67). West Lafayette, IN: Parlor Press.

Fulwiler, T., & Young, A. (Eds.). (1990). *Programs that work: Models and methods for writing across the curriculum*. Portsmouth, NH: Boynton/Cook.

Galin, J. (2010, March). *Improving rather than proving: Self-administered sustainability mapping of WAC programs*. Paper presented at the Sixty-First Annual Convention of the Conference on College Composition and Communication, Louisville, KY.

George Mason University. (2001). Faculty survey on student writing. Retrieved from http://wac.gmu.edu/wp-content/uploads/Faculty_Survey.pdf

George Mason University. (2016). Writing across the curriculum. Retrieved from http:/wac.gmu.edu

Goldstein, J., Hazy, J. K., & Lichtenstein, B. B. (2010). *Complexity and the nexus of leadership: Leveraging nonlinear science to create ecologies of innovation.* New York, NY: Palgrave Macmillan.

Goldstein, L. M. (2005). *Teacher written commentary in second language writing classrooms.* Ann Arbor, MI: University of Michigan Press.

Gottschalk, K., & Hjortshoj, K. (2004). *The elements of teaching writing: A resource for instructors in all disciplines.* Boston, MA: Bedford/St. Martin's.

Granovetter, M. S. (1973). The strength of weak ties. *American Journal of Sociology, 78*(6), 1360–80.

Hardi, P., & Zdan, T. (1997). *Assessing sustainable development: Principles in practice.* Winnipeg, Manitoba, Canada: International Institute for Sustainable Development. Retrieved from https://www.iisd.org/pdf/bellagio.pdf

Hazy, J. K., Goldstein, J. A., & Lichtenstein, B. B. (Eds.). (2007). *Complex systems leadership theory: New perspectives from complexity science on social and organizational effectiveness.* Mansfield, MA: ISCE Publishing.

Herrington, A. J., & Curtis, M. (2000). *Persons in process: Four stories of writing and personal development in college.* Urbana, IL: National Council of Teachers of English.

Hillyard, C. (2012). Comparative study of the numeracy education and writing across the curriculum movements: Ideas for future growth. *Numeracy: Advancing Education in Quantitative Literacy, 5*(2), art. 2. Retrieved from http://scholarcommons.usf.edu/numeracy/vol5/iss2/art2

Hirsh, L. (2014). Writing intensively: An examination of the performance of L2 writers across the curriculum at an urban community college. In T. M. Zawacki & M. Cox (Eds.), *WAC and second language writers: Research towards linguistically and culturally inclusive programs and practices* (pp. 151–80). Fort Collins, CO: The WAC Clearinghouse and Parlor Press. Retrieved from https://wac.colostate.edu/books/l2/chapter6.pdf

Holdstein, D. H. (2000). "Writing across the curriculum" and the paradoxes of institutional initiatives. *Pedagogy, 1*(1), 37–52.

Holling, C. S. (1973). Resilience and stability of ecological systems. *Annual Review of Ecology and Systematics, 4*(1), 1–23.

Howard, R. M. (1988). "In situ" workshops and the peer relationships of composition faculty. *WPA: Writing Program Administration, 12*(1–2), 39–46.

Hyland, F. (1998). The impact of teacher written feedback on individual writers. *Journal of Second Language Writing, 7*(3), 255–86.

International Network of Writing-Across-the-Curriculum Programs. (2014). Statement of WAC principles and practices. Retrieved from https://wac.colostate.edu/principles/statement.pdf

Ison, R. (1993). Participative ecodesign: A new paradigm for professional practice. In G. C. Curran (Ed.), *Epidemiology proceedings of Australian Veterinary Association conference and scientific presentations of Epidemiology Chapter annual general meeting* (pp. 41–50). Tamworth, New South Wales, Australia: Australian College of Veterinary Sciences.

Jackson, M. C. (1985). Social systems theory and practice: The need for a critical approach. *International Journal of General Systems, 10*(2–3), 135–51.

Janopoulos, M. (1995). Writing across the curriculum, writing proficiency exams, and the NNS college student. *Journal of Second Language Writing, 4*(1), 43–50.

Johns, A. M. (1991). Interpreting an English competency exam: The frustrations of an ESL science student. *Written Communication, 8*(3), 379–401.

Johnson, S. (2010). Listening to feedback. In B. Barrios (Ed.), *Emerging: Contemporary readings for writers* (1st ed.) (pp. 190–215) Boston, MA: Bedford/St. Martin's.

Jolliffe, D. A. (2001). Writing across the curriculum and service learning: Kairos, genre, and collaboration. In S. H. McLeod, E. Miraglia, M. Soven, & C. Thaiss (Eds.), *WAC for the new millennium: Strategies for continuing writing-across-the-curriculum programs* (pp. 86–108). Urbana, IL: National Council of Teachers of English. Retrieved from https://wac.colostate.edu/books/millennium/chapter4.pdf

Knoke, D. (2009). Social network analysis: Theory and methods [Power Point slides]. Retrieved from https://www.soc.umn.edu/~knoke/pages/INTRODUCTION_to_NETWORK_ANALYSIS.ppt

Kristensen, P. (2004). The DPSIR framework. Presented at Workshop on Vulnerability of Water Resources in Africa, UNEP Headquarters,

Nairobi, Kenya, 27-29 September, 2004. Retrieved from http://wwz
.ifremer.fr/dce/content/download/69291/913220/file/DPSIR.pdf.

Laane, W. E. M., & Peters, J. S. (1993). Ecological objectives for management purposes: Applying the Amoeba approach. *Journal of Aquatic
Ecosystem Health*, 2(4), 277–86.

LaFrance, M. (2015). Making visible labor issues in Writing Across the
Curriculum: A call for research. *Forum: Issues about Part-Time and
Contingent Faculty*, 19(1), A13–A16.

Leadership Council of the Sustainable Development Solutions Network.
(2015). *Indicators and a monitoring framework for the sustainable
development goals: Launching a data revolution*. Retrieved from
http://unsdsn.org/wp-content/uploads/2015/05/FINAL-SDSN-
Indicator-Report-WEB.pdf

Leki, I. (1995). Coping strategies of ESL students in writing tasks across
the curriculum. *TESOL Quarterly*, 29(2), 235–60.

Leki, I. (1999). "Pretty much I screwed up": Ill-served needs of a permanent resident. In L. Harklau, K. M. Losey, & M. Siegal (Eds.),
*Generation 1.5 meets college composition: Issues in the teaching
of writing to U.S.-educated learners of ESL* (pp. 17–43). Mahwah,
NJ: Erlbaum.

Leki, I. (2001). "A narrow thinking system": Nonnative-English-
speaking students in group projects across the curriculum. *TESOL
Quarterly*, 35(1), 39–67.

Leki, I. (2003a). A challenge to second language writing professionals:
Is writing overrated? In B. Kroll (Ed.), *Exploring the dynamics of
second language writing* (pp. 315–32). Cambridge, England: Cambridge University Press.

Leki, I. (2003b). Living through college literacy: Nursing in a second
language. *Written Communication*, 20(1), 81–98.

Leki, I. (2007). *Undergraduates in a second language: Challenges and
complexities of academic literacy development*. New York, NY:
Erlbaum.

Leon, J. [Complexity Labs]. (2014, April 18). *Complexity science: 2
complexity theory* [Video file and transcript]. Retrieved from https://
www.youtube.com/watch?v=P00A9IZ7Pog

Levy, D. L. (2000). Applications and limitations of complexity theory
in organization theory and strategy. In J. Rabin, G. J. Miller, &

References

W. B. Hildreth (Eds.), *Handbook of strategic management* (2nd ed.) (pp. 67–87). New York, NY: Marcel Dekker.

Maimon, E. P. (1992). Preface. In S. H. McLeod & M. Soven (Eds.), *Writing across the curriculum: A guide to developing programs* (pp. ix–xiv). Newbury Park, CA: SAGE. Reprinted by WAC Clearinghouse, 2000. Retrieved from https://wac.colostate.edu/books/mcleod_soven/preface.pdf

Mallett, K. E., & Zgheib, G. (2014). Campus internationalization: A center-based model for ESL-ready programs. In T. M. Zawacki & M. Cox (Eds.), *WAC and second language writers: Research towards linguistically and culturally inclusive programs and practices* (pp. 387–413). Fort Collins, CO: The WAC Clearinghouse and Parlor Press. Retrieved from https://wac.colostate.edu/books/l2/chapter16.pdf

Matsuda, P. K., & Cox, M. (2009). Reading an ESL writer's text. In S. Bruce & B. Rafoth (Eds.), *ESL writers: A guide for writing center tutors* (2nd ed.) (pp. 39–47). Portsmouth, NH: Boynton/Cook.

McAdam, D., McCarthy, J. D., & Zald, M. N. (1988). Social movements. In N. J. Smelser (Ed.), *Handbook of sociology* (pp. 695–737). Newbury Park, CA: SAGE.

McLeod, S. H. (Ed.). (1988a). *Strengthening programs for writing across the curriculum.* San Francisco, CA: Jossey-Bass. Reprinted by WAC Clearinghouse, 2002. Retrieved from http://wac.colostate.edu/books/mcleod_programs/

McLeod, S. H. (1988b). Translating enthusiasm into curricular change. In S. H. McLeod (Ed.), *Strengthening programs for writing across the curriculum* (pp. 5–12). San Francisco, CA: Jossey-Bass. Reprinted by WAC Clearinghouse, 2002. Retrieved from https://wac.colostate.edu/books/mcleod_programs/mcleod.pdf

McLeod, S. H., & Maimon, E. (2000). Clearing the air: WAC myths and realities. *College English, 62*(5), 573–83.

McLeod, S. H., & Miraglia, E. (2001). Writing across the curriculum in a time of change. In S. H. McLeod, E. Miraglia, M. Soven, & C. Thaiss, C. (Eds.), *WAC for the new millennium: Strategies for continuing writing-across-the-curriculum programs* (pp. 1–27). Urbana, IL: National Council of Teachers of English. Retrieved from https://wac.colostate.edu/books/millennium/chapter1.pdf

McLeod, S. H., Miraglia, E., Soven, M., & Thaiss, C. (Eds.). (2001). *WAC for the new millennium: Strategies for continuing writing-*

across-the-curriculum programs. Urbana, IL: National Council of Teachers of English. Retrieved from https://wac.colostate.edu/books/millennium/new.pdf

McLeod, S. H., & Shirley, S. (1988). Appendix: National survey of writing across the curriculum programs. In S. H. McLeod (Ed.), *Strengthening programs for writing across the curriculum* (pp. 103–30). San Francisco, CA: Jossey-Bass.

McLeod, S. H., & Soven, M. (1991). What do you need to start—and sustain—a writing-across-the-curriculum program? *WPA: Writing Program Administration, 15*(1–2), 25–33.

McLeod, S. H., & Soven, M. (Eds.). (1992). *Writing across the curriculum: A guide to developing programs.* Newbury Park, CA: SAGE. Reprinted by WAC Clearinghouse, 2000. Retrieved from http://wac.colostate.edu/books/mcleod_soven/

Meadows, D. H. (1998). *Indicators and information systems for sustainable development: A report to the Balaton Group.* Hartland Four Corners, VT: Sustainability Institute.

Melzer, D. (2013). Using systems thinking to transform writing programs. *WPA: Writing Program Administration, 36*(2), 75–94.

Merrill, J., Caldwell, M., Rockoff, M., Gebbie, K., Carley, K., & Bakken, S. (2008). Findings from an organizational network analysis to support local public health management. *Journal of Urban Health, 85*(4), 572–84.

Midgley, G. (1996). What is this thing called CST? In R. L. Flood & N. R. A. Romm (Eds.), *Critical systems thinking: Current research and practice* (pp. 11–24). New York, NY: Plenum Press.

Milgram, S. (1967). The small world problem. *Psychology Today, 2,* 60–67.

Miraglia, E., & McLeod, S. (1997). Whither WAC? Interpreting the stories/histories of enduring WAC programs. *WPA: Writing Program Administration, 20*(3), 46–65.

Monroe, J. (Ed.). (2006). *Local knowledges, local practices: Writing in the disciplines at Cornell.* Pittsburgh, PA: University of Pittsburgh Press.

National Council of Teachers of English. (2010). Position statement on the status and working conditions of contingent faculty. Retrieved from http://www.ncte.org/positions/statements/contingent_faculty

National Council of Teachers of English. (2013). *NCTE framework for 21st century curriculum and assessment.* Retrieved from http://www.ncte.org/positions/statements/21stcentframework

National Council of Teachers of English, & Council of Writing Program Administrators. (2008). *NCTE–WPA white paper on writing assessment in colleges and universities.* Retrieved from http://www.ncte.org/positions/statements/nctewpawritingassess

National Council of Teachers of English, Council of Writing Program Administrators, & National Writing Project. (2011). *Framework for success in postsecondary writing.* Retrieved from http://www.ncte.org/positions/statements/collwritingframework

New England Association of Schools and Colleges & Commission on Institutions of Higher Education. (2016). Standards for accreditation. Retrieved from https://cihe.neasc.org/standards-policies/standards-accreditation/standards-effective-july-1-2016

Norberg, J., & Cumming, G. (Eds.) (2008). *Complexity theory for a sustainable future.* New York, NY: Columbia University Press.

Northeast Writing Across the Curriculum Consortium. (2016). Mission. Retrieved from http://newacctest.wac.colostate.edu/mission/

Northeastern University. (2011). *NU Writing Journal.* Retrieved from http://www.northeastern.edu/writing/nu-writing-journal/

Northouse, P. G. (2001). *Leadership: Theory and practice* (2nd ed.). Thousand Oaks, CA: SAGE.

Oregon State University. (2016). WIC survival guide chapter 3: Department writing guides. Retrieved from the Writing Intensive Curriculum program website: http://wic.oregonstate.edu/department-writing-guides

Patton, M. D. (2011). Mapping the gaps in services for L2 writers. *Across the Disciplines, 8*(4). Retrieved from http://wac.colostate.edu/atd/ell/patton.cfm

Phillips, T. (2014). Developing resources for success: A case study of a multilingual graduate writer. In T. M. Zawacki & M. Cox (Eds.), *WAC and second language writers: Research towards linguistically and culturally inclusive programs and practices* (pp. 69–91). Fort Collins, CO: The WAC Clearinghouse and Parlor Press. Retrieved from https://wac.colostate.edu/books/l2/chapter2.pdf

Plymouth State University. (2016). *Out of WAC Newsletter*. Retrieved from https://www.plymouth.edu/office/writing-center/wac/out-of-wac-newsletter/

Reiff, M. J., Bawarshi, A., Ballif, M., & Weisser, C. (2015a). Writing program ecologies: An introduction. In M. J. Reiff, A. Bawarshi, M. Ballif, & C. Weisser (Eds.), *Ecologies of writing programs: Program profiles in context* (pp. 3–18). Anderson, SC: Parlor Press.

Reiff, M. J., Bawarshi, A., Ballif, M., & Weisser, C. (Eds.) (2015b). *Ecologies of writing programs: Program profiles in context*. Anderson, SC: Parlor Press.

Rhodes, T. (2009). *Assessing outcomes and improving achievement: Tips and tools for using the rubrics*. Washington, DC: Association of American Colleges and Universities.

Roberge, M. (2009). A teacher's perspective on generation 1.5. In M. Roberge, M. Siegal, & L. Harklau (Eds.), *Generation 1.5 in college composition: Teaching academic writing to U.S.-educated learners of ESL* (pp. 3–24). New York, NY: Routledge.

Russell, D. R. (2002). *Writing in the academic disciplines: A curricular history*. Carbondale, IL: Southern Illinois University Press.

Salisbury University. (2015). Welcome to writing across the curriculum. Retrieved from http://www.salisbury.edu/wac/

Segall, M. T., & Smart, R. A. (2005). *Direct from the disciplines: Writing across the curriculum*. Portsmouth, NH: Boynton/Cook.

Selfe, C. L. (1997). Contextual evaluation in WAC programs. In K. B. Yancey & B. Huot (Eds.), *Assessing writing across the curriculum: Diverse programs and practices* (pp. 51–68). Greenwich, CT: Ablex.

Senge, P. M. (1990). *The fifth discipline: The art and practice of the learning organization*. New York, NY: Doubleday.

Siczek, M., & Shapiro, S. (2014). Developing writing-intensive courses for a globalized curriculum through WAC–TESOL collaborations. In T. M. Zawacki & M. Cox (Eds.), *WAC and second language writers: Research towards linguistically and culturally inclusive programs and practices* (pp. 329–46). Fort Collins, CO: The WAC Clearinghouse and Parlor Press. Retrieved from https://wac.colostate.edu/books/l2/chapter13.pdf

Simpson, S., Clemens, R., Killingsworth, D. R., & Ford, J. D. (2015). Creating a culture of communication: A graduate-level STEM communication fellows program at a science and engineering university.

Across the Disciplines, 12(3). Retrieved from http://wac.colostate .edu/atd/graduate_wac/simpsonetal2015.cfm

Smart, R. A. (2013). *Double Helix:* History and origins. *Double Helix: A Journal of Critical Thinking and Writing, 1*(1), 1–2.

Southern Connecticut State University. (2016). *WAC newsletter.* Retrieved from http://www.southernct.edu/academics/wac/newsletter .html

State University System of Florida. (2016). Academic program inventory: Inventory of SUS-related discipline-specific accrediting bodies. Retrieved from https://prod.flbog.net:4445/pls/ apex/f?p=136:82:0::NO:

Sternglass, M. S. (1997). *Time to know them: A longitudinal study of writing and learning at the college level.* Mahwah, NJ: Lawrence Erlbaum.

Taylor, M. (2002). *The moment of complexity: Emerging network culture.* Chicago, IL: University of Chicago Press.

ten Brink, B. J. E. (1991). The AMOEBA approach as a useful tool for establishing sustainable development? In O. Kuik & H. Verbruggen (Eds.), *In search of indicators of sustainable development* (pp. 71–87). Dordrecht, The Netherlands: Kluwer Academic Publishers.

ten Brink, B. J. E., Hosper, S. H., & Colijn, F. (1991). A quantitative method for description and assessment of ecosystems: The AMOEBA approach. *Marine Pollution Bulletin, 23,* 265–70.

Texas A&M University–San Antonio. (2016). Fast facts about Texas A&M University–San Antonio. Retrieved from http://www .TAMUSA.edu/about/fastfacts.html

Thaiss, C. (2001). Theory in WAC: Where have we been, where are we going? In S. H. McLeod, E. Miraglia, M. Soven, & C. Thaiss, C. (Eds.), *WAC for the new millennium: Strategies for continuing writing-across-the-curriculum programs* (pp. 299–325). Urbana, IL: National Council of Teachers of English. Retrieved from https:// wac.colostate.edu/books/millennium/chapter12.pdf

Thaiss, C. (2006). Still a good place to be: More than 20 years of the national network of WAC programs. In S. H. McLeod & M. I. Soven (Eds.), *Composing a community: A history of writing across the curriculum* (pp. 126–41). West Lafayette, IN: Parlor Press.

Thaiss, C., Bräuer, G., Carlino, P., Ganobcsik-Williams, L., & Sinha, A. (Eds.). (2012). *Writing programs worldwide: Profiles of academic writing in many places.* Fort Collins, CO: WAC Clearinghouse and Parlor Press. Retrieved from https://wac.colostate.edu/books/wpww/

Thaiss, C., & Porter, T. (2010). The state of WAC/WID in 2010: Methods and results of the U.S. survey of the international WAC/WID mapping project. *College Composition and Communication, 61*(3), 534–70.

Townsend, M. (1994). Writing across the curriculum. In A. C. Purves (Ed.), *Encyclopedia of English studies and language arts: A project of the National Council of Teachers of English* (vol. 2) (pp. 1299–302). New York, NY: Scholastic Leadership Policy Research.

Townsend, M. (2008). WAC program vulnerability and what to do about it: An update and brief bibliographic essay. *The WAC Journal, 19*, 45–61.

Truscott, J. (1999). The case for "The case against grammar correction in L2 writing classes": A response to Ferris. *Journal of Second Language Writing, 8*(2), 111–22.

Tsui, A. B. M., & Ng, M. (2000). Do secondary L2 writers benefit from peer comments? *Journal of Second Language Writing, 9*(2), 147–70.

Uhl-Bien, M., Marion, R., & McKelvey, B. (2007). Complexity leadership theory: Shifting leadership from the industrial age to the knowledge era. *The Leadership Quarterly, 18*(4), 298–318.

United Nations World Commission on Environment and Development. (1987). *Report of the world commission on environment and development: Our common future.* Retrieved from http://www.un-documents.net/our-common-future.pdf

University of California, Santa Barbara. (2008). Writing Research Across Borders. Retrieved from http://www.writing.ucsb.edu/wrconf08/

University of Central Florida. (n.d.). Program annual reports. Retrieved from the Department of Writing and Rhetoric website: http://writingandrhetoric.cah.ucf.edu/reports.php

University of Minnesota Twin Cities. (2015). *Open pathway quality initiative institutional report template.* Retrieved from http://academic.umn.edu/provost/reviews/tc_institutional/UMTCQualityInitiative.pdf

University of Missouri. (2016a). *Mission statement.* Retrieved from the Campus Writing Program website: http://cwp.missouri.edu/about/index.php

University of Missouri. (2016b). *Publications*. Retrieved from the Campus Writing Program website: http://cwp.missouri.edu/publications/

University of Vermont. (2016). *Annual reports*. Retrieved from the Writing in the Disciplines Program website: https://www.uvm.edu/wid/?Page=annualreport.html&SM=submenu1.html

Valencia College Institutional Research. (2015). *Valencia college statistical history fact book 2014/2015*. Retrieved from http://valenciacollege.edu/academic-affairs/institutional-effectiveness-planning/institutional-research/Reporting/internal/documents/Completed2014-15StatHistoryFactBook.pdf

WAC Clearinghouse. (n.d.a). *Across the Disciplines*. Retrieved from https://wac.colostate.edu/atd/

WAC Clearinghouse. (n.d.b). WAC Graduate Student Organization. Retrieved from https://wac.colostate.edu/go/

WAC Clearinghouse. (n.d.c). The International WAC Network. Retrieved from http://wac.colostate.edu/network/

WAC Clearinghouse. (n.d.d). A brief history of the WAC Network. Retrieved from http://wac.colostate.edu/network/history.cfm

Walker, B., & Salt, D. (2006). *Resilience thinking: Sustaining ecosystems and people in a changing world*. Washington, DC: Island Press.

Walvoord, B. E. (1992). Getting started. In S. H. McLeod & M. Soven (Eds.), *Writing across the curriculum: A guide to developing programs* (pp. 9–22). Newbury Park, CA: SAGE. Reprinted by WAC Clearinghouse, 2000. Retrieved https://wac.colostate.edu/books/mcleod_soven/chapter2.pdf

Walvoord, B. E. (1996). The future of WAC. *College English*, *58*(1), 58–74.

Walvoord, B. E., & McCarthy, L. P. (1991). *Thinking and writing in college: A naturalistic study of students in four disciplines*. Urbana, IL: National Council of Teachers of English.

Wasserman, S., & Faust, K. (1994). *Social network analysis: Methods and applications*. Cambridge, England: Cambridge University Press.

White, E. M. (1990a). The damage of innovations set adrift: Change for the worst. *AAHE Bulletin*, *43*(3), 3–5.

White, E. M. (1990b). Language and reality in writing assessment. *College Composition and Communication*, *41*(2), 187–200.

Whittlesley, V. (2005). Student learning outcomes assessment and the disciplinary accrediting organizations. *Assessment Update, 17*(4), 10–12.

Yancey, K. B., Baker, E., Gage, S., Kistler, R., Lee, R., Szymanski, N., Taczak, K., & Taylor, J. (Eds.). (2009). Writing across the curriculum and assessment: Activities, programs, and insights at the intersection [Special issue: WAC and Assessment]. *Across the Disciplines*, 6. Retrieved from https://wac.colostate.edu/atd/assessment/

Yancey, K. B., & Huot, B. A. (Eds.). (1997). *Assessing writing across the curriculum: Diverse approaches and practices.* Greenwich, CT: Ablex.

Young, A. (2003). Writing across and against the curriculum. *College Composition and Communication, 54*(3), 472–85.

Young, A. (2006). *Teaching writing across the curriculum* (4th ed.). Upper Saddle River, NJ: Pearson Education. Retrieved from http://wac.colostate.edu/books/young_teaching/

Young, A., & Fulwiler, T. (1990). Afterword: The enemies of writing across the curriculum. In T. Fulwiler & A. Young (Eds.), *Programs that work: Models and methods for writing across the curriculum* (pp. 287–94). Portsmouth, NH: Boynton/Cook.

Zawacki, T. M., & Cox, M. (Eds.). (2014). *WAC and second language writers: Research towards linguistically and culturally inclusive programs and practices.* Fort Collins, CO: The WAC Clearinghouse and Parlor Press. Retrieved from http://wac.colostate.edu/books/l2/

Zawacki, T. M., & Gentemann, K. M. (2009). Merging a culture of writing with a culture of assessment: Embedded, discipline-based writing assessment. In M. C. Paretti & K. M. Powell (Eds.), *Assessment of writing* (pp. 49–64). Tallahassee, FL: Association for Institutional Research.

Zawacki, T. M., Reid, E. S., Zhou, Y., & Baker, S. E. (2009). Voices at the table: Balancing the needs and wants of program stakeholders to design a value-added writing assessment plan [Special issue: WAC and Assessment]. *Across the Disciplines*, 6. Retrieved from https://wac.colostate.edu/atd/assessment/zawackietal.cfm

Zhu, W. (2001). Interaction and feedback in mixed peer response groups. *Journal of Second Language Writing, 10*(4), 251–76.

INDEX

Note: An "f" following a page number indicates a figure and a "t" indicates a table.

Indicators. *See* Sustainability indicators (SIs)
Institutional diagrams, 91–92, 92f
Institutional network maps, 93–96, 94f, 95f
Integration, 47, 49, 67
Interconnectivity, 118–24. *See also* Points of leverage
International Network of Writing-Across-the-Curriculum (INWAC) Programs, 11, 190, 220t, 226, 231
International WRAB conference, 222t, 226
INWAC "Statement of WAC Principles and Practices," 11
Ison, R., 137
IWAC conference, 220t, 224, 226

Jackson, Michael, 33
Johnson, S., 29

Kennesaw State University, 175
Kopp, Bryan, 77, 82–83, 87–88, 94, 98

LaFrance, Michelle, 125, 231
Lancaster, Zak, 140, 145–47, 157, 163, 166
Language and Learning Across the Disciplines (journal), 220t
Leadership
  complex systems leadership theory (CSLT), 74, 199–200
  distributed, 201–2
  future research on, 217–18
  mentorship, 190–91, 229–30, 231–32
  sustainability of, 74–75, 198–204, 228–31
  vignettes, 170–77

as WAC principle, 46, 48–49
in whole systems methodology, 56–57
Leadership theories, 199
Leki, Ilona, 126–27
Leon, J., 28, 30, 31
Leverage. *See* Points of leverage
Levy, D.L., 29
Lichtenstein, B. B., 200
Limitations, 211–12
Listservs, 181, 190, 220t, 224
Lynn, R., 125

Macro-level focus, 15–16, 25, 69–70, 155–59
Maimon, Elaine, 110, 111, 156
Mallett, Karyn, 128
Mapping. *See also* Organizational network analysis (ONA); Social network theory
  AMOEBA diagrams, 54, 54f, 62
  institutional diagrams, 91–92, 92f
  institutional network maps, 93–96, 94f, 95f
  process maps, 92–93
  of WAC, as field, 225f
Marion, R., 200
McAdam, D., 14
McCarthy, J. D., 14
McKelvey, B., 200
McLeod, Susan
  on faculty development, 111, 156
  guides for WAC directors by, 10–11
  survey data, 126
  on sustainable leadership, 172
  on traits of enduring WAC programs, 12–13, 198
  WAC for the New Millennium, 15–16
  on WAC programs as localized, 110

development; WAC
programs
Writing-related organizations,
189–91
Writing to communicate, 9
Writing to learn, 9

Yancey, Kathleen Blake, 193–94
Young, Art, 10, 11–12, 121, 228

Zald, M. N., 14
Zawacki, Terry Myers, 172,
173–75, 186, 187, 194,
231
Zdan, T., 44–45, 48, 58
Zgheib, Ghania, 128
Zoltek, Stanley, 172

AUTHORS

Michelle Cox is the inaugural director of the English Language Support Office in Cornell University's Knight Institute. Previously, she was faculty at Bridgewater State University and Dartmouth College. She has taught undergraduate and graduate courses on writing, writing theory, and writing pedagogy; launched and directed a Writing Across the Curriculum program; and is currently developing a writing and speaking support program for international graduate and professional students. She earned her PhD in composition studies from the University of New Hampshire in 2006. Her publications include coedited collections—*Second Language Writing in the Composition Classroom: A Critical Sourcebook* (2006), *Reinventing Identities in Second Language Writing* (2010), *WAC and Second Language Writers: Research towards Linguistically and Culturally Inclusive Programs and Practices* (2014), and *Supporting Graduate Writers: Research, Curriculum, and Program Designs* (2016)—as well as book chapters and articles on WAC theory and administration, graduate student writing, and second language writing. Cox is past chair of the Consortium on Graduate Communication and current chair of the CCCC Standing Group on Writing Across the Curriculum, and is on the editorial boards of *Across the Disciplines*, the *WAC Clearinghouse*, and *College English*. She is currently co-leading the formation of the Association for Writing Across the Curriculum as a 501c3 organization

Jeffrey R. Galin is associate professor at Florida Atlantic University and founder and director of FAU's University Center for Excellence in Writing, Writing Across the Curriculum program, and Community Center for Excellence in Writing. He has taught undergraduate and graduate courses on writing, writing theory and pedagogy, intellectual property, multimodal composition, and writing program administration. He earned his PhD in critical and cultural studies with specialization in composition

at the University of Pittsburgh in 1995. He has coedited *The Dialogic Classroom: Teachers Integrating Computer Technology, Pedagogy, and Research* and *Teaching/Writing in the Late Age of Print*. He has published articles in *College Composition and Communication, Computers and Composition*, and *Kairos*, as well as in social work, chemical education, and honors council journals. He has also published chapters on issues of copyright fair use and multimodal teaching in several edited book collections. Galin is past chair of the Intellectual Property Caucus of CCCC and the CCC Intellectual Property Committee. He is incoming chair of the CCCC Standing Group on Writing Across the Curriculum and is on editorial boards of *Across the Disciplines*, the *WAC Clearinghouse*, and *Kairos: A Journal of Rhetoric, Technology, and Pedagogy*. He is currently co-leading the formation of the Association for Writing Across the Curriculum as a 501c3 organization and the development of the three-day WAC Institute.

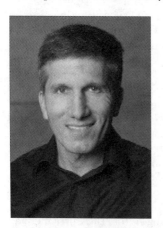

Dan Melzer is the director of first-year composition at the University of California, Davis. Previously, he was the director of Writing Across the Curriculum and the University Reading and Writing Center at California State University, Sacramento. He earned his PhD in rhetoric and composition at Florida State University in 2002. He teaches undergraduate courses in first-year composition and advanced composition, and graduate courses in rhetoric and composition theory and practice. His publications include a scholarly monograph, *Assignments Across the Curriculum: A National Study of College Writing*; the textbooks *Exploring College Writing* and *Everything's a Text* (coauthored with Deborah Coxwell-Teague); and articles on WAC theory and administration in the journals *College Composition and Communication, Writing Program Administration*, and *The WAC Journal*. Melzer is past-chair of the CCCC Standing Group on Writing Across the Curriculum and is on the editorial board of the *WAC Clearinghouse*. He is currently co-leading the formation of the Association for Writing Across the Curriculum as a 501c3 organization.

CONTRIBUTORS

Chris M. Anson is Distinguished University Professor and director of the Campus Writing and Speaking Program at North Carolina State University, where he teaches graduate and undergraduate courses in language, composition, and literacy and works with faculty across the disciplines to enhance writing and speaking instruction. He has published 18 books and more than 125 articles and book chapters relating to writing and has spoken widely across the United States and in 31 other countries. He is past chair of the Conference on College Composition and Communication and past president of the Council of Writing Program Administrators. His full CV is at www.ansonica.net.

Maury Elizabeth Brown is a PhD candidate in rhetoric and writing at Old Dominion University and an assistant professor of English at Germanna Community College. She is also the co-founder of a role-playing in education company, Learn Larp, LLC. She researches collaborative composing using Google Apps for Education, and she seeks to empower her students through the writing process and help them find their voices.

Maggie Cecil directs the California State University, San Bernardino Writing Centers, in addition to teaching part time for the Department of English. She is an active and dedicated hospice volunteer, specializing in pet therapy and is regularly accompanied on hospital, assisted living, and residential visits by her current registered therapy dog, Winter.

Michael J. Cripps is associate professor of rhetoric and composition in the Department of English at the University of New England, where he directs composition. He has been involved in WAC and WID initiatives in several university systems over the last two decades, most notably in the City University of New York, where he served as WAC coordinator at York College/CUNY for a number of years. His research is in writing program administration and its intersection with such aspects of composition studies as new media, professional development, peer review, and, more recently, developmental writing.

Beth Daniell taught graduate and undergraduate courses in rhetoric and writing for many years. Before her retirement, she served as director of general education in English and as director of the WAC Program in the College of Humanities and Social Science at Kennesaw State University in the northern Atlanta suburbs. She is author of *A Communion of Friendship: Literacy, Spiritual Practice, and Women in Recovery* and coeditor of *Women and Literacy: Local and Global Inquiries for a New Century* and *Renovating Rhetoric in Christian Tradition*. She enjoyed her work in WAC at Clemson University and at Kennesaw State and learned a great deal about teaching and about writing from the professors she worked with at both places.

Deanna Dannels is professor of communication and associate dean of Academic Affairs in the College of Humanities and Social Sciences at North Carolina State University. Her research explores theoretical and curricular protocols for teacher training and development; as well as frameworks for designing, implementing, and assessing oral communication across the disciplines. As associate dean, Dannels works to support the college's intellectual community through advancing undergraduate and graduate programs, facilitating disciplinary and interdisciplinary scholarship, supporting diversity initiatives for graduate and undergraduate students, and promoting high impact educational experiences that contribute to student success.

Violet ("Vi") A. Dutcher is professor of rhetoric and composition and teaches writing and speech courses at Eastern Mennonite University, where she also directs the university's Writing Program. Her research and writing focus is in community literacy practices, particularly in Old Order Amish women's literacy events. She is currently working on a book manuscript that identifies and explores the literacy practices of specific communities of Old Order Amish women. She is a consulting editor for *The Conrad Grebel Review* and a member of the Feminist Caucus of the Conference on College Composition and Communication.

Carol Peterson Haviland is emerita professor of English and Writing Center WAC/WID director at California State University, San Bernardino. Retired in Portland, Oregon, she works to support younger scholars' voices and contributions and to promote feminist and translingual pedagogies as she volunteers in her grandson's preschool. She encourages those who speak for "correct English" to listen to the ways all English acquirers speak and write, including young children who quickly see that *writed* and *drawed* are logical past tenses that puzzle only the audiences who do not wish to understand them.

Composition teacher **Marla L. Hyder** developed and led a successful WAC program at College of Lake County in northern Illinois from 2013 to 2016. In 2016, Hyder moved with her family to Washington State, where she joined Everett Community College's Ocean Research College Academy (ORCA), a one-of-a-kind running start program centered on the local marine environment. ORCA's interdisciplinary approach mirrors Hyder's WAC/WID work: in addition to teaching composition, humanities, and literature classes, she collaborates closely with other faculty and joins students and faculty on ORCA's research vessel and at STEM conferences. The WAC program continues to thrive at College of Lake County under new leadership.

Bryan Kopp is Writing Programs coordinator in the Center for Advancing Teaching and Learning and assistant professor of English at the University of Wisconsin–La Crosse. He is also associate director of the Lesson Study Project, an initiative that supports collaborative teaching improvement across the disciplines. He teaches undergraduate writing and rhetoric courses as well as professional and technical writing. His speciality areas include genre studies, cultural studies, and the scholarship of teaching and learning.

Zak Lancaster is assistant professor of English at Wake Forest University, where he coordinates the Writing Associates program, a WAC/WID initiative. His research focuses on writing across the disciplines and the language of stance and evaluation. His work has appeared in *Across the Disciplines*, *College Composition and Communication*, *Journal of Writing Research*, *Journal of English for Academic Purposes*, and *Written Communication*.

Mary McMullen-Light directed the WAC Program at Metropolitan Community College–Longview for more than 20 years, collaborating with faculty in general education, career, and technical programs across the college to create a culture of writing that fully embraced the two prongs of WAC: writing to learn and learning to write. She served on the Board of Consultants for the International WAC Network and contributed to the "Statement of WAC Principles and Practices." McMullen-Light has presented at the International WAC Conference and CCCC. She began working at Johnson County Community College as research coordinator for outcomes assessment in 2014 and is currently serving in the institutional effectiveness branch.

Michael J. Michaud teaches courses in rhetoric and composition at Rhode Island College (RIC) in Providence. His work has appeared in *Teaching English in the Two Year College, Enculturation, Writ-*

ing and Pedagogy, Composition Forum, Writing on the Edge, and *College Composition and Communication,* and is forthcoming in *Technical Communication Quarterly* (with Sarah Read). In addition to first-year composition, Michaud teaches courses in professional writing, digital and multimodal writing, and composition theory. He is the founder and lead teacher of an annual faculty seminar on writing pedagogy at RIC. His current book project investigates the reformer Donald M. Murray, examining Murray's contributions to the teaching of writing at the University of New Hampshire and in the emergent field of composition and rhetoric from 1963 to 1987.

Kerri K. Morris is associate professor at Governors State University, where she was hired to direct Writing Across the Curriculum and to help build the university's first general education program. Her background is in historical rhetoric with a special interest in the epideictic genre. She is also interested in WAC research and rhetorics of health. Morris is at heart a writing teacher and a writer.

Mary Lou Odom is professor of English and director of the Writing Center and Writing Across the Curriculum at Kennesaw State University, where she teaches graduate courses in rhetoric and composition and mentors graduate teaching assistants. Her current areas of research include using connections between the reading and writing practices of college students to inform pedagogy, as well as exploring the role of ethics in writing center administration. Most recently, her scholarship has appeared in *WLN: A Journal of Writing Center Scholarship* and *Across the Disciplines.*

Timothy Patrick Oleksiak is assistant professor of English at University of Massachusetts Boston where he teaches courses in rhetoric and composition and new media authoring. His research interests center on queer rhetoric and composition theory and the way LGBTQ rhetors use silence and listening as strategies for rhetorical negotiation. During the fall 2018 semester, he assumes direction of the Professional and New Media Writing Concentration. Oleksiak loves people, food, and opera in equal measure and is overjoyed when he can combine all three. Other identifications include husband, table-top gamer, and drag enthusiast.

Juli Parrish is a teaching associate professor and directs the Writing Center at the University of Denver, which has a student staff of about 40 and offers writing support and workshops to undergraduates, graduate students, staff, and faculty across the curriculum. She has published in *Across the Disciplines* and *Transformative Works and Cultures,* and her current research explores the ways that communities of writers create and negotiate rhetorical traditions both in and out of academic settings. Parrish also coedits the open access journal *Literacy in Composition Studies.*

Holly L. Ryan is associate professor of English and Writing Center co-ordinator at Pennsylvania State University, Berks in Reading. She serves as a Writing Across the Curriculum committee member and supports the writing fellows—undergraduate writing tutors in the disciplines—on her campus. Additionally, she serves as associate editor of *Prompt: A Journal of Writing Assignments*, an interdisciplinary journal focused on writing in and across the disciplines.

Eliana Schonberg was the founding director of the University of Denver's University Writing Center and is now the director of the Thompson Writing Program Writing Studio at Duke University. She was a co-founding editor of *Praxis* and is currently a coeditor of the *Writing Center Journal*. Her work has appeared in *Across the Disciplines, Writing Center Journal, Praxis: A Writing Center Journal*, and *WLN: A Journal of Writing Center Scholarship*. Her scholarship addresses questions of transfer, collaboration, and translation, whether disciplinary or linguistic.

Chris Thaiss is professor emeritus of writing studies at the University of California, Davis. Before becoming Clark Kerr Presidential Chair and director of the University Writing Program at Davis in 2006, he helped build the WAC Program, Writing Center, First-Year and Advanced Writing Programs, and MA Teaching of Writing Program over his 30 years at George Mason University, where he also chaired the Department of English. He cherishes the exceptional colleagues, fellow teachers, and students who have inspired him at Davis and Mason, as well as colleagues across the United States and transnationally, all of whom make writing studies such a wonderfully innovative discipline. His latest book project, based on his Davis courses, is a textbook titled *Writing Science in the 21st Century*.

Barbara E. Walvoord has founded and directed four centers for WAC, assessment, and teaching/learning: Central College in Iowa, Loyola College in Maryland (where she was named 1987 Maryland English Teacher of the Year for Higher Education), the University of Cincinnati, and the University of Notre Dame. She has consulted or led workshops at more than 400 institutions of higher education on writing across the curriculum, assessment, and teaching and learning. Publications include *Assessing and Improving Student Writing in College: A Guide for Institutions, General Education, Departments, and Classrooms* (2014), *Assessment Clear and Simple: A Practical Guide for Institutions, Departments, and General Education* (2nd ed., 2010), and *Effective Grading: A Tool for Learning and Assessment in College* (with coauthor Virginia Johnson Anderson, 2nd ed., 2010).

Christian Weisser is professor of English at Penn State Berks. He serves as coordinator of both the Professional Writing Program and the Writing Across the Curriculum Program. For more than a decade, he has served as the editor of *Composition Forum*, a peer-reviewed scholarly journal in rhetoric and composition. Weisser's research focuses on the relationships between rhetoric and location; his current work investigates the rhetoric of sustainability in higher education. Weisser has published eight books and numerous articles on writing and rhetoric. He teaches courses in technical, business, and electronic writing; composition theory; and environmental and sustainability rhetoric.

Stephen Wilhoit is professor in the English department at the University of Dayton, where he also serves as director of faculty career enhancement in the Ryan C. Harris Learning Teaching Center. Over the past 15 years, he has led semester-long WAC seminars for faculty and staff at the university in addition to programs related to effective teaching practice, learning outcomes assessment, faculty research, and vocational discernment. He has authored two writing textbooks and a guide for new graduate teaching assistants in English departments and writing programs.

Terry Myers Zawacki is emerita professor and former director of Writing Across the Curriculum at George Mason University, where she was recognized for significant long-term contributions to the overall excellence of the university. Her publications include *Engaged Writers and Dynamic Disciplines* and the coedited collections *WAC and Second Language Writers; Writing Across the Curriculum: A Critical Sourcebook;* and the forthcoming *Re/writing the Center: Approaches to Supporting Graduate Students in the Writing Center,* as well as articles and chapters on WAC, writing centers, assessment, WID and L2 writers, international L2 writers, and challenges around dissertation writing. She is lead editor of the book series International Exchanges on the Study of Writing at the WAC Clearinghouse.

This book was typeset in Sabon by Barbara Frazier.
The typeface used on the cover was Neue Haas Grotesk
Display Pro 65 Medium.
The book was printed on 50-lb. White Offset paper
by Versa Press, Inc.